Love and revolution

Manchester University Press

Contemporary Anarchist Studies

A series edited by

Laurence Davis, *University College Cork, Ireland*
Uri Gordon, *Independent Scholar, UK*
Nathan Jun, *Independent Scholar, USA*
Alex Prichard, *University of Exeter, UK*

Contemporary Anarchist Studies promotes the study of anarchism as a framework for understanding and acting on the most pressing problems of our times. The series publishes cutting-edge, socially engaged scholarship from around the world – bridging theory and practice, academic rigor and the insights of contemporary activism.

The topical scope of the series encompasses anarchist history and theory broadly construed; individual anarchist thinkers; anarchist informed analysis of current issues and institutions; and anarchist or anarchist-inspired movements and practices. Contributions informed by anti-capitalist, feminist, ecological, Indigenous and non-Western or Global South anarchist perspectives are particularly welcome. So, too, are manuscripts that promise to illuminate the relationships between the personal and the political aspects of transformative social change, local and global problems, and anarchism and other movements and ideologies. Above all, we wish to publish books that will help activist scholars and scholar activists think about how to challenge and build real alternatives to existing structures of oppression and injustice.

International Editorial Advisory Board:

Recent books in the series

Love and revolution

A politics for the deep commons

Matt York

MANCHESTER UNIVERSITY PRESS

The right of Matt York to be identified as the author of
this work has been asserted by them in accordance with the
Copyright, Designs and Patents Act 1988.

Published by Manchester University Press
Oxford Road, Manchester M13 9PL

www.manchesteruniversitypress.co.uk

British Library Cataloguing-in-Publication Data
A catalogue record for this book is available from the British
Library

ISBN 978 1 5261 6433 9 hardback
ISBN 978 1 5261 9152 6 paperback

First published 2023
Paperback published 2025

The publisher has no responsibility for the persistence or
accuracy of URLs for any external or third-party internet
websites referred to in this book, and does not guarantee
that any content on such websites is, or will remain, accurate
or appropriate.

EU authorised representative for GPSR:
Easy Access System Europe – Mustamäe tee 50,
10621 Tallinn, Estonia
gpsr.requests@easproject.com

Typeset by Newgen Publishing UK

Dedicated to Jacqueline,
for everything...

Contents

Foreword by John P. Clark   *page* viii
Acknowledgements   xiii

Part I: Locating (r)evolutionary love

Introduction   3
1 The anarchy of love   12
2 Collective visioning: Utopia as process   41

Part II: A collective vision

3 The dystopian present   55
4 The deep commons   84
5 Activating the Agapeic web   114
6 The collective heart: Co-constituting free society   149
Conclusion   167

Bibliography   174
Index   193

Foreword

This is a very important and timely work. Indeed, nothing could be timelier. As I write, another global climate summit has just come and gone. For the twenty-sixth time, the Principalities and Powers have failed to act decisively to prevent what is, in effect, the End of the World. We are told repeatedly that this is because of a certain lack of 'ambition'. Perhaps, it is really because of a certain lack of love.

This work is part of a great tradition of reflection on the social, political, spiritual and philosophical meaning of love. A perennial theme in the world's cosmologies, mythologies, philosophies and theologies is that love offers us the answer to the most basic questions. What is the meaning of life? How can we realise the flourishing of humanity and nature? How can we attain the greatest good? How can we avoid the greatest evils?

The tradition that points to love for an answer is vast. We can look to Shakyamuni Buddha's teachings of compassion and loving-kindness, to Daoist sage Laozi's precept of deep love, to the Agapeic teachings of the Gospels, and to the love-centred poetry of Rumi, to mention only a few of the most famous examples. These are, in turn, rooted in an even more primordial legacy of stories and teachings concerning the primacy of love in Indigenous, kinship-centred, relational societies over the millennia.

What we call 'modern civilization' has been aberrant in straying so far from this age-old focus on love in the constitution of being, nature and humanity. Matt York's work helps take us back to our primordial awareness of the centrality of love. In doing so, it is, in a very deep sense, a work of hope. It expresses the hope, and even more, the aspiration, that by reawakening our awareness of the many dimensions of love, and by exploring new possibilities for the realisation of engaged love, we can discover how to act well, and act effectively, at this decisive moment in geohistory and in our own lives.

This work poses the question of what could possibly possess the power to transform, and indeed, to terminate, an imperious, self-perpetuating and seemingly inescapable system of universal destruction. The import of the work is that in an age of mass extinction and looming threat of global eco-logical collapse, our engaged love – for the Earth, for the land and for all our fellow beings that dwell there – may be the last and best hope.

For such an engaged love to emerge, York says, we must 'become ter-restrials once more'. In fact, our present level of knowledge of geohistory and of bioscience offers us new possibilities for becoming terrestrials in a deeper sense than ever before, should this science be combined with eco-logical wisdom and unbounded compassion. Yet, tragically, within today's techno-bureaucratic society of mass consumption, the average human being drifts ever further away from living and thinking like a terrestrial being. This work aims at reversing this disordered condition.

Becoming terrestrial relates to York's extremely important idea of the deep commons. While the concept of the commons has become increas-ingly important in recent times, York proposes a much more expansive and far-reaching conception than most. In one very concise formulation, he describes it as the ensemble of 'our more-than-human psycho-socio-material relations'. One might say that it means being not only in the world but of the world, on all the deepest levels, so that we can ultimately 'co-constitute' a terrestrial 'community of communities'. We might say that such co-constitution is one way of defining the goal of (r)evolutionary love.

York discusses four major traditional forms of love: *éros*, which he links to desire and passion; *storgē*, which he identifies as 'familial affection', *philía*, which he relates to friendship and kinship, and *agápe*, which he defines as 'empathetic love for the many'. He offers us abundant evidence that love in its diverse forms is a powerful force, but he also shows us that its power can be exerted in widely divergent directions. On the one hand, it has 'the potential to encourage alternative and liberatory forms of relation-ship beyond separateness and competition', and to be the basis for a 'radical solidarity'. However, it also has enormous potential 'to legitimise xenopho-bic nationalisms, patriotisms and fascisms'. If anyone thinks of the power of love as some naïve or sentimental illusion, they might reflect for a moment on the power it wields when it takes on some of these demonic forms.

As York shows, this radical divergence in love's manifestations has a deeply rooted ontological basis. The loving person and community expe-rience the very being of things in a way that is radically different from persons and communities who experience things from a dominating and appropriating perspective. We might say that our mode of being-in-the-world is always a certain form of libidinal being-in-the-world. However, such being can take many courses of becoming. It can go in the direction of spirit, of commonality, and of unity-in-diversity, or in the direction of ego, of alienation, and of antagonistic splitting. York describes this dichotomy in terms of first, an 'ontology of separation' that is connected to the illusion of 'an imagined separate autonomous self' and which lies at the core of domination, and second, what he calls 'an ontology of entanglement and immanence' that is 'intimately interrelational' and can form the basis for (r)evolutionary love and the deep commons.

York's analysis is particularly noteworthy for giving due recognition to the contribution of Indigenous cosmovisions to the development of the needed ontology. He points to Indigenous values that express 'an inextricable interrelationality with the non-human world, a refusal of anthropocentrism, an acknowledgement of interactive ecologies shared by human and non-human beings, and a deeply process-oriented ontology'. In a sense, we might say that 'ontology is destiny'. Our ontological experience, our most fundamental mode of apprehending the being and becoming of all beings, conditions everything else. And all attempts at social transformation will come to naught if they do not move our basic ontology very much in the direction of what York admires in many Indigenous cosmovisions. This appreciation of the achievements of Indigenous societies illustrates one of the major points in the book.

One of the central truths that it conveys is that our hopes for the power of love and for humanity's ability to exercise this power are evidence based. York points out that we have abundant evidence of how humanity's cooperative impulses and capacities for mutual aid can be unleashed in times of crisis. This is what scott crow, co-founder of Common Ground, the large anarchist-inspired disaster recovery organisation, has labelled 'Emergency Heart'. York points out that it has been extensively documented that in the face of natural disasters such as earthquakes, hurricanes, and floods, 'new egalitarian social structures arise in a moment'. Such crisis experience gives us grounds for optimism, as we enter into the period of deepest and most sustained crisis in the history of humanity.

This experience is related to a phenomenon that George Katsiaficas has called the 'Eros Effect'. According to this concept, inspired in part by the philosopher Marcuse, éros is, on the deepest ontological level, a cosmic force for unification, reconciliation, attraction and convergence, and on the phenomenal level, a powerful social and psychological reality that is manifested intensely at crucial points in history. It signals the moment when evolutionary love also becomes revolutionary love. Underlying this effect is an 'inherent feeling of connection with others' and an 'instinctual love for freedom'. When it is manifested at a given historical juncture, 'cooperation replaces competition, equality replaces hierarchy and power gives way to truth'.

If we relate this idea more specifically to the classical anarchist tradition, we find that it has a close affinity to the great communitarian anarchist Gustav Landauer's concept of spirit in history. As Landauer expresses this idea: 'It is in revolution's fire, in its enthusiasm, its brotherhood, its aggressiveness that the image and the feeling of positive unification awakens; a unification that comes through a connecting quality: love as force'.[1]

Ideas such as 'emergency heart', 'the Eros Effect', and 'love as force' should be very heartening. Yet, they somehow seem rather distant at this point in history. We are at a moment of resignation, and perhaps fear, in which awareness of the power they point to has receded to the margins of the social imagination. We, collectively, seem unable to ask the simple question, 'What can a social body do?'

Our level of social amnesia is striking, since we have many inspiring examples of the politically transformative power of (r)evolutionary love, even within the lifetime of some of us. Satyagraha, the practice of the movement that successfully overthrew the British Empire in India, is usually described as 'non-violent resistance', but Gandhi also identified it more evocatively as 'love force'. Martin Luther King Jr. called the vision that guided and animated the civil rights movement in its campaigns of civil disobedience 'the Beloved Community'. One can also point to the often revolutionary Christian base communities of Latin America, which, in the hundreds of thousands, have been motivated by a strong ethos of justice and, above all, love. These communities have been described as creating a new 'civilization of love'. This book helps us keep in mind this history of (r)evolutionary love and speaks for the realisation of that civilization, or perhaps better, that Beloved Community.

A final great strength of the work that must be mentioned is the author's incorporation of the collective visioning process, which expresses in concrete practice some of the most basic values that have been mentioned. York realises, in a way that most academic and theoretical researchers and writers do not, that the methodology is the message, and the message is the methodology. Accordingly, collective visioning is a collaborative approach that incorporates such liberatory and communitarian dimensions as mutual aid, solidarity, cooperation, respect for the knowledge and experience of others, dialogue, careful listening and mindfulness.

The project is a model of meaningful diversity. It included activists who came from fourteen countries and five continents, in diverse positions between the core and periphery of Empire, and who had a wide range of social movement engagement, including 'anti-capitalist and ecological activism, anarchist organising, indigenous struggles, feminist activism, refugee solidarity work, food sovereignty projects, cooperatives and permaculture projects.' Thus, the research project was not only extensive in relation to its global scope, but also intensive in relation to the range of participants' experiences. In integrating this wealth of experience, it incorporates an important dimension of collective creativity.

At the very end of the book, the author addresses the issue of 'reconnecting'. In this he gives us, I think, a key to grasping the central message of the work. It asks us whether we are capable of overcoming such barriers to connection as denial, disavowal, ideology and false consciousness. It asks whether we are capable of connecting with lost parts of ourselves, with other persons, with other beings, with other communities, and with the Earth. It asks, in short, whether we are capable of making the kind of connections that allow us to develop wisdom and compassion, mindful care, and engaged love.

From a slightly different perspective, the central message of this indispensable work is to confront us with the following question: how might it be possible for the (r)evolutionary community of love to be the primary political agent, the (r)evolutionary subject of history? It seems to me that there is no more important question than this one today.

John P. Clark, emeritus professor of philosophy,
Loyola University, eco-communitarian anarchist
author and activist, director of La Terre Institute
for Community and Ecology, New Orleans

Note

1 Gustav Landauer, 'Revolution', in *Revolution and other writings: A political reader*, ed. and trans. G. Kuhn (Oakland, CA: PM Press, 2010), p. 170.

Acknowledgements

I am deeply grateful to all of the many people who have helped to make this book a reality. Foremost, I would like to express my sincere gratitude to Laurence Davis for his support throughout the entire process of researching and writing *Love and Revolution*, and without whose patient mentorship, expertise and kindness this project would not have been possible. And likewise, my appreciation goes to John Clark for his invaluable support and encouragement of the work, and for agreeing to write the foreword for the book. Many thanks are also due to Órla O'Donovan, Caitríona Ní Dhúill, Clodagh Harris, Theresa Reidy and Chiara Bonfiglioli, whose generous feedback and advice has proved indispensable. In addition, I would like to thank the editors of the Contemporary Anarchist Studies book series for their critical engagement and insightful suggestions – all of which have greatly improved the quality of the work. Similarly, the detailed and important points raised by the anonymous reviewers have led to significant improvements to the final manuscript. I also gratefully acknowledge the prompt and professional support I have received from the Manchester University Press publishing team, and in particular my editors Thomas Dark and Laura Swift. Sections of the chapter 'The anarchy of love' have been developed from an article originally published in the *Radical Philosophy Review*, and I would therefore also like to thank the editorial team and reviewers who worked with me on this material at that time.

I have been thinking about the themes explored in this book for a very long time and have had the good fortune to develop these ideas at a number of conferences and seminars in recent years, including the Political Theory Specialist Group panel at the Political Studies Association of Ireland Conference; the Transnational Institute of Social Ecology Conference, Athens; the 'Theorising Politics and International Relations in the 21st Century' and Political and Social Movements Specialist Group panels on consecutive years at the UK Political Studies Association Conference; the Anarchist Studies Network 6th and 7th International Conferences; the conference 'Acting As If – Prefigurative Politics in Theory and Praxis', and the 21st Conference of the European Utopian Studies Society. To all of those who have dialogued with me, critiqued my work, introduced new ideas and encouraged me to dig deeper, I am truly grateful.

From a movement perspective, I am particularly indebted to my co-researchers and comrades who undertook the collective visioning process with me, including Denise Alcantar, Nisreen Khashman, Federico Venturini, Di Bligh, Jean Halley, Mark Øvland, Skhumbuzo Mlibeni, Kirsten Kratz, Mohamed Mussa, Kathryn Tulip, Isla McLeod, Harris Akampurira, and the many others who have preferred to remain anonymous. It is your experience, commitment, solidarity and joy that has brought this book to life. And finally, to my father Peter York, for teaching me that the best politics is always grounded in community, and for everything else.

Part I

Locating (r)evolutionary love

Introduction

'In short, love is the great, solemn, I would almost say the only purpose of humanity'.

– Pierre-Joseph Proudhon[1]

My own introduction to political activism was via the direct-action network *Reclaim the Streets* (RTS) in the mid-1990s. RTS had emerged when *Earth First!* and the UK anti-roads movement met the burgeoning rave scene of the time, organising massive street parties which liberated public spaces to create temporary autonomous zones (TAZ) beyond state control. The carnival atmosphere of these actions enacted a spontaneous, autonomous and participatory politics that aimed to prefigure the free society that so many of us yearned for by 'rescuing communality from the dissection table of capitalism'.[2] And it was at one such street party on a sunny afternoon in a newly reclaimed Cowley Road in East Oxford, that something really beautiful happened. A local police officer who had been sent to intervene in our action had clearly succumbed to the sheer joy of it all and was moved to join us in dancing to the pulsating beats of Spiral Tribe.[3] Grinning from ear to ear and hugging his fellow ravers, at one point he even allowed one new Rastafarian friend to wear his 'wooden top' helmet as each waved their arms in the air reaching towards the heavens in sheer abandon. All this to the cheers of onlookers young and old who had gathered to watch, with many of them similarly moved to join us in this celebration of life. Eventually, after what seemed to be possibly the most fulfilling twenty minutes of this man's life, he was 'rescued' by his fellow officers and taken to safety, and one assumes an awkward debrief back at the station. The sound system was confiscated, crowds eventually dispersed and the Cowley Road returned to its traffic-filled, exhaust-fume-saturated normality.

But the question remained – what on earth had happened to this poor unfortunate officer of the law? What was this communal field co-constituted in the TAZ that had led to such a remarkable transformation of being? For me and my comrades who were there on the day there was no doubt – *the answer was love.* And we were by no means alone in this way of framing our struggle. Throughout history there have been many such examples of political actors revolutionising love to align with specific political and social ideals. And as we will discover in the course of this book, such a love continues to be a common embodied experience for many contemporary activists, materialising as political direct action, as long-term processes of struggle, and as a radical solidarity embedded in a Deep Commons. It is the experience of Jack at Ende Gelände, of Hassan on the streets in Syria, of Tom at the G20 protests in Toronto, of Maria and her permaculture community in Mexico, of Angelo and his comrades occupying squares in Brazil, of Lowanna and her sisters 'love bombing' the Tasmanian government, and of Dembe and his affinity group in Kampala. It is the empathic matrix of mirror neurons described by Frans De Waal, the experience of *O'on* or 'collective heart' that infuses Zapatista social reproduction in Chiapas, and the 'level of real love' that Abdullah Öcalan argues will be necessary for the construction of a free democratic society.

Unfortunately, when it comes to contemporary political theory more generally the subject of love most often evokes an embarrassed response with the topic suggesting a conservatism, a denial of politics and 'an aura of naïveté and sentimentality'.[4] As Robin Kelley argues: 'Freedom and love may be the most revolutionary ideas available to us, and yet as intellectuals, we have failed miserably to grapple with their political and analytical importance'.[5] Is it therefore possible to locate and define what it is we mean by love, and what it might mean for those of us in pursuit of a free society? And if so, is it possible to do so in an unapologetically political context? As a useful starting point, classical Greek philosophy isolated four distinct conceptions of love: *Éros, Storgē, Philía* and *Agápe*, each of which this book will argue can legitimately be considered as inherently political. Through this enquiry we will explore how both *éros* (desire/passion) and *storgē* (familial affection) have acutely divergent potentialities – the potential for abuse, inequality and domination or the potential to encourage alternative and liberatory forms of relationship beyond separateness and competition. Similarly, we will examine how *philía* (friendship/kinship) and *agápe* (charity/empathetic love for the many) at once offer the potential to act as a basis for building a radical solidarity or of being subverted to legitimise xenophobic nationalisms, patriotisms and fascisms. But while these four facets of love clearly possess liberatory potential in their own right, this book will argue that it is the *(r)evolutionary love* that we will proceed to examine that might prove the most politically transformative due to its catalytic relationship with each of them. In the process, the agency of such a love will be shown to offer a direct (and directable) causal effect on our multiple entangled relations, and to the extent to which they will lead to intimate or social relations of domination or liberation. We will explore how this radical interrelationality might thus serve as the basis for a co-emergent relational ethics of solidarity and care. And furthermore, how such an approach is uniquely anarchistic as it rejects the abstractions of more transcendent ethical forms, and the constitution of rigid norms, constraining rules and forms of coercion that are otherwise required for the maintenance of more universal ethical systems.

But before we commence our search for a free society it will be useful to first examine the etymology of this word *free* that we are using to define it. The word derives from the old English *freo* and Proto-Germanic *friaz* which mean 'not in bondage' and 'acting of one's own will'. Furthermore, and of great relevance to this enquiry, the source of these words can then be found in the root *fri* meaning 'love', developed through the Gothic *frijon* – 'to love'; the Old English *freod* – 'affection, friendship', and *friga* – 'love'; and the Old Norse *friðr* – 'love, friendship'. This historical evolution from 'love' to 'free' can be traced to the notion of 'beloved' being applied to the free members of one's clan.[6] Freedom then, in the original sense of the word, was clearly located in a sense of loving community. This was not only a *freedom from* certain conditions or oppressions, or a *freedom to* take certain actions, but a *freedom with* others – and a freedom grounded in love.

And one further clarification is required before we proceed, regarding the means with which love might then be animated in order to arrive at such freedom. Revolutionary and evolutionary theories of social change have commonly been considered as contradictory yet contingent parts of a 'slow march of progress', each leading to the other in a perpetual cycle of alternation. The book will question this perceived polarity and propose *(r)evolution* as an alternative model for radical social change. This should not be mistaken for a kind of tacit reformism, or a postponement of the revolutionary transformation the world is currently crying out for. (R)evolution – as it is formulated here – is more in line with Proudhon's concept of 'permanent revolution' which, unlike the Marxist-Trotskyist use of the term that maintains the need for a vanguard party seizing state control,[7] involves 'the people alone, acting upon themselves without intermediary'[8] in order to break the cycle of partial revolutions which are examined at length in Chapter 5 of this book. Consequently, we will explore how social reproduction is firmly grounded in loving-caring relations, and how such relations offer a stream of continuation from the old to the new – offering possibilities for averting the usual post-revolutionary vacuum in which the counterrevolution occurs and free society is repeatedly stolen from us. And so, as stressed by eco-activist Jack in the second part of the book, our struggles must remain dynamic or risk being 'in opposition to life and the dynamism of who we are'. For him, as for many of the other activists contributing to this enquiry, it is therefore essential that we remain in movement:

'an ongoing dance – grounded in the moment'. From this perspective, and as long argued by both anarchists and feminists, everyday life should no longer be considered as outside the political sphere, but as the very ground from which it springs – a (r)evolution of the here-and-now that will be explored at depth in later chapters.

Locating itself within a strong tradition of knowledge co-production between political activists and the academy, a process of *Collective Visioning* has grounded this book. It has involved a group process of intentionally generating a vision that is unapologetically utopian while remaining grounded in grassroots struggle – operationalising imagination as a productive power in the pursuit of new knowledge and praxis. Participants of this collective visioning process have included activists from South Africa, Mexico, *Trouwunna* (Tasmania, Australia), Ireland, UK, Syria, Uganda, Germany, Italy, Canada, the Netherlands, Turkey, USA and Jordan, with movement engagement including anti-capitalist and ecological activism, anarchist organising, Indigenous struggles, feminist activism, refugee solidarity work, food sovereignty projects, cooperatives and permaculture projects.

While not all of the activists participating in this collective visioning self-identified as Anarchist (with a capital A), the majority shared a common anarchist critique of contemporary governance and politics and a commitment to anarchistic forms of organising in opposition to the constantly evolving institutional structures of contemporary global capitalism: autonomy from the state; horizontalism and direct democracy; direct action; the occupation of public space as Temporary Autonomous Zones; a prefigurative politics; and the practice of mutual aid. And as we will discover, far from the negative stereotypes which have been inserted into the public psyche of 'bomb-throwing fanatics', 'eccentric utopians' or 'idle scoundrels',[9] this re-emergence and reimagining of anarchist praxis in recent decades has led to a vibrant, dynamic, effective and sustainable movement which challenges the hegemony of global capitalism, and even occasionally wins. From the New Left student movement of the late 1960s, the worldwide disarmament movement of the 1980s, the alter-globalisation movement of the late 1990s and early 2000s, the movement wave of 2011 which gave rise to the Arab Spring, Spanish Indignados and Occupy, through Indigenous-led struggles globally, and more recently from Rojava to Paris, Hong Kong to Algeria, Sudan to Beirut, and the worldwide environmental and racial justice movements – this wave of (r)evolutionary love continues to offer our greatest hope for countering the ravages of global capitalism and averting the ecological disaster we are careering towards, while simultaneously co-constituting free society in the here-and-now.

Resonating with and complementing this anarchistic impulse, the majority of activists involved in this collective vision have expressed a profound sense of connection to nature – an intimate entanglement with(in) a more-than-human plurality as opposed to more commonly held core beliefs relating to the separation of humans and the natural world. Such ways of seeing, thinking and feeling align with a contemporary posthumanist world-view[10] – that all bodies, human and non-human, come to being through the world's 'intra-activity', and that the very nature of life itself is one of intimate entanglement.[11] And furthermore, these entangled posthuman perspectives share a deep affinity with internationally shared Indigenous conceptions of what it is to be human: an inextricable interrelationality with the non-human world, a refusal of anthropocentrism, an acknowledgement of interactive ecologies shared by human and non-human beings, and a deeply process-oriented ontology[12] – a method for framing the world that can trace its origins back through multiple Indigenous traditions. And so, it is here where this book locates our struggle for a free society: in the entangled plurality that has emerged as a theme in this collective visioning process, through contemporary posthumanist enquiry, through anarchist theory and praxis before it, and through Indigenous ontologies over millennia, in our more-than-human psycho-socio-material relations – in the deep commons.

Outline of this book

This book is organised in two parts. Part I introduces us to the distinctive lineage of (r)evolutionary love this book explores, and then to the collective visioning process in which this particular work has been grounded. And Part II deals with the fruits of this collective vision – synergised and formulated into an ideological framework: Critique, Utopia and Praxis. It is in this second part of the book that the voices of the activists are brought to life.

Chapter 1 – 'The anarchy of love' – will first isolate and trace a distinct lineage of (r)evolutionary love that has acted to animate radical social transformation throughout history. Starting with the anarchists of the late nineteenth and early twentieth centuries, we will also follow their Marxist revolutionary cousins; feminist perspectives on love; the anti-colonial revolutionaries of the twentieth century; the civil rights activists of the 1960s; and in recent years the number of anarchist political philosophers and social movement theorists who have explored whether love can be utilised as a useful key concept for a new political theory of global revolution. Next, in order to further define the (r)evolutionary love this book explores, we will undertake a close analytical reading of the works of influential anarchist revolutionary and theorist Emma Goldman and autonomist theorist Michael Hardt, who have both pursued such a political concept of love. And through exploring themes of love as domination, love as transformation and love as freedom, we will examine the relevance and potentialities of this political force for contemporary ecological, anti-capitalist, feminist and anti-racist activists. We will explore how the disorienting of conventional political schemas and the expansive trajectory of their political imaginary prealign Goldman and Hardt with aspects of emerging work in posthumanism in which a number of scholars are starting to extend their thinking about love to include non-humans, the environment, technology and even matter itself – to which the chapter then turns. And it is further proposed that as we come to more fully understand the depths of our profoundly entangled interrelationality, it is anarchist thought that may well prove to be the political philosophy for our times. It is the willingness of anarchist theory and praxis to remain open to the dynamic and creative dialectical relationship between the apparent opposites of individuality and community, between the one and the whole, and without the reification or negation of either mode of being, that places it in a truly unique position.

Chapter 2 – 'Collective visioning: Utopia as process' – then briefly locates this enquiry within a strong tradition of knowledge co-production between political activists and the academy: from the workers' enquiries of the nineteenth century; experiments in direct democracy of the early twentieth century; the participatory research methods that emerged from the *campesino* movements of Africa and Latin America in the 1960s; Italy's *Operaismo* and Argentina's *Argentinazo*; and more recently the Zapatista-inspired *encuentros* and the dialogical spaces of the World Social Forum. We then outline the specific collective visioning approach used for this book and meet the participants themselves, exploring how the process works to reveal images of future worlds, and of the seeds of liberation already existing in the present. This method, as we will discover, utilises utopia *as process* – transitioning the functionality of utopia from noun to verb, and operationalising imagination as a productive power in the pursuit of new knowledge and praxis.

Moving to the second part of the book, Chapter 3 – 'The dystopian present' – will first look at Big Data Capitalism and the algorithmic conditions in which we find ourselves increasingly immersed, and the subsequent assault on free will, imagination and agency that we now collectively face. We will then examine the causes of our current ecological and climate emergency, exploring the relationship between this bewildering act of ecocide, the rampant materialism that is reified in contemporary society, and the consequent mental health epidemic gripping the planet. And as we draw closer to a wider discussion and analysis of (r)evolutionary love in the following chapters, we will revisit the theme of love as domination and the exploitative abusive relations, xenophobic nationalisms and patriotisms that it can be observed to manifest as. Finally, we will discuss how, if at all, we might begin to turn this tide in pursuit of free society. The chapter will argue that an ontology of separation causes love to manifest as domination – in the service of an imagined separate autonomous self. Conversely, and as we will explore in the remaining chapters, an ontology of entanglement and immanence potentiates the (r)evolutionary love this book pursues, manifesting as non-domination and in service of both the *I* and the *WE* – as intimately interrelational.

Grounded in themes emerging from the collective visioning process, Chapter 4 – 'The deep commons' – will then explore the conditions of empathic entanglement that act as the basis for societal formation, and the radical loving-caring praxes which underpin many contemporary struggles. And by extending popular conceptions of the commons to include these more-than-human psycho-socio-material relations, the deep commons will be proposed as a ground through which this (r)evolutionary love might circulate in order for new political (inter)subjectivities to manifest. This enquiry adopts the same philosophical starting point as previous green anarchisms, that is 'to rethink human society's sense of itself and its place in the wider ecology',[13] while taking great care to navigate a path that avoids both the potential anthropocentric bias of social ecology and the holism of deep ecology. The apparent binary tension between personal autonomy and social solidarity that exists in much of contemporary political/philosophical thought will be re-examined in light of these more-than-human loving entanglements, and Indigenous concepts of the deep commons will be considered as alternatives to our current colonial, capitalist and anthropocentric political imaginaries. The concept of degrowth will then be examined in pursuit of the temporal shift to a slower pace of life required to avert our impending ecological disaster.

But while the deep commons might offer a new lens though which to better understand both the nature of our current intertwined systems of oppression and their alternative as free ecological society, the question remains – what forms of praxis will take us to the latter? Rather than focusing merely on a rejection of the state and capitalism, activists involved in the collective visioning took as their starting point a more expansive view of the interdependent and entangled nature of their own and others multiple struggles. There exists a long political lineage of such theory and praxis within the anarchist tradition, encompassing a wide range of issues linking anti-capitalist, feminist, anti-racist and ecological politics intersectionally, and expanding our understanding of what constitutes social transformation – from merely abolishing hierarchical institutions alone, to a far more comprehensive redefinition of social patterns across all spheres of life. Thus, in Chapter 5 – 'Activating the Agapeic web' – we will first explore (r)evolutionary love as a radical solidarity – producing spontaneous mutual aid at times of rapid social change, and acting to establish affinity both in and across movement organisations. Next, we will examine how throughout history revolutionary movements have been co-opted by political parties in order to gain power for their own self-interest rather than completing the task of dismantling the institutions of state domination. The perceived antinomy of revolutionary and evolutionary theories of social change will then be questioned and the central concept of *(r)evolution* unpacked and proposed as an alternative model for radical social transformation. And drawing on contemporary anarchist debates, the temporal gap between current struggles and imagined futures is problematised, prefigurative praxes critiqued and a politics of immanence suggested in remedy. And finally, the question of how a free society might respond to the potential of violence and ongoing political contestation will be examined, arguing that (r)evolutionary love might offer the ethical/relational basis for the development of new processes of agonistic pluralism to augment consensus-based approaches.

Chapter 6 – 'The collective heart: Co-constituting free society' – argues that the agency of (r)evolutionary love thus offers a direct (and directable) causal effect on our multiple entangled relations, and the extent to which they will lead to intimate and social relations of domination or liberation. Strategically developing political praxes grounded in this love might therefore provide the basis upon which to co-constitute free society here-and-now – as an imaginative/responsive ongoing process rather than reverting to default capitalistic, patriarchal, racist or anthropocentric modes of reproduction, and thus provide a means of sustaining such a system in the absence of domination. But (many will undoubtedly ask) how realistic can such a profound reconfiguration actually be? And the answer, somewhat unsurprisingly given the sheer scale of struggle visible today, is that there are in fact many living, vibrant examples of such societal formations across the world right now which might inspire us. The chapter will first turn to the Zapatista revolution as one such example, and specifically the Indigenous concept of *O'on* or 'collective heart', examining its central role in the social reproduction of their communities and organisational structures. A critique of contemporary international relations theory and its reification of the state as sole political actor will follow. And finally, using the example of the extraordinary experiment in horizontal participatory democracy taking place in the Autonomous Administration of North and East Syria as a starting point, the deep commons will be proposed as a location in which to co-constitute the global 'community of communities' envisaged by generations of anarchist thinkers as a liberatory alternative to the current system.

Notes

1 Pierre-Joseph Proudhon, *Système des contradictions économiques ou Philosophie de la misère* (Paris: Garnier Frères, 1850), quotation trans. David Berry, 'Revolution as redemption: Daniel Guérin, religion and spirituality', in A. Christoyannopoulos and M.S. Adams (eds) *Essays in anarchism and religion: Volume III* (Stockholm: Stockholm University Press, 2020), p. 152.

2 Do Or Die, 'Reclaim the Streets!', *Do or Die – Voices from Earth First!* 6 (2003), 6.

3 Spiral Tribe is a musical and arts collective and free party sound system that organised parties, festivals and raves in the 1990s at a time when the UK government was enforcing legislation to eradicate the free festival and rave movement. See: https://sp23.org/about/ (accessed 10 May 2022).

4 Margaret E. Toye, 'Towards a poethics of love: Poststructuralist feminist ethics and literary creation'. *Feminist Theory* 11:1 (2010), 40.

5 Robin Kelley, *Freedom dreams: The black radical imagination* (Boston, MA: Beacon Press, 2003), p. 11.

6 See: www.etymonline.com/word/free (accessed 17 April 2022).

7 See: Karl Marx and Frederick Engels, 'Address of the central committee to the communist league', London, March 1850; and Leon Trotsky, *The permanent revolution*, 1931. Available online: www.marxists.org/archive/trotsky/1931/tpr/pr-index.htm (accessed 10 May 2022).

8 Pierre-Joseph Proudhon, *Toast to the revolution*, 1848, p. 9. Available online: https://libcom.org/files/pierre-joseph-proudhon-toast-to-the-revolution.pdf (accessed 15 May 2022).

9 Giorel Curran, *21st century dissent: Anarchism, anti-globalisation and environmentalism* (New York: Palgrave Macmillan, 2006), p. 2.

10 Rosi Braidotti, *The posthuman* (Cambridge: Polity Press, 2013, see chapter 'Post-anthropocentrism: Life beyond the species', pp. 55–104).

11 Karen Barad, 'Matter feels, converses, suffers, desires, yearns and remembers', in R. Dolphijn and I. Van der Tuin (eds) *New materialism: Interviews and cartographies* (Ann Arbor, MI: Open Humanities Press, 2012), p. 69.

12 Simone Bignall and Daryle Rigney, 'Indigeneity, posthumanism and nomadic thought: Transforming colonial ecologies', in R. Braidotti and S. Bignall (eds) *Posthuman ecologies: Complexity and process after Deleuze* (London: Rowman and Littlefield, 2019), p. 160.

13 Andy Price, 'Green anarchism', in C. Levy and M. Adams (eds) *The Palgrave handbook of anarchism* (Cham, Switzerland: Palgrave Macmillan, 2019), p. 287.

1

The anarchy of love

'Whether love last but one brief span of time or for eternity, it is the only
creative, inspiring, elevating basis for a new race, a new world'.
                                                            – Emma Goldman[1]

Populated by interconnecting organisations with a diverse array of
ideologies, methodologies, identities and cultural norms, there is a pressing
need for a framework of plurality within our current wave of ecological,
anti-capitalist, feminist and anti-racist activism which avoids the dominations and hierarchies of previous structures, resists co-option and subversion by neoliberal forces, maintains its constituent diversity, and yet allows
for the construction of a cohesive collective identity. Through analysing the
causes behind some three dozen revolutions in the Global South between
1910 and the present, John Foran speculates about the future of revolutions in an age of globalisation and argues that love is the emotion that
'most strongly underlies the vital force that impels many ordinary people
into extraordinary acts, across time and place'.[2] Such a love, Foran claims,
expresses hope and optimism, and might provide a constructive counterpoint to the powerful forces of domination. Although often omitted by
conventional political histories, there are many examples of activists who
have dared struggle to change the established order by revolutionising love
to align with specific political and social ideals. It is here where the lines
between the personal and the political blur, where we have seen glimpses of
potentiality for love as a radically transformative revolutionary force. And it
is here where we might discover that love has always performed an intimate
catalytic role within revolutionary politics.

Before we turn to the collective vision itself, it will be necessary for us to
first define the specific conception of love the book explores. This chapter will
therefore begin by isolating and tracing a distinct lineage of (r)evolutionary
love that has acted to animate radical social transformation throughout
history. Starting with the anarchists of the late nineteenth and early twentieth centuries, we will also engage with their Marxist revolutionary cousins;

feminist perspectives on love; the anti-colonial revolutionaries of the twentieth century; the civil rights activists of the 1960s; and in recent years the number of anarchist and autonomist political philosophers and social movement theorists who have explored whether love can be utilised as a useful key concept for a new political theory of global revolution. In order to further narrow the focus of our enquiry, a close reading of the works of anarchist revolutionary Emma Goldman and autonomist theorist Michael Hardt[3] will then be undertaken, and specifically their pursuit of such a love – drawing on, and making links with contemporary ideas of love as a political concept for radical social transformation in the twenty-first century. Following an exploration of their ideas we will turn to emerging work in posthumanism which further extends political thought around love to include non-humans and the environment. Through exploring themes of *love as domination*, *love as transformation*, *love as freedom* and *love beyond Anthropos*, we will examine the relevance and potentialities of such a political force for contemporary activism, arguing that as we come to more fully understand the depths of our profoundly entangled interrelationality, it is anarchist thought that may well prove to be the political philosophy for our times.

(R)evolutionary love: a radical lineage

Love has proved to be a prominent and recurring theme in the writings of many anarchist theorists and activists. Gustav Landauer claimed that love 'sets the world alight and sends sparks through our being', and that it is the 'deepest and most powerful way to understand the most precious that we have'.[4] And similarly Errico Malatesta claimed that anarchists 'seek the triumph of freedom and of love'.[5] He argued for love as a central motivating force not only in anarchism but for all those possessing an 'anarchist spirit' which aims at 'the good of all, freedom and justice for all, solidarity and love among the people'.[6] He asserted that such a spirit was not an exclusive characteristic of self-declared anarchists, but a central inspiration for 'all people who have a generous heart and an open mind'. Love similarly played a key role in the politics of Christian anarchists such as Leo Tolstoy, who embraced the precept to 'love your enemies' as a key political praxis and thus developed a clear, defined philosophy which he believed 'all have it within their power to fulfil'. Tolstoy's anarcho-pacifism and rejection of the state were grounded in this philosophy – that through love it was possible to 'make no distinction between one's own and other nations', and therefore to 'avoid the natural results of these distinctions, such as being at enmity with other nations, going to war, taking part in war, arming for war, etc.'.[7] From Tolstoy's perspective then, Christian teachings on love were quite literally 'outlawing patriotism'.[8] Similarly, Dorothy Day's political praxis consisted of 'love in action'.[9] For her a true revolutionary should 'become love' and must 'love beyond the state'.[10] At the heart of Day's political vision was a community created through love, and a love sustained by community. And the depth of her love led to an experience of profound interconnection with, and empathy towards, the multitude of other beings with whom she shared her world (a common experience for many contemporary activists to be explored later in this book):

> I was no longer a young girl, part of a radical movement seeking justice for the oppressed. I was the oppressed. I was that drug addict, screaming and tossing in her cell, beating her head against the wall. I was that shoplifter who for rebellion was sentenced to solitary … I was that mother whose child had been raped and slain. I was the mother who had borne the monster who had done it.[11]

In the first and second wave feminism of the nineteenth and twentieth centuries political theories of love tended to focus upon a critique of heterosexual romantic love relations within patriarchal societies,[12] and often in a fierce criticism of (state and church controlled) marriage as perpetuating gender inequality and masculine domination.[13] Alongside this critique, however, a number of anarcho-feminist activists and theorists also proposed love as a potential site for resistance to – and transformation of – patriarchal society itself.[14] Emma Goldman's concept of 'free love', for instance, called upon the revolutionaries of the time to 'ignite their inner desires'.[15] And it was her strong conviction that revolution and love must never be mutually exclusive that led to her defence of causes such as sexual freedom, birth control and marriage reform for which even many of her fellow anarchists derided her, and that contributed to her eventual deportation from the USA to Soviet Russia in 1919 and subsequent exile from Russia in 1921.[16] A contemporary of Goldman, Marxist revolutionary and Bolshevik Alexandra Kollantai (who played a leading role in the revolutionary struggles of the time and was a key participant in the formation of the early Union of Soviets, becoming the first head of the new Department of Social Welfare)[17] similarly found love to be a profoundly social and political emotion which was 'not in the least a private matter concerning only two loving persons' but possessed a uniting element 'valuable to the collective'.[18] Such positions argued the necessity of carrying out ideological struggle concerning the structure of gender and sexual relations in tandem with social and economic struggles, and were highly contentious for their time.

Even Marx proposed that love, in contrast to money, operates through proper exchanges: 'If we assume man to be man and his relation to the world to be a human one, then love can be exchanged only for love, trust for trust, and so on'.[19] Money on the other hand, he claimed, distorts such relations – exchanging 'every quality for every other quality and object, even if it is contradictory' – and thus undermines our ability to create relationships with each other and to form cohesive social bonds. Love, then, was positioned by Marx as providing a superior foundation for social organisation than money and current capitalist formations. But although, as the activist and philosopher Ewa Majewska argues,[20] this interest in love as expressed by Marx might work to undermine and possibly challenge the hegemony of monetary exchange (and thus point to an alternative to capitalism), there are, as Michael Hardt also points out,[21] limitations to Marx's considerations of love as merely a form of exchange, missing what might be the most important aspect of love as a political force – how it can transform us – as we will go on to discuss. In *Eros and Civilisation*, Herbert Marcuse worked to synthesise Marxist theory with the psychoanalytic theory of the time, and that of Sigmund Freud in particular.[22] Rather than positioning class struggle as the central means of liberation, however, he considered the liberation of spirit – of éros – as the true source of freedom. Turning Freud's thesis that 'civilised morality is the morality of repressed instincts' on its head, Marcuse argued that a mature civilisation will only be achieved by 'harmonizing instinctual freedom and order: liberated from the tyranny of repressive reason'.[23] And once freed, he argued, our instincts would then tend towards 'free and lasting existential relations' and generate a 'new reality principle'.[24] For Marcuse the domestication of sexuality and love in the form of possessive private relations had long acted to suppress our instinctual urge for freedom at a societal level. Thus a liberation of our instinctual desires, rather than leading to a 'society of sex maniacs' would allow for a 'transformation of the libido' that bridges the gap between the personal and social spheres previously maintained through such repression – nothing less than a complete societal transformation that releases 'the free play of individual needs and faculties'.[25] And also from the Marxist tradition, Erich Fromm took a similarly robust political position on love, claiming that 'the principle underlying capitalist society and the principle of love are incompatible'.[26] He argued that by necessity love is a 'marginal phenomenon' in our modern 'production-centred' and 'commodity greedy' societies, and that radical changes in our social structures will be necessary in order to change this.[27] Echoing Marcuse, he explained:

> Society must be organised in such a way that man's social, loving nature is not separate from his social existence, but becomes one with it. If it is true … that love is the only sane and satisfactory answer to the problem of human existence, then any society which excludes, relatively, the development of love, must in the long run perish of its own contradiction with the basic necessities of human nature.[28]

In the first half of the twentieth century, love also occupied a central role in the Indian independence movement, which like all modern revolutions had certainly suffered from internal flaws – not least its widespread acceptance of the caste system, with Gandhi himself accused of discrimination against the *Dalit* community.[29] At its height, however, the 'Gandhian revolutionary love'[30] which guided the Indian independence movement undoubtedly transformed social consciousness, social relations and power relations among the people of India. The independence movement's organisational structures were infused with a (r)evolutionary love, with the ashram communities allowing activists to prefigure and establish alternative social structures and ways of life before the end of British rule, and to experiment with loving practices prior to engaging in non-violent direct action.[31] And decades later, Marxist revolutionary and guerrilla leader Ernesto Che Guevara made a three-month trip to Africa to offer his knowledge and experience as a guerrilla to the ongoing conflict in the Congo. During this time, he urged his comrades to embrace such a love, claiming that 'the true revolutionary' was in fact guided by 'great feelings of love'.[32] In reading a little deeper, however, we notice a parallel desire to escape the limitations of what Guevara referred to as 'the level where ordinary people put their love into practice'.[33] And so the 'great feelings of love' he claimed are necessary for the true revolutionary appear to be firmly situated in the public domain. He thus defers the 'love practices' involved in affective and caring labour to the 'ordinary people', one assumes mainly women, in order to unlock the mobility and freedom required for 'genuine' revolutionary activity. Such a theory and practice of love fails to acknowledge the different subject positions held within a group, movement or society itself, not to mention the transformative potential inherent in such *ordinary* (or as we shall argue – (r)evolutionary) loving-caring practices, and is therefore incomplete and will be further interrogated in the following chapters.

In the 1960s and 1970s US civil rights movement, activists such as Ella Baker and Martin Luther King Jr. saw themselves as part of a 'beloved community' and aimed at a concept of social justice based in love and equality for all humans.[34] King asserted that a mistakenly bi-polar relationship between love and power, which identified love with a 'resignation of power' and power with a 'denial of love', had become accepted wisdom. He proceeded to remedy this misperception by arguing that power without love is 'reckless and abusive' and that love without power is 'sentimental and anaemic'.[35] King's (r)evolutionary love was by no means idealistic, however, and he consistently linked the spiritual revolution he called for to an analysis of the three evils he felt afflicted American society: 'the giant triplets of racism, extreme materialism, and militarism'.[36] And less than a decade after King's assassination the Combahee River Collective similarly positioned their black feminist project as evolving from 'a healthy love for ourselves, our sisters, and our community which allows us to continue our struggle and work'.[37] This emergence of love as a radical ethic and political methodology for black feminism in the 1970s served to lay the groundwork for coalition building in and across the movements of the time. Likewise, a central theme of the work of feminist theorist bell hooks has been the construction of an activist approach to social transformation that recognises the intersections between gender, race and class – which again imagines love as a powerful transformative political ethic. hooks is convinced that the realisation of such a love ethic can happen only as we relinquish our obsession with power and domination, and makes the argument that 'domination cannot exist in any social situation where a love ethic prevails'.[38]

Adopting a similarly expansive vision, Chela Sandoval's *Methodology of the Oppressed* aims to reinvent love as a political technology: 'a body of knowledges, arts, practices and procedures for re-forming the self and the world'.[39] Sandoval's postcolonial feminism positions love as central to a new decolonising theory and method for a new period of radical activism in pursuit of an 'internationalist, egalitarian, non-oppressive, socialist-feminist democracy'.[40] Carolyn Ureña further builds on Sandoval's work to theorise *decolonial love* as an ongoing political and ethical act, and one which poses a direct challenge to systems of power that perpetuate coloniality.[41] Colonial love, Ureña argues, is based on an imperialist, dualistic logic which fetishises the beloved object and participates in the oppression and subjugation of difference. Decolonial love by contrast is framed as originating from below and operates between those rendered *other* by hegemonic forces. She proposes that such a concept promotes love as an active, intersubjective process, and in so doing articulates an 'anti-hegemonic, anti-imperialist affect and attitude' that can guide the actions that work to dismantle oppressive regimes. It has been noted by Majewska that such work by feminists of colour is often depreciated for supposed lack of theoretical structure.[42] She asserts however that contrary to these opinions, the focus on subjectivity as central to these feminist theories has a great deal to offer critiques of capitalism. In full agreement, such a focus will be maintained throughout the course of this book.

And, in recent years, a growing number of anarchist and autonomist political philosophers and social movement theorists have similarly revisited the question of whether love can be utilised as a useful key concept for a new political theory of global revolution. This body of work exploring love as a catalyst for a deep and far-reaching transformation of contemporary society focuses on the long-term process of transforming power in our institutions and everyday lives. Jamie Heckert and Richard Cleminson for instance called for a queering of anarchism that includes practices of care of the self, care for each other, and care of the earth – all of which they describe as acts of 'revolutionary love'.[43] And Heckert later enquires: 'What political systems might we love? What politics might nurture our capacity to love: to care for ourselves and each other and to recognise our fundamental equality, dynamic interdependence and inherent beauty?'[44] Antonio Negri and Michael Hardt (and particularly Hardt, as we will explore in depth in the following sections) have similarly argued that love might form a 'social body' that is more powerful than individual bodies, constructing 'a new and common subjectivity'.[45] And building on this work, Richard Gilman-Opalsky has called for a 'communism of love' – arguing that our current capitalist forms of exchange value are unable to appreciate what human beings value the most – experiences and relationships of love.[46] What is thus envisioned by these theorists is a radically different type of (r)evolutionary movement not merely aiming at the seizure of political power through violent means, but, as Laurence Davis explains, with the 'liberation of imagination, desire and human creative potential' in our day-to-day lives, a (r)evolutionary practice which is 'patient, constructive, organic and open ended'.[47] Simultaneously theorising love as political and as praxis challenges the boundaries between private and public, between personal and social, and draws connections between the emotional and the political in non-binary ways, thus creating openings for the formation of new desires, new imaginaries and new forms of collective practice.

As we now turn to a close reading of the works of Goldman and Hardt and their ideas concerning such a love, it is clear that they possess materially distinctive subject positions, having inhabited profoundly different worlds. A working-class Jewish immigrant to the US from Eastern Europe in the late nineteenth century, Goldman's ideas grew out of and played a key role in developing the burgeoning anarchist movement in North America and Europe at the first part of the twentieth century. Very much grounded in direct action, she was involved in feminist struggles, the labour movement and anti-war campaigning. Arrest was such a common occurrence for Goldman that she carried a book with her to political rallies so that she would have something to read in jail.[48] Hardt however is a contemporary academic, professor of literature and political philosopher. He is best known for his collaboration with Antonio Negri on the *Empire* trilogy, which proved influential for the vibrant alter-globalisation movement at the turn of the millennium, and thus works within and contributes to the autonomist Marxist tradition of thought. Yet as we will explore, in spite of these vastly different cultural and historical contexts in which Goldman's and Hardt's ideas were developed, the confluence of their theories of love as a revolutionary force is quite remarkable. Both theorise the inextricable interrelationality of the personal and political, illuminating the processes through which love manifests as domination within intimate asymmetrical power relations, and as patriotisms, populisms, nationalisms, fascisms and religious fundamentalisms. Yet both also pursue a theory and praxis of love which aims to challenge and transform such dominations while simultaneously constituting the free society which is their ultimate shared political goal – as we will now explore.

Love as domination

Feminist theory has made a robust exploration of the multiple forms of unequal and exploitative exchanges that are possible within intimate and social relations in the name of love. From this perspective love is dangerous, love wounds, love perpetuates asymmetrical gendered power relations, and as such can be appropriated as a vehicle for domination. And so, as Eleanor Wilkinson suggests – any truly political understanding of love therefore requires us to first and foremost acknowledge the 'messiness, ambiguities, and unruliness of affective life'.[49]

Goldman was well known for her ruthless criticism of church- and state-sanctioned marriage throughout her life and works, in line with her anarchist principles. For her, such an institution perpetuates a 'perversion of love' rather than its 'ideal form'.[50] In the 1911 article 'Marriage and love', Goldman argues that conventional marriage is primarily an economic arrangement, an 'insurance pact' which differs from ordinary life insurance agreements only in it being 'more binding, more exacting'.[51] Leaving little doubt in her condemnation of the institution, she claims that Dante's motto on the gate of hell – 'Ye who enter here leave all hope behind' – applies equally to marriage, a pact which a woman must pay for with 'her name, her privacy, her self-respect, her very life, until death doth part'.[52] Goldman concedes that some marriages might be based purely on love and that in some cases love might continue throughout married life, but maintains that love does so regardless of marriage, not because of it. Rather than a union based on love, Goldman saw an institution in service of 'the only God of practical American life' which is 'can the man make a living? Can he support a wife?'[53] For this central reason, argues Goldman, the state and church approve of no other ideal because it is through institutionalised marriage that they can exert an optimum level of control over women, men and society. There have clearly been widespread advances in equal opportunity legislation in many countries over the past century which have (at least in limited ways) addressed much of the starker gender inequalities as described by Goldman. In seeing the beginnings of this emancipation in her own lifetime, however, vitalised through the rapid introduction of women to the industrial sector, Goldman remained cynical: 'Six million women wage workers; six million women, who have equal right with men to be exploited, to be robbed, to go on strike; aye, to starve even'.

Goldman's critique of marriage and love illuminated the inextricable interrelationality of the personal and the political. This theoretical achievement allowed her to reposition intimate asymmetrical power relations from a private matter dismissed by most revolutionary groups to a public concern worthy of political struggle.[54] Goldman was acutely aware of the distinct privileges and oppressions that both marriage and the emerging rights based equality offered to women from different classes, aligning women's social freedom with financial profit within a patriarchal, capitalist system.[55] As a woman from a working class, immigrant background, Goldman's indifference to the suffrage movement and commitment to intersectionality arose from an embodied, lived experience of multiple forms of domination, and her passionate (r)evolutionary love armed her with a counterforce unconstrained by patriarchal or capitalist power. And such a counterforce might offer inspiration for a coherent, radical political praxis for contemporary activists who likewise find themselves marginalised in modern liberal societies within which freedom, as in Goldman's time, remains aligned to capital and intimately relational to class, gender and race.

Hardt similarly critiques the 'corruption' of romantic love which he sees as a process of 'becoming the same' requiring the couple to 'merge into unity'.[56] He describes how the contemporary dominant notion of romantic love requires adherence to a mandatory sequence of 'couple – marriage – family', closing the couple into a unit that corrupts the common. This 'family love', argues Hardt, applies pressure to love only those closest to you within the family, and requires the exclusion or subordination of those who fall outside.[57] Hardt is further concerned about how such a familial logic is reproduced through political organisation and exclusive social bonding, leading to manifestations of patriotism and 'love of nation'.[58] Hardt fiercely rejects such patriotism, or love of nation/race, as a corrupt, identitarian form of love.[59] Such patriotic love attempts to push aside difference and multiplicity to form a united national people and a national identity, in turn bringing into being *the other*. From this perspective populisms, nationalisms, fascisms and religious fundamentalisms are not so much based on hatred, as might commonly be understood, but on a 'horribly corrupted form of identitarian love'. Consequently, it has now become increasingly common for right-wing fascist hate groups to rebrand themselves as organisations of love, claiming to act out of love for their own kind and for the nation, rather than out of hatred for strangers and others.[60] And we can see in contemporary politics globally how such an appropriation of love as a justification for hate can (and frequently does) frame those who oppose such groups (such as anti-fascist, anti-racist, anti-war activists) as working against the nation, and consequently against love.

Goldman similarly saw patriotism as a 'menace to liberty' and 'the last resort of scoundrels'.[61] She described in detail how the 'love of one's birthplace' is co-opted and subverted, how this 'superstition' is created and maintained through a 'network of lies and falsehoods'. She argued that state powers had for centuries been engaged in 'enslaving the masses'[62] and had in the process made a thorough study of the social psychology of patriotism, becoming skilled in redirecting strong feelings arising in relation to internal state oppression towards patriotic fervour and obedience. On the logic of patriotism, Goldman ridiculed the 'peace-loving people' who claim to hate bloodshed and are opposed to violence, yet in the name of love of country 'go into spasms of joy over the possibility of projecting dynamite bombs from flying machines upon helpless citizens'.[63] This 'patriotic lie', Goldman argued, must be undermined in order for a true internationalism to exist, and for the 'truly free society' she so yearned for to finally emerge.[64]

Love as transformation

The works of both Goldman and Hardt repeatedly highlight the seeming antinomies of personal/political, individual/communal, and of a (r)evolutionary love grounded in existing struggles while simultaneously envisioning a utopian beyond – positions often met with significant criticism. Goldman's critique of marriage and her scandalous public advocacy of free love meant that her own intimate life commanded a great deal of attention, both then and now.[65] A number of feminist scholars have criticised Goldman's lack of consistency between her anarchist ideals of personal freedom in intimate relations and her own apparent longing for loving and stable relationships with men, expressing disappointment in their feminist role model. Candace Falk sees in Goldman a 'pattern of denial'[66] which meant that she could not acknowledge 'how deeply conflicted she felt about many of her most adamant public stands', and that it was her 'contradictory longing for the security of husband, children, and a home', while simultaneously rejecting the forms in which such stability was commonly manifested, that kept her from being able to work honestly on a popular revision of the article 'Marriage and love'.[67] Alice Wexler similarly laments the gap between Goldman's private life and 'her legend'.[68]

It seems curious however that it surprises such scholars that Goldman might experience the desires, obsessions, insecurities, fragilities and complexities that the vast majority of us are similarly called upon to navigate as emotional-sexual-social human beings. Goldman describes vividly her difficulty in managing the tensions between her unyielding commitment to revolutionary politics and her basic human need for intimate personal relationship in her autobiography *Living My Life*. Reflecting on her relationship with fellow anarchist and lover Edward Brady she conceded that the personal would always play a dominant part in her life: 'I was not hewn of one piece like Sasha[69] or other heroic figures. I had long realized that I was woven of many skeins, conflicting in shade and texture. To the end of my days, I shall be torn between the yearning for a personal life and the need of giving all to my ideal'.[70] It is particularly striking however that although Hardt's work receives significant criticism, which we will address later in this section, as a man his personal life and the tensions between it and his writings have not been scrutinised in the same way as Goldman's. In fact, a review of his work has been unable to discover any such critique. And so, rather than a betrayal of her anarcho-feminist principles, such apparent contradictions might be more fairly reframed as evidence of Goldman's dual commitment to imagining new worlds while being grounded in the existing one – thus anchoring her 'radical imagination' in 'material, yet extraordinary experience'.[71]

Such criticisms are also in danger of obscuring Goldman's wider political vision of the transformative power of love. Although she made a sustained, fierce critique of the institution of (state/church-controlled) marriage, her core interest was in the transformation of intimate relationships rather than their eradication. In her 1896 essay 'Anarchy and the sex question' she continues to rail against the 'unnatural unions which are not hallowed by love' and the 'chain which has been put around their necks by the law and Church'.[72] Goldman then proceeds however to present 'an anarchist's dream' of what a free marriage could be, one in which 'each will love and esteem each other, and will help in working not only for their own welfare, but, being happy themselves, they will desire also the universal happiness of humanity'.[73] Goldman's vision of free love was not as Rochelle Gurstein describes, aligned to the 'sexual realism – anaemic and cynical – of advertising and pornography',[74] but a free love which exhorted people to 'live in the open air'. She imagined an anarchist love which extended far beyond (but not excluding) the family, a love which informed the construction of a free and equal society, by free individuals.

Goldman has similarly faced criticism for her perceived silence on the subject of racial oppression.[75] Yet in spite of this, it remains relatively simple to find numerous examples of her addressing the oppression of African Americans through her personal letters, essays and the journals she published.[76] Rather than overlooking racial oppression, as such critics have claimed, she positioned violence against African Americans as part of the wider violence of capitalism against workers.[77] And so for Goldman, it was global anarchism rather than the struggle for legal reform that would act as the 'great liberator of man from the phantoms that have held him captive',[78] and, indeed, for her only love offered the 'creative, inspiring, elevating basis for a new race, a new world'.[79] There are of course limitations to Goldman's race analysis and her move to reduce such oppressions to class oppression – as the monumental (yet strikingly incomplete) transformations fought for and won by the US civil rights movement demonstrate, but we might also unpick potential insights for contemporary politics, and particularly the limits of liberalism. Goldman consistently rejected legal reforms which failed to address the systemic inequalities produced through capitalism and the state. While there have been widespread and welcome advances in equal opportunity/affirmative action legislation concerning race and gender, there has not, and likely never will be, similar legislation regarding class – which remains inextricably linked to both.[80] Chris Rossdale contends that we are 'more desiring of domination' than we might wish to acknowledge, and suggests that through reading Goldman we might develop a radical politics which truly seeks to 'unsettle our endless complicity in domination' and recognising that this task is never fully complete, a struggle that we must 'dance to death'.[81] In the pursuit of a truly (r)evolutionary race, gender *and* class liberation, the concept of love offered by Goldman might offer both the scale of vision required to disorient conventional political schemas and the frame within which a radical reimagining of society might occur.

Hardt's theoretical ideas around the *corruption* of love through a process of 'becoming the same' have also received significant criticism from contemporary feminist scholars who argue that they work to uphold dominant scripts of masculine mobility and freedom. Such a script positions the home and intimate sphere (and by association, women) as confining men and holding them back from 'real' political action.[82] As Ann Ferguson reminds us, the tensions and contradictions between love relations as experienced by individuals, couples, parents and wider social groups in our hegemonic racist capitalist patriarchy clearly persist,[83] and therefore from this perspective Hardt's multitude will tend not to be women with young children, sick relatives or elders to care for. Furthermore, Rosemary Hennessy contends that Hardt's notion of a liberating biopolitics obscures the unmet need that capitalism produces and its relationship to political agency.[84] Arriving at a partial degree of alignment with Hardt, however, Hennessy subsequently proposes that love might act as the ground for a praxis that transforms such unmet need into political action – but as a praxis *grounded in* rather than *breaking free* of the loving-caring relations which fundamentally co-constitute society on a daily basis. And this book agrees that such a relocation of *where* liberation might ultimately be achieved is of central importance. In fact, this dichotomy between the immanence of traditionally feminine labours and the apparent opportunity for transcendence found in traditionally male activities, has been a continued focus for feminist theorists from De Beauvoir's *Second Sex* through to contemporary debates. De Beauvoir very clearly framed immanence and transcendence respectively as passive and active modes of being, with women's liberation equated with the realisation of such transcendence: 'towards the totality of the universe and the infinity of the future'.[85] A number of feminist theorists have critiqued this approach, however, and pointed to a masculinist bias implicit in this formulation, with the pitting of immanence against transcendence disclosing a glorification of traditional male activities and consequently a denigration of traditionally female labours as unproductive.[86] Part II of this book will thus argue at some depth for liberation to be realised *through* a politics of immanence and not by somehow escaping it.

Without doubt, social constructionism has performed a central and important role in feminist theory, highlighting capitalism and patriarchy as crucial for understanding women's oppression, and challenging essentialist and determinist claims concerning static or inescapable roles of women in society. However, by adopting a social constructionist approach without questioning its inherent mechanistic understanding of matter as both passive and separable, Rachel Tillman argues that some forms of feminism have 'refused nature', rather than 'reconceptualising it' – perpetuating a Cartesian subject/object divide and attempting to subsume nature into culture.[87] Many contemporary scholars in the posthumanities have therefore proposed a *new materiality* in which the relationship between humans, other agents and material reality is framed as one of intra-action, as opposed to interaction.[88] This shift in perspective reframes the individual from a sovereign and separable unit to a contingent, profoundly entangled set of relationalities – offering potential for the co-constitution of political agency through the formation of new subjectivities and new intersubjectivities. And such a dynamism is generative not merely in the sense of bringing new objects into the world but in 'bringing forth new worlds', of engaging in 'an ongoing reconfiguring of the world'.[89] Rosi Braidotti – a feminist theorist and leading figure in the new posthumanities – in fact positions herself alongside Hardt as part of a community of Spinozist scholars working on 'the politics of life itself as a relentlessly generative force', requiring an 'interrogation of the shifting interrelations between human and nonhuman forces'.[90] This is of course not to claim that such a political conceptualisation of love could not be used to mask issues of power and domination,[91] because clearly it could. But I would suggest that in this instance Hardt might be read not as seeking to negate current social relations of domination, but as attempting to 'discover and live' a love which creates 'spaces of liberation' which have the power to co-create alternatives to capitalist and patriarchal society.[92]

Through challenging the anthropocentric bias of contemporary political thought, the emergence of posthumanism therefore presents exciting opportunities for a reimagining of the frame within which radical social transformation might occur. However, as Lauren Berlant contends – a 'properly transformational' political concept of love will require the courage to take a leap into a project of better relationality that fully acknowledges the unpredictable part of love's various temporalities.[93] Such a project will require us to open spaces for really dealing with the discomfort of the radical contingency that a genuine democracy will demand. And given the (not unfounded) criticism that there has been a distinct tendency to privilege the thought of 'white, male, universalizing philosophers'[94] at the expense of works located in particular gendered, racialised and socially situated relationships, it is therefore important for this enquiry to make absolutely clear the necessity at the heart of such a reimagining for further theorisation of praxes which: (1) ensure access to, and the doing of loving-caring labours are equally shared and distributed; that (2) dismantle structures and practices of domination, inequality and abuse (of human and more-than-human); and that (3) promote positive gender, class and ethnic relations, extending the resultant affective field to a care and respect for more-than-human beings and our shared world.

Contemporary identity projects based on class, race, gender and sexuality, warns Hardt, can also operate on a conception of sameness and unification, expelling differences in the interest of 'what unites'.[95] Forms of resistance that reclaim and affirm identities which have become the focus of oppression have been – and continue to be – necessary and effective forms of struggle, and it is therefore important for us to be alert in avoiding any critique of 'love of the same' becoming reactionary and exclusionary of those for whom identity politics has offered a lifeline.[96] Yet Hardt once again, like Goldman before him, sets sight on a longer-term goal in the pursuit of freedom, which is to 'abolish the very identifications on which oppressive social hierarchies are built'.[97] In analysing the complexities of identity politics within feminist activism for instance, Agatha Beins uses the term 'radical other' to describe the increasing self-representation of people involved in revolutionary movements in the Global South and notes how the subsequent racial politics within feminist groups has provided a language and imagery symbolising a wider revolutionary movement.[98] Taking a contemporary socialist-feminist perspective, Ferguson agrees that the solidarity required to fight sexism cannot just be between women and women, but must extend to people of all genders and sexualities fighting capitalism, racism, religious phobism and other forms of ethnicism, as well as heterosexism.[99] Intersectionality thus provides a useful analytical approach to understanding how an experience of domination or oppression is dependent on one's positionality. But as Jennifer Nash argues, even intersectionality is inextricably linked to the production and maintenance of identity categories.[100] Identity politics and intersectionality thus serve to fix us to the present, and simply 'changing the political grammar of our contemporary political moment' will not remove us from 'the script that is always already in place'.[101] Rather than sticking to this script, Nash argues that as practitioners of 'love politics' we should collectively dream of an as yet unwritten future, a world 'ordered by love, by a radical embrace of difference, by a set of subjects who work on/against themselves to work for each other'. Such a vision does not negate the numerous ways in which structures of domination continue to act upon individuals and groups, rather it is a rational, critical response to the 'violence of the ordinary' and the sheer persistence of inequality that urgently calls for a 'politics of the visionary'.[102]

Contemporary activism, with its tendency to favour forms of praxis that are oppositional rather than creatively propositional, might well learn from Goldman and Hardt's theoretical offerings. Their (r)evolutionary love, through illuminating the inextricable interrelationality of individual and public affect, aims at transforming the political subjectivities and intersubjectivities of women and men and in so doing creating revolutionary subjects. Clare Hemmings describes Goldman's counter-politics as a place of 'intense feeling and reimagined relationships' and a 'space for exemplary joy against the odds'.[103] Viewed in this way, the affective processes upon/between individual or social bodies might act as a vehicle for a (r)evolutionary love to both transform domination relations and constitute free society simultaneously. Work I facilitated in South Africa concerning transformative education and masculinities indicated similar value to love as a lens through which to understand and transform the processes that reproduce domination while simultaneously providing the frame, motivation and energy required for (r)evolutionary social change.[104] We found that through introducing the concept of love (in this case via the Southern African concept of Ubuntu)[105] as a habit of mind, at a level of functioning where moral consciousness, social norms and world view are produced, substantial changes in the subjectivities and intersubjectivities of participants were experienced. Further, due to the emphasis on love and solidarity within the Ubuntu concept, newly formed attitudes, beliefs and behaviours reflected these values, allowing culturally congruent transformation to occur which promoted radical and nonviolent social change, and significant reframing of schemas concerning patriarchy, power and violence.

Love as freedom

The convergence of Goldman and Hardt's ideas of love as a political concept can be traced to a wider alignment of their political positions conforming to an anarchist (r)evolutionary narrative which is anti-capitalist and transcends party and state. Goldman envisions her (r)evolutionary love as the 'creative, inspiring, elevating basis for a new race, a new world'.[106] Throughout her numerous defeats at the hand of the state, her imprisonment and eventual exile, Goldman consistently, patiently and with an unyielding zeal found the energy to resist and rebel against domination. And this was perhaps her greatest act of (and victory in the name of) love. In a 1931 letter to Alexander Berkman, she writes how: 'the still voice in me will not be silenced, the voice which wants to cry out against the wretchedness and injustice in the world'.[107] At the core of Goldman's anarchist politics was an unwavering belief that if the world was ever to give birth to a society free from class, gender or race-based forms of systemic inequality, having moved beyond domination and oppression, that 'love will be the parent'.[108]

In alignment, Hardt's revolutionary love is the element that animates all other theoretical elements of his political theories, the *multitude* of the poor, the social productivity of *biopolitical labour*, and the *exodus* from capitalist command, into one coherent project.[109] Such a love remains beyond the control of capital, refuses to be privatised and is inherently open to all, clearly contradicting capitalist values which reduce all things to profits.[110] He pursues a love which serves as the 'central, constitutive mode and motor of politics', an essential (and greatly under-theorised) concept for contemporary political thought.[111] For him, this (r)evolutionary love is the 'event that arrives from the outside and breaks time in two',[112] shattering the structures of this world and creating 'a new world'. In relation to political struggle Hardt rejects a reason/emotion opposition, arguing that reason cannot be devoid from passions and affects,[113] and, like Goldman and her anarchist contemporaries, he positions solidarity, caring for others and cooperation as central human survival mechanisms. He contends that when we band together in social solidarity, we form a 'social body' that is more powerful than individual bodies, constructing 'a new and common subjectivity'.[114] Hardt's (r)evolutionary love produces affective networks, schemes of cooperation and social subjectivities. Rather than being spontaneous or passive as it is often presented, Hardt proposes love to be 'an action, a biopolitical event, planned and realised in common'. He takes a Spinozan perspective of love as an ontological event which marks a rupture with existing being to create new being, a production of the common that 'constantly aims upward', a creative expansion with ever more power, culminating in 'the love of nature as a whole, the common in its most expansive figure'. In what can only be described as an anarchistic turn, Hardt's common thus refuses all external authority, with society organised collectively – 'an orchestra with no conductor'.[115]

Similarly for Goldman, love is the revolutionary force she holds above all others in her pursuit of a free society: 'Love, the strongest and deepest element in all life, the harbinger of hope, of joy, of ecstasy; love, the defier of all laws, of all conventions; love, the most powerful moulder of human destiny'.[116] She remarks on the notion of free love and questions if love could be anything other, claiming it can 'dwell in no other atmosphere'. Goldman understands that such a love is revolutionary because it remains elusive to capitalist and patriarchal control. Reflecting on the challenge presented to capitalism by such a love she remarks how 'all the millions in the world have failed to buy love',[117] and how love is 'the element that would forego all the wealth of money and power and live in its own world of untrammelled human expression'.[118] She perceives a similar relationship between love and military oppression, noting how 'man has conquered whole nations, but all the power on earth has been unable to subdue love'.[119] She also provides a taste of the potentiality of love utilised as a dual power strategy, claiming that 'all the laws on the statutes, all the courts in the universe, cannot tear it from the soil, once love has taken root'.

Just as Goldman had illuminated the inextricable interrelationality between the personal and the political in order to transform the political subjectivities and intersubjectivities of women and men, and in so doing created revolutionary subjects, Hardt similarly realises that love 'composes singularities' not in unity but as a 'network of social relations'.[120] Bringing together these two faces of love – 'the constitution of the common and the composition of singularities' argues Hardt, is the central challenge for understanding love as a political act. Using the example of the Gezi encampment at the centre of the 2013 wave of demonstrations and civil unrest in Turkey, he describes how many of the activists involved had experienced this protest as love – as a transformative encounter.[121] Hardt claims that this transformative nature of love is central when considering love as a political concept. More than merely recognising solidarity and forming a coalition of the same, love transforms, love creates something new. In unity, through examining events such as the Arab Spring, Occupy Movement and New Left, Srećko Horvat suggests that we explore what connects these events in a deeper sense, which he also proposes to be love:

> What connects them, more than anything, is something that can't be reduced to pure facts. What can't be reduced is this feeling of presence beyond classification or definitions; a presence of submergence; the feeling that you are completely alone but not abandoned, that you are more alone and unique than

ever before, but more connected with a multitude than ever as well, in the very same moment. And this feeling can be described as love. Revolution is love if it wants to be worthy of its name.[122]

This apparent paradox concerning feelings of heightened individuality *and* solidarity during moments of revolutionary rupture, animated by a spirit of love, are further examined in the next section through the entangled empathy in which identity and agency are co-constituted by our social and material entanglements across multiple interrelations. And consequently, a deeper analysis of the seeming antinomies of personal/political, individual/ communal, and of a (r)evolutionary love grounded in existing struggles while simultaneously envisioning a utopian beyond, will form a central aspect of the final chapters of this book.

George Katsiaficas' work on developing the concept of the 'Eros Effect' through a deep analysis of revolutionary events (from the global revolutions of 1968 through to the Occupy Movement and Arab Spring) concludes that the 'activation' of such events are based more upon an inherent feeling of connection with others and an instinctual 'love for freedom' than with the specific economic or political conditions they oppose.[123] When this 'Eros Effect' is activated, their 'love for' and 'solidarity with' each other suddenly replace previously dominant values and norms – cooperation replaces competition, equality replaces hierarchy and 'power gives way to truth'. But (as Katsiaficas enquires) can we make ourselves fall in love? Can we simply will ourselves to remain in love? Hardt pursues these same questions and concludes that such transformative events will not simply repeat themselves. He does suggest, however, that we can learn from such events, from the transformative power of love, and create habits which prolong or reproduce such encounters. New political constitutions of this kind will not be generated using conventional political logic. Neither 'we the people' nor any singular identity can act as founder, for such a politics does not aim at unity.[124] For Hardt, a political constitution arising through and grounded in a (r)evolutionary love must generate encounters between different social multiplicities, producing new plural relationships. And in reframing the conventional genesis of political constitution from unity to multiplicity, from fixed structure to dynamic process, Hardt's (r)evolutionary love manages (theoretically at least) to prolong and extend the force of the revolutionary event to form and repeatedly transform social and political institutions, translating the 'force of the event' into a 'temporal process'.[125]

Hardt's (r)evolutionary love is not a unifying force aimed at some kind of love monoculture – a love year zero. Like Goldman he envisions free individuals living in cooperative social relations and in so doing constituting the common, the free society. In this way, love is not anti-political by ignoring the differences necessary for political contestation. Love could function as an 'antagonistic engagement of differences that form stable bonds' and which remain based on multiplicity.[126] Of course, any political realist worth their salt would argue that such a society is as impossible now as it was in the time of Goldman. Through identifying the so called 'corrupt' forms of love, however, Hardt brings into question the primacy of competition as the core driver of human nature in favour of love, solidarity, caring for others and cooperation – human traits long held by anarchist and feminist theorists as the key mechanisms for human survival and prosperity. And so, if, as many Social Darwinists might claim, self-centred competition is truly the primary human drive, then we would indeed need to yield to domination in order to restrain our fundamental human natures. Positioning love as primary however suggests that it holds the power to combat such corruptions, and therefore a (r)evolutionary love has no need to 'accept the rule of a lesser evil'.[127] Hardt cautions that we should not imagine that we can defeat the forces of domination once and for all, and clearly such 'corruptions' of love will continue long into the future, but this does offer great optimism for political contestation and the struggle for radical social change. Like Goldman before him, Hardt is ultimately interested in *what human nature can become*. If evil, as he contends, is secondary to love, then 'the battle is ours to fight and win'.

Love beyond Anthropos

The (r)evolutionary love of both Goldman and Hardt succeeds in displacing the realist notion of sovereignty at either the individual or social level, making clear the intimate relationality of social formation. This disorienting of conventional political schemas and the expansive trajectory of their political imaginary prealign Goldman and Hardt with some of the emerging theoretical work in posthumanism in which a number of scholars are starting to extend their thinking about love to include non-humans, the environment, technology and even matter itself – challenging the anthropocentric bias of contemporary political thought.

Posthumanism positions the (human) subject as fully immersed in a network of non-human relations.[128] This emerging field calls for a 'love of the world'[129] leading to an ethics of 'political cohabitation' grounded in a respect for and responsibility towards our more-than-human plurality. Such a 'nontotalising, nonhomogenising earth ethics'[130] calls upon us to embrace our shared life on this planet with a multitude of others. The responsibility to engender response, or facilitate the ability to respond, in others and the

environment, is the primary obligation of this new ethics. Our usual separation of epistemology from ontology assumes an inherent difference between
human and non-human, subject and object, mind and body, matter and
discourse. In remedy, Barad proposes the use of an 'onto-epistem-ology' –
as a better way to think through how we understand specific intra-actions
to matter.[131] The Anthropocene has coincided with an era of high technological mediation which challenges anthropocentrism from within.[132] This
decentring of Anthropos challenges the separation of *bios* (life as the prerog-
ative of humans), from *zoe* (the life of non-human entities). What has come
to the fore instead is 'a nature-culture continuum'[133] which reconceptualises
the self as embodied, embedded, relational and extended. Our frame of reference therefore becomes the world, in all its 'open-ended, interrelational,
transnational, multisexed, and transspecies flows of becoming'.[134] And in
relation to this current period of crises, the more than human interrelationality being described by these theorists offers a frame within which a
(r)evolutionary love might work to animate the scale of activism necessary
to avert our imminent anthropogenic ecocide.

This emerging field explores how all bodies, human and non-human,
come to matter through the world's 'intra-activity' and concludes that the
very nature of materiality itself is one of entanglement.[135] From this perspective what we commonly take to be individual entities are not 'separate
determinately bounded and propertied objects', but rather are (entangled
parts of) phenomena that extend across time and space.[136] Ethics therefore
shifts focus from finding the correct response to an externalised other to an
obligation to be responsive to the other, who is not entirely separate from
what we call the self. In pursuit of a (r)evolutionary love, such an entangled
empathy[137] presents a robust relational framework through which identity
and agency are co-constituted by our social and material entanglements,
with our individual subjectivities forming as an expression of entanglements
in multiple relations across 'space, species, and substance'.[138] We therefore
care about others because they are fundamentally part of our own agency.
An example of this empathic entanglement can be seen through the story
of environmental activist Julia Butterfly Hill who in the late 1990s spent
two years living in a redwood tree she named *Luna*. Her goal was to save it
from being cut down by a logging company. She succeeded in saving both
Luna and a surrounding three-acre swath of trees, becoming an inspiring
symbol of environmental direct action in the process. She later reflected on
her motivation for taking this action and on what had sustained her through
the two-year period:

> I realized I didn't climb the tree because I was angry at the corporations and the
> government; I climbed the tree because when I fell in love with the redwoods,

I fell in love with the world. So, it is my feeling of connection that drives me, instead of my anger and feelings of being disconnected.[139]

There is however a danger that the alleged *newness* of this theoretical work might mask the fact that many Indigenous peoples have never forgotten the entanglement of human and non-human beings, largely denied in Western post-enlightenment thought. Kim TallBear explains how within many Indigenous ontologies even objects and forces such as stones, thunder and stars are considered to be 'sentient and knowing persons' thus extending the frame of what is living (and consequently what might be loved) far beyond the human.[140] Such a radical solidarity is congruent with the many theorists and activists throughout history who have revolutionised love to align with their pursuit of freedom. This expansive, creative, disorienting (r)evolutionary love that is emerging through posthumanism and entanglement theory is – we might argue – the very same force that animated Goldman's radical politics a century ago. And so, in this post-neoliberal era of increasing authoritarianism, xenophobic nationalisms and ecological collapse, finding ways to fulfil the promise of a political theory and praxis grounded in (r)evolutionary love constitutes a pressing political project for all of us engaged in authentic contemporary struggles for radical social change.

Of course, on the face of it such a profound state of entanglement might present a terrifying prospect for many. As we have already examined, certain feminist debates have taken a far more critical view of entangled relations, with the immanent nature of traditionally feminine labours serving as a prison that in turn withholds the possibility of transcendence and liberation. From this perspective the radically entangled nature of being that the post-humanities direct us towards could clearly be seen as highly problematic. But perhaps counterintuitively this book argues that freedom can (in fact must) be realised *through* immanence and not by somehow escaping it. And it is at this point where the limitations of concept and language prove particularly challenging. Readers will note that throughout this enquiry I refer to this state of contingent relationality by using a number of terms: entanglement, co-emergence, immanence and the deep commons, among others. This might of course disclose a lack of literary dexterity or philosophical sophistication on the part of the author, but I am by no means alone in struggling to find a suitable signifier for that which seems to remain ultimately unnameable. Joel Kovel, for instance, considered to be a founder of eco-socialism, spoke of the 'plasma of being' – a state in which there is no real separation between *things* – only one 'single, endlessly perturbed, endlessly becoming body'.[141] At the level of this plasma of being there is therefore no differentiation between subject and object. Yet paradoxically, as Kovel points out, a being who was identical with all other beings would logically be 'no being at all'.[142] Resonating with this paradox, Timothy Morton's work on *The Mesh* finds a similarly perplexing contradiction: 'At the DNA level, the whole biosphere is highly permeable and boundaryless ... And yet we have bodies with arms, legs, and so on, and every day we see all kinds of life-forms floating and scuttling around, as if they were independent'.[143]

But it is in the *Mūlamadhyamakakārikā* (fundamental verses on the middle way), a text written in the second century CE by the Buddhist philosopher and dialectician Nāgārjuna that we might perhaps find the most accomplished analysis of this existential conundrum. According to Nāgārjuna, no phenomena (including human phenomena) exist independently – and thus all are *empty* of intrinsic existence. For as he explains: 'you are not the same as or different from conditions on which you depend. You are neither severed from nor forever fused with them'.[144] All phenomena, he therefore argues, originate in dependence on all other phenomena. And it is the harmony of this empty nature of things and the co-emergence of all phenomena that illuminates a mode of being which eschews both essentialism and nihilism. Nāgārjuna argues that such existential insight is an essential component in our search for freedom and that our liberation ultimately hinges on two kinds of truth: 'Partial truths of the world, and truths which are sublime. Without knowing how they differ, you cannot know the deep; without relying on conventions, you cannot disclose the sublime; without intuiting the sublime, you cannot experience freedom'.[145] His vision is thus one of uncompromising immanence. But for Nāgārjuna, rather than this absence of intrinsic existence resulting in a lack of meaning or agency, it signifies the vibrant presence of transformative potentiality and freedom in every moment. It positions freedom squarely as an integral aspect of the present.

As modern science begins to catch up with the insights Nāgārjuna articulated nearly two millennia ago, and as we come to more fully understand the depths of our profoundly entangled interrelationality, it is thus anarchist thought that may well prove to be the political philosophy for our times. Landauer for instance located his own liberation at the heart of this paradox: 'I reject the certainty of my I so that I can bear life. I try to build myself a new world, knowing that I do not really have any ground to build it on'.[146] Similarly for contemporary anarchist theorist Tomás Ibáñez, liberatory power is created within, and emerges from, the entirety of the social sphere because it is immanent to it. Consequently, revolution is (and must remain) both anchored in, and transformative of the here-and-now. For him, this immanent symbiosis lies at the very heart of contemporary anarchism, which is constantly being reinvented through practices of struggle and therefore must inevitably remain in movement.[147] This willingness of anarchist theory and praxis to remain open to the dynamic and creative dialectical relationship between the apparent opposites of individuality and community, between the one and the whole, and without the reification or negation of either mode of being, places it in a unique and auspicious position. And it is for this reason that the voices of the activists involved in the collective visioning process will be brought into dialogue with classical and contemporary anarchist theory in the second part of this book.

Notes

1 Emma Goldman, 'Marriage and love', in E. Goldman, *Anarchism and other essays* (Los Angeles, CA: Enhanced Media Publishing, 2017), p. 102.
2 John Foran, *Taking power: On the origins of Third World revolutions* (Cambridge: Cambridge University Press, 2005), p. 274.
3 While much of Hardt's thinking around love has been undertaken with co-author of the *Empire* trilogy Antonio Negri, he has considerably broadened this work and written extensively on the subject as a solo author – hence the focus on the work of Hardt, with no intention to diminish or obscure the considerable theoretical contributions of Negri.
4 Gustav Landauer, 'Through separation to community', in G. Kuhn (ed. and trans.) *Revolution and other writings: A political reader* (Oakland, CA: PM Press, 2010), pp. 106–107.
5 Errico Malatesta, *Life and ideas: The anarchist writings of Errico Malatesta*, ed. V. Richards (Oakland, CA: PM Press, 2015), p. 60.
6 Ibid., p. 110.
7 Leo Tolstoy, *What I believe*, trans. C. Popoff (n.p., 2005 [1886]). Available online: https://archive.org/details/WhatIBelieve_109 (accessed 5 May 2022).
8 Alexandre Christoyannopoulos, *Christian anarchism: A political commentary on the gospel* (Exeter: Imprint Academic, 2011), p. 95.
9 Terrance A. Wiley, *Angelic troublemakers: Religion and anarchism in America* (New York: Bloomsbury Academic, 2014), p. 69.
10 Ibid., p. 106.
11 Dorothy Day, *From Union Square to Rome*, 1939. Available online: www.catholicworker.org/dorothyday/articles/201.pdf (accessed 16 May 2022).
12 See for instance: Simone De Beauvoir, *The second sex*, trans. H.M. Parshley (London: Vintage, 1997); Shulamith Firestone, *The dialectic of sex: The case for feminist revolution* (New York: Bantam Books, 1971).
13 For example: Goldman, 'Marriage and love'; Juliet Mitchell, *Psychoanalysis and feminism* (New York: Pantheon Books, 1974).
14 Emma Goldman, 'Anarchy and the sex question', in T. Anderson (ed.) *Publications by Emma Goldman* (CreateSpace Independent Publishing Platform, 2017).
15 Kate Zittlow-Rogness and Christina R. Foust, 'Beyond rights and virtues as foundation for women's agency: Emma Goldman's rhetoric of free love'. *Western Journal of Communication* 75:2 (2011), 148.

16 Vivian Gornick, 'Love and Anarchy: Emma Goldman's passion for free expression burns on'. *The Chronicle of Higher Education*, 2011. Available online: www.chronicle.com/article/love-and-anarchy/ (accessed 7 May 2022).

17 Teresa L. Ebert, 'Alexandra Kollontai and red love'. *Solidarity US*, 1999. Available online: www.solidarity-us.org/site/node/1724 (accessed 12 March 2022).

18 Alexandra Kollontai, *Selected writings of Alexandra Kollontai* (A. Holt, ed. and trans.), (New York: Horton, 1977), p. 108.

19 Karl Marx, 'Economic and philosophical manuscripts', in *Early writings*, trans. R. Livingstone and G. Benton (London: Penguin, 1975), p. 379.

20 Ewa Majewska, 'Precarity and gender: What's love got to do with it?' *Praktyka Teoretyczna* 4:38 (2020), 27.

21 Michael Hardt, 'For love or money'. *Cultural Anthropology* 26:4 (2011), 679.

22 Herbert Marcuse, *Eros and civilization: A philosophical enquiry into Freud* (Boston, MA: Beacon Press, 1966).

23 Ibid., pp. 196–197.

24 Ibid., p. 197.

25 Ibid., p. 202.

26 Erich Fromm, *The art of loving* (London: Thorsons, 1995), p. 103.

27 Ibid.

28 Ibid., p. 104.

29 Arundhati Roy, 'The Mahatma Ayyankali lecture'. Presentation given to the international seminar *Re-imagining struggles at the margins: A history of the unconquered and the oppressed*. University of Kerala, Thiruvananthapuram, 17 July 2014.

30 Sean Chabot, 'Love and revolution'. *Critical Sociology* 34:6 (2008), 816.

31 Joan V. Bondurant, *Conquest of violence: The Gandhian philosophy of conflict* (Berkeley, CA: University of California Press, 1971), p. 180.

32 Ernesto Che Guevara, *Che Guevara reader: Writings on politics and revolutions*, ed. David Deutschmann (Melbourne: Open Press, 2003), p. 225.

33 Ibid.

34 Ann Ferguson and Margaret Toye, 'Feminist love studies – Editors' introduction'. *Hypatia* 32:1 (2017), 15.

35 Martin Luther King Jr., 'Where do we go from here?' Speech made at the *11th Annual Southern Christian Leadership Conference*, Atlanta, Georgia, 16 August 1967.

36 Frank Ascaso, 'Why MLK should be remembered as a revolutionary'. *Black Rose Anarchist Federation*, 2019. Available online: https://blackrosefed.org/why-mlk-should-be-remembered-as-a-revolutionary/ (accessed 12 May 2022).

37 Combahee River Collective, 'The Combahee River Collective statement', 1977. Available online: https://americanstudies.yale.edu/sites/default/files/files/Keyword%20Coalition_Readings.pdf (accessed 5 May 2022).

38 bell hooks, *All about love: New visions* (New York: Harper Collins, 2000), p. 93.

39 Chela Sandoval, *Methodology of the oppressed* (Minneapolis, MN: University of Minnesota Press, 2000), p. 4.

40 Ibid., p. 5.

41 Carolyn Ureña, 'Loving from below: Of (de)colonial love and other demons'. *Hypatia* 32:1 (2017), 87.

42 Ewa Majewska, 'Love in translation: Neoliberal availability or a solidarity practice?', in A. G. Jonasdottir and A. Ferguson (eds) *Love: A question for feminism in the twenty-first century* (London: Routledge, 2014), p. 212.

43 Jamie Heckert and Richard Cleminson, *Anarchism and sexuality: Ethics, relationships and power* (New York: Routledge, 2012); see also: Jamie Heckert, Deric Michael Shannon and Abbey Willis, 'Loving-teaching: Notes for queering anarchist pedagogies'. *Educational Studies* 48:1 (2012), 12–29.

44 Jamie Heckert, 'Loving politics: On the art of living together', in C. Levy and S. Newman (eds) *The anarchist imagination: Anarchism encounters the humanities and social sciences* (London: Routledge, 2019), p. 133.

45 Michael Hardt and Antonio Negri, *Commonwealth* (Cambridge: Harvard University Press, 2011), p. 180.

46 Richard Gilman-Opalsky, *The communism of love: An inquiry into the poverty of exchange value* (Chico, CA: AK Press, 2020).

47 Laurence Davis, 'Love and revolution in Ursula Le Guin's *Four Ways to Forgiveness*', in J. Heckert and R. Cleminson (eds) *Anarchism and sexuality: Ethics, relationships and power* (New York: Routledge, 2011), p. 114.

48 Kathy E. Ferguson, *Emma Goldman: Political thinking in the streets* (Plymouth: Rowman and Littlefield, 2013), p. 2.

49 Eleanor Wilkinson, 'On love as an (im)properly political concept'. *D: Society and Space* 35:1 (2017), 66.

50 Clare Hemmings, *Considering Emma Goldman: Feminist political ambivalence and the imaginative archive* (Durham, NC: Duke University Press, 2018), p. 45.

51 Goldman, 'Marriage and love', p. 97.

52 Ibid.

53 Ibid., p. 99.

54 Leyna Lowe, 'Revolutionary love: Feminism, love, and the transformative politics of freedom in the works of Wollstonecraft, Beauvoir, and Goldman', in A. G. Jónasdóttir and A. Ferguson (eds) *Love: A question for feminism in the twenty-first century* (London: Routledge, 2014), p. 193.

55 Zittlow-Rogness and Foust, 'Beyond rights and virtues as foundation for women's agency', p. 154.

56 Hardt and Negri, *Commonwealth*, p. 183.

57 Ibid., p. 183.

58 Ceren Özselçuk, 'Fifteen years after the Empire: An interview with Michael Hardt'. *Rethinking Marxism* 28:1 (2016), 130.

59 Hardt and Negri, *Commonwealth*, p. 182.

60 Sara Ahmed, *The cultural politics of emotion* (Edinburgh: Edinburgh University Press, 2004), 122–123.

61 Emma Goldman, 'Patriotism: A menace to liberty', in E. Goldman, *Anarchism and other essays* (Los Angeles, CA: Enhanced Media Publishing, 2017), p. 49.

62 Ibid., p. 53.

63 Ibid.

64 Ibid., p. 57.
65 Ferguson, *Emma Goldman: Political thinking in the streets*, p. 177.
66 Candace Falk, *Love, anarchy and Emma Goldman: A biography* (New York: Holt, Rinehart, and Winston, 1984), p. 402.
67 Ibid., p. 135.
68 Alice Wexler, *Emma Goldman: An intimate life* (New York: Pantheon, 1984), p. 278.
69 The name Sasha refers to Alexander Berkman (21 November 1870 – 28 June 1936) – a lover and lifelong friend of Goldman, who was a leading member of the anarchist movement in the early twentieth century and famous for both his political activism and his writing. In 1918 Berkman and Goldman were both deported from the US to Russia under the Anarchist Exclusion Act.
70 Emma Goldman, *Living my life* (London: Penguin Books, 2006), p. 104.
71 Keally McBride, 'Emma Goldman and the power of revolutionary love', in J. Casas Klausen and J. Martel (eds) *How not to be governed: Readings and interpretations from a critical anarchist left* (Plymouth: Lexington Books, 2011), p. 164.
72 Goldman, 'Anarchy and the sex question', pp. 1–2.
73 Ibid., p. 3.
74 Rochelle Gurstein, 'Emma Goldman and the tragedy of modern love'. *Salmagundi* 135/136 (2002), 87.
75 See: Richard Drinnon, 'Introduction', in E. Goldman, *Anarchism and other essays* (New York: Dover Publishers, 1969), pp. xi–xii; and Christine Stansell, *American moderns: Bohemian New York and the creation of a new century* (New York: Henry Holt and Co., 2000), p. 131.
76 See: Ferguson, *Emma Goldman: Political thinking in the streets*, 212; Martha Gruening, 'Speaking of democracy', in P. Glassgold (ed.) *Anarchy! An anthology of Emma Goldman's Mother Earth* (Washington, DC: Counterpoint, 2001), pp. 400–404; and Peter Glassgold, 'Introduction: The life and death of Mother Earth', in P. Glassgold, *Anarchy! An anthology of Emma Goldman's Mother Earth*, p. xxxiv.
77 Ferguson, *Emma Goldman: Political thinking in the streets*, p. 217.
78 Emma Goldman, 'Anarchism: What it really stands for', in E. Goldman, *Anarchism and other essays* (Los Angeles, CA: Enhanced Media Publishing, 2017), p. 12.
79 Goldman, 'Marriage and love', p. 102.
80 Ferguson makes this same argument in *Emma Goldman: Political thinking in the streets*, p. 240.
81 Chris Rossdale, 'Dancing ourselves to death: The subject of Emma Goldman's Nietzschean anarchism'. *Globalizations* 12:1 (2015), 129.
82 Eleanor Wilkinson, 'Love in the multitude? A feminist critique of love as a political concept', in A. G. Jónasdóttir and A. Ferguson (eds) *Love: A question for feminism in the twenty-first century*, p. 238.
83 Ann Ferguson, 'Feminist love politics: Romance, care, and solidarity', in A. G. Jónasdóttir and A. Ferguson (eds) *Love: A question for feminism in the twenty-first century* (London: Routledge, 2014), p. 259.

84 Rosemary Hennessy, 'Bread and roses in the common', in A. G. Jónasdóttir and A. Ferguson (eds) *Love: a question for feminism in the twenty-first century* (London: Routledge, 2014), p. 267.
85 De Beauvoir, *The second sex*, p. 471.
86 See Andrea Veltman, 'Transcendence and immanence in the ethics of Simone De Beauvoir', in M. A. Simons (ed.) *Philosophy of Simone De Beauvoir: Critical essays* (Bloomington, IN: Indiana University Press, 2006), p. 122.
87 Rachel Tillman, 'Toward a new materialism: Matter as dynamic'. *Minding Nature* 8:1 (2015), 31.
88 See for example: Karen Barad, *Meeting the universe halfway: Quantum physics and the entanglement of matter and meaning* (Durham, NC: Duke University Press, 2007).
89 Ibid., p. 170.
90 Rosi Braidotti, 'The politics of "life" itself and new ways of dying', in D. Coole and S. Frost (eds) *New materialisms: Ontology, agency, politics* (Durham, NC: Duke University Press, 2010), p. 206.
91 As Wilkinson argues in 'On love as an (im)properly political concept', p. 68.
92 Michael Hardt, 'Pasolini discovers love outside'. *Diacritics* 39:4 (2009), 128.
93 Lauren Berlant, *Cruel optimism* (Durham, NC: Duke University Press, 2011), p. 684.
94 See: Catriona Sandilands, 'Feminism and biopolitics: A cyborg account', in S. MacGregor (ed.) *Routledge handbook of gender and environment* (New York: Routledge, 2017), p. 231.
95 Hardt, 'For love or money', p. 677.
96 Wilkinson, 'On love as an (im)properly political concept', p. 62.
97 Pier Paulo Frassinelli, 'Biopolitical production, the common, and a happy ending: On Michael Hardt and Antonio Negri's *Commonwealth*'. *Critical Arts* 25:2 (2011), 126.
98 Agatha Beins, 'Radical others: Women of colour and revolutionary feminism'. *Feminist Studies* 41:1 (2015), 157.
99 Ferguson, 'Feminist love politics, p. 252.
100 Jennifer C. Nash, 'Practicing love: Black feminism, love-politics, and post intersectionality'. *Meridians: Feminism, Race, Transnationalism* 2:2 (2013), 5.
101 Ibid., p. 18.
102 Ibid.
103 Clare Hemmings, 'In the mood for revolution: Emma Goldman's passion'. *New Literary History* 43 (2012), 542.
104 Matt York, 'Transforming masculinities: A qualitative study of a transformative education programme for young Zulu men and boys in rural Kwazulu-Natal'. *Journal of Pan African Studies* 7:7 (2014), 55–78.
105 The concept of *Ubuntu* is best expressed through the *Nguini* proverb '*Umuntu ngu-umuntu ngobantu*' meaning 'I am because we are'. This sense of collective solidarity characterises Ubuntu through love, caring, tolerance, respect, empathy, accountability and responsibility.
106 Goldman, 'Marriage and love', p. 102.
107 Goldman, cited in: Ferguson, *Emma Goldman: Political thinking in the streets*, p. 304.

108 Goldman, 'Marriage and love', p. 102.

109 Hardt and Negri, *Commonwealth*, p. 179.

110 Majewska, 'Love in translation', p. 208.

111 Michael Hardt, *The procedures of love* (Ostfildern, Germany: Hatje Cantz Verlag, 2012), p. 5.

112 Ibid., p. 4.

113 Özselçuk, 'Fifteen years after the empire', p. 130.

114 Hardt and Negri, *Commonwealth*, p. 180.

115 Michael Hardt and Antonio Negri, *Multitude: War and democracy in the age of empire* (London: Penguin Books, 2005), p. 338.

116 Goldman, 'Marriage and love', p. 101.

117 Ibid.

118 Emma Goldman, 'What I believe', in T. Anderson (ed.) *Publications by Emma Goldman* (CreateSpace Independent Publishing Platform, 2017), p. 18.

119 Goldman, 'Marriage and love', p. 101.

120 Hardt and Negri, *Commonwealth*, p. 184.

121 Özselçuk, 'Fifteen years after the empire', p. 132.

122 Srećko Horvat, *The radicality of love* (Cambridge: Polity Press, 2016), p. 6.

123 George Katsiaficas, 'Eros and revolution'. Paper prepared for the *Critical Refusals Conference of the International Herbert Marcuse Society*, Philadelphia, 28 October 2011.

124 Hardt, *The procedures of love*, p. 9.

125 Ibid., p. 12.

126 Özselçuk, 'Fifteen years after the empire', p. 133.

127 Hardt and Negri, *Commonwealth*, p. 198.

128 Braidotti, *The posthuman*.

129 Kelly Oliver, *Earth and world* (New York: Columbia University Press, 2015), p. 104.

130 Ibid., p. 240.

131 Karen Barad, 'Posthumanist performativity: Toward an understanding of how matter comes to matter'. *Gender and Science* 28:3 (2003), 829.

132 Rosi Braidotti, 'The critical posthumanities; or, is Medianatures to Naturecultures as Zoe is to Bios?' *Cultural Politics* 12:3 (2016), 388.

133 Ibid., p. 381.

134 Ibid., p. 388.

135 Barad, 'Matter feels, converses, suffers, desires, yearns and remembers', p. 69.

136 Karen Barad, 'Nature's queer performativity'. *Qui Parle* 19:2 (2011), 125.

137 See: Lori Gruen, *Entangled empathy: An alternative ethic for our relationships with animals* (New York: Lantern Books, 2015).

138 Lori Gruen, 'Expressing entangled empathy: A reply'. *Hypatia* 32:2 (2017), 458.

139 Julia Butterfly Hill, 'The Taoist and the activist', interview with Dr. Benjamin Tong for *Lunch with Bokara*, KCET Television, 7 July 2005. Available online: www.kcet.org/shows/lunch-with-bokara/episodes/the-taoist-and-the-activist (accessed 12 March 2022).

140 Kim TallBear, 'An indigenous reflection on working beyond the human/not human'. *GLQ: A Journal of Lesbian and Gay Studies* 21:2–3 (2015), 234.

141 Joel Kovel, *History and spirit: An inquiry into the philosophy of liberation* (Boston, MA: Beacon Press, 1991), p. 161.
142 Ibid.
143 Timothy Morton, 'The Mesh', in S. Lemenager, T. Shewry and K. Hiltner (eds) *Environmental criticism for the twenty-first century* (New York: Routledge, 2011), p. 27.
144 Nāgārjuna, cited in: Stephen Batchelor, *Verses from the centre: A Buddhist vision of the sublime* (New York: Riverhead Books, 2001), p. 115.
145 Ibid., p. 123.
146 Landauer, 'Through separation to community', p. 97.
147 Tomás Ibáñez, *Anarchism is movement* (London: Freedom Press, 2019), p. 49.

2

Collective visioning: Utopia as process

'ΈΙΜΑΣΤΕ ΕΙΚΟΝΑ ΑΠΟ ΤΟ ΜΕΛΛΟΝ' ('We are an image from the future.')

– Graffiti from the 2008 Greek riots[1]

Through our examination of political actors across the twentieth century and new theory in the academy today we have now been able to isolate a distinctive lineage of (r)evolutionary love which acts to animate radical social transformation. But surprisingly, as a rich and varied debate around the theorisation of love as politically transformative develops, very little work has been undertaken to link the experiences and practices of activists on the ground to this emerging theory. And while Goldman's theories were strongly practice based and grounded in lived experience, contemporary dialogues concerning the politics of love in radical social transformation remain largely confined to the realm of academia. The theories we have examined illuminate a vibrant, intellectually rigorous theoretical resource which can and should be drawn on by contemporary ecological, anti-capitalist, feminist and anti-racist movements. But it further suggests that any such work will be usefully complemented by the voices of activists on the ground in order to augment and advance current knowledge – a process requiring both theory informing practice *and* practice informing theory.

Historically, social movements have provided a rich source of knowledge about forms of oppression and injustice, generating debate around the ways in which society is structured, and offering further possibilities for agency in social change processes – with the knowledge produced through struggle often challenging those holding power and society itself. It is, however, a relatively recent development for social movements to be explicitly recognised by the academy as producers of knowledge in their own right, despite their lead role in shaping a number of academic disciplines including women's studies, black and postcolonial studies, peace studies, queer studies and others.[2] The idea of co-research with social movement activists can be traced back at least to Karl Marx. In 1880, Marx designed a questionnaire in order to ignite an enquiry into the conditions of the French proletariat. Rather than merely attempting to extract useful information, the questionnaire, entitled 'A Workers' Inquiry',[3] aimed at analysing the characteristics of exploitation itself, and encouraged workers to think about oppositional modes against their own exploitation – a method oriented towards encouraging the critical reflection of workers themselves in a process of knowledge co-production.[4] The agency of such a process was evidenced in the early twentieth century with the working class appropriation of anarchist theory informing the new models of direct democracy which came into being during the Russian revolutionary movement of October 1917, preceding the imposition of authoritarian rule.[5]

In the 1960s, Participatory Action Research (PAR) methods grew out of the anti-imperialist and anti-colonial revolutionary movements so prevalent at that time. The PAR process involves participants working together to understand a context-specific problematic situation, seeking to 'liberate' the group through developing a collective understanding of the situation in order to then take action. While closely associated with Latin America and Freirian popular education,[6] experimentation with PAR in support of social organising was also prevalent in South Asia and a number of African countries – empowering social struggles in rural areas and supporting the emergence of strong *campesino* (peasant farmer) movements. A lineage of leading militant figures involved in this proliferation of PAR in the Global South includes Fals Borda in Colombia, Mohammed Anisar Rahman in Bangladesh and Sithembiso Nyoni in Zimbabwe. By the late 1960s PAR had reached Europe and North America, where experiments with the methodology aimed at the empowerment of marginalised urban communities.[7] On the cusp between this movement and a reimagining of the workers' enquiries first used by Marx was the *Operaismo* or Autonomist Marxist Workerism in Italy. *Operaismo* developed new analytical tools in order to search for resistance against the new forms of capitalist organisation at the time, with the co-research methodologies firmly grounded in and growing out of actual working-class life and struggle.[8] This Italian Autonomism became a major influence on the work of Hardt and Negri, and in turn upon militant research collectives arising through the 'revolt of Argentina' or *Argentinazo* from 2001 onwards.[9] Another example of such PAR-inspired processes were the Wages for Housework campaigns which began in the early 1970s, also in Italy. The emerging struggles and debates within this feminist movement informed the pamphlet *The Power of Women and the Subversion of Community*,[10] which in turn served as a catalyst for the Wages for Housework campaign to extend into a global feminist social movement – from praxis, to theory, to an augmented praxis, and so on.

Through the final decades of the twentieth century to the present day, new waves of social movement mobilisation offering resistance to neoliberal globalisation and a critique of its inherent limitations and inequalities has continued this tradition. And it has been possible to observe a 'qualitative shift' in the methodologies of these movements during this period, with their practices becoming increasingly reflexive.[11] From the Latin American *encuentros* (international gatherings) that brought Indigenous rights, alter-globalisation, ecological, anarchist and feminist activists together for face-to-face discussion and solidarity building, to the open spaces for activist dialogue/movement building of the World Social Forum – such processes have worked to operationalise the 'epistemic diversity' found in and across the movements in pursuit of an emancipatory 'cosmopolitan ecology of knowledges'.[12] Ultimately, for radical social change to be realised not through taking power, but through making/transforming power – as discussed in the previous chapter, the activation of what Negri calls 'constituent imagination' is necessary at both local and global levels.[13]

A recent study conducted with activists across Europe found that although this utopian imagination is considered to be a central aspect of their struggles, processes which harness this collective imaginary are rarely used as a method for designing strategy and tactics.[14] And so by way of response to this apparent deficit, a process of collective visioning has been used to develop the work presented in the remainder of this book. The approach has been adapted from participatory methods used within the global Occupy movement as a tool for collaboration and collective action. It involves a group process of intentionally generating a vision that is unapologetically utopian while remaining grounded in grassroots struggle – to be enacted in the here-and-now.[15] In alignment with the new forms of knowledge co-production we have just explored, such collective visioning acts to reveal 'glimpses of a future world'[16] – and (perhaps more importantly) of the seeds of liberation already existing in the present. For Ernst Bloch, such imagination is 'productive of the revolution', and revolution is 'the changing of the world'[17] – positioning imagination not as mere fantasising, but as a process inherently attuned to 'objectively real possibility'[18] and therefore to the 'properties of reality which are themselves utopian' (which already contain the future). Similarly Katarzyna Balug positions imagination as the central driver of cognition and perception, concluding that society can therefore 'only create that which its members can imagine'.[19] Without engaging in such future-oriented discussion on values, goals and visions it will never be possible to 'take over' that very future.[20] Utopian political imaginaries have largely been rejected by conventional politics since the end of the Second World War on the grounds that such thought is 'abstract' and 'metaphysical', and that a utopian desire for justice and perfection might well rupture the ordered fragility of the international status quo.[21] From this perspective, to be utopian is to be 'hopelessly impractical, or dangerously idealistic, or both'.[22] And such a negation of imagination has led many political theorists to narrow their focus exclusively to the empirical *now* – thus constraining contemporary political imagination to a fixed (neoliberal) present. Tom, one of the collective visioning participants, reflects on this situation:

> There are a lot of people who say that it's easier to imagine the end of the world than it is to imagine the end of capitalism, and I think that means that their world-view has been so thoroughly dominated by capitalism that this really is the case. For some reason idealism and utopianism are framed as a bad thing. The declaration that we cannot think an end to capitalism is not just defeatist – it shows that a lot of the leftist tradition has failed and it's done.

The argument here does not aim to negate the importance of a political praxis which is responsive to the present and rooted in everyday experience, or as the Zapatistas put it: *preguntando caminamos* ('walking we ask questions') – but simply to acknowledge that without visions of how the world might be different, struggles will stagnate and decline.[23] Might it therefore be possible to develop a mode of praxis which imagines futures that realign movement trajectory while simultaneously grounding itself in present moment realities – an imaginative/responsive ongoing process? Ruth Levitas suggests reframing utopia as method, an 'imaginary reconstitution of society' which addresses both the new society and the transition to it – thus maintaining a 'double standpoint' between present and future and, she suggests, 're-reading the present from the standpoint of the future'.[24] Taking this logic even further, Laurence Davis draws a clear distinction between *transcendent utopias* which imagine and strive for perfection in an impossible future, and what he terms *grounded utopias* which imagine qualitatively better forms of living latent in the present – transforming the restrictions of the 'here and now' into an 'open horizon of possibilities'.[25] Davis believes that we may well be witnessing a paradigm shift in utopian thinking in this early part of the twenty-first century, with a new conception of utopia as an 'empirically grounded, dynamic, and open-ended' feature of the 'real world' of history and politics.[26] He builds on Friedrich Kümmel's idea of time as a temporal coexistence between past, future and present, with the relation of these temporal components not merely conceived as one of succession but also as one of conjoint existence.[27] And he presents a concept of time in which 'the future represents the possibility, and the past a basis, of a free life in the present'.[28] From this perspective such grounded utopias both emerge out of, and support the further development of, historical movements for social change – and thus are not 'fantasised visions of perfection to be imposed on an imperfect world'[29] but rather provide the space for a utopian reimagining of current (and therefore future) social relations which are firmly grounded in contemporary grassroots struggle. Consequently, through collective visioning this book utilises utopia *as process* – transitioning the functionality of utopia from noun to verb and operationalising imagination as a productive power in the pursuit of new knowledge and praxis.

The process has involved the thoughts, feelings, ideas and imaginings of a global cross section of ecological, anti-capitalist, feminist and anti-racist activists from fourteen countries, with a specific and sustained effort being made to maintain a diverse representation of participants from both the Global South and North in order to encourage a 'cosmopolitan ecology of knowledges'.[30] We have therefore strived for an epistemic diversity in the (co)production of new theory, with full cognisance of the long history of oppression/suppression against so much of the knowledge(s) produced in the South – on which the Western academy has built its current hegemony of imperial knowledge and consequently the systems driving our current socio-ecological crises. The following participants (pseudonyms have been used)[31] represent the core group involved in this collective visioning:

- **Maria, Mexico:** Involved in eco-activism for many years, Maria has co-initiated a women's led permaculture project in rural Mexico with food sovereignty projects taking shape across a number of local Indigenous communities. She is currently focusing her energies on developing a directly democratic eco-community based on permaculture principles.
- **Tom, Canada:** As an anarchist, Tom became active in the Occupy movement in Toronto, as well as being a non-native ally to grassroots Indigenous movements. He has since been involved in longer term projects such as tenant organising, sustainable community gardening for food sovereignty/food autonomy, decolonisation projects, rewilding projects and anti-pipeline struggles.
- **Lowanna, *Trouwunna* (Tasmania, Australia):** A *Trawlwulwuy* woman from *Tebrakunna* country, north-east Tasmania, and an Indigenous rights activist and researcher. Lowanna has been a long-term activist and campaigner in decolonial and anti-racist struggles, and in challenging state violence against Indigenous Australian communities.
- **Rosie, UK:** First became involved in direct action as part of *Reclaim the Streets* and the anti-roads movement in the UK in the 1990s. She was also part of an affinity group using direct action tactics in opposition to the introduction of GM crops to the UK. More recently she has concentrated on supporting social justice and environmental groups with training and capacity building.
- **Hassan, Syria:** During the Arab Spring wave of uprisings, Hassan became involved in the fledgling Syrian revolutionary movement. He was an organiser in the early days of the revolution – coordinating activists to gather in public squares and calling for an end to the regime. Following

the violent government backlash, Hassan's life became endangered and he was forced to flee, making his way into Turkey before crossing by boat to Greece. He is currently living with his family in Ireland, where he has refugee status.

- **Alice, UK:** Negotiating her roles as both lone parent and eco-activist, Alice is a member of an affinity group that engages in direct action tactics in order to highlight the current ecological and climate emergency and challenge the institutions that cause it – occupying government buildings and public spaces in acts of non-violent, creative civil disobedience. She has a particular interest in degrowth and rewilding, and facilitates grief circles for those coming to terms with the current ecocide.

- **Dembe, Uganda:** Orphaned at the age of six, Dembe was raised by his grandmother in a deep rural community which experienced chronic social and economic deprivation, radicalising him at an early age. He has co-initiated a number of grassroots activist groups in Kampala engaged in ecological and anti-capitalist struggle. More recently he has been involved in forming and developing transnational activist networks to build solidarity and learn from each other's movements.

- **Katie, USA:** An activist, researcher and author, Katie has a long history of engagement with feminist and anti-racist struggles in the USA. As a vegan she is also dedicated to animal liberation activism, and it is through exploring the (violent) relationship between human and non-human animals that her activism and research coalesce.

- **Angelo, Italy:** First became involved in activism through an anarchist social centre in 2001. His activism had been sparked by the G8 summit in Genoa where Carlo Giuliani was killed. After spending time in Brazil, where he was active in social movements and the national protests of 2013, he returned to Italy, where he has since been involved in a militant research collective. Angelo is also currently active in developing a transnational network of social-ecological activists.

- **Anna, Germany:** An eco-activist who has become increasingly dedicated and committed to this struggle over the past decade. She is co-initiator of a direct-action eco-activist network. Anna is also active in the German climate coalition *Ende Gelände* and has been involved in learning from Occupy and other social movements in Germany and Europe to fertilise new movement repertoires.

- **Jack, UK:** First became involved in direct action at the *Preston New Road* anti-fracking campaign with *Reclaim the Power*, engaging in a rolling resistance to shut down the site gates. His subsequent participation with *Ende Gelände* in Germany inspired him to full-time activism. His affinity group has been involved in a number of recent high visibility actions to draw attention to the current ecological and climate emergency – occupying government buildings and public spaces in the process.

- **Msizi, South Africa:** Growing up in a deep rural area in KwaZulu-Natal, Msizi's activism has been informed by the stark inequalities and fractured communities which are the legacy of colonialism and apartheid. He is a community organiser who has played a central role in local struggles for housing, access to healthcare and poverty alleviation. Msizi also facilitates training for groups of men around masculinities, gender equality and social change, and has been active in local and national campaigns to end gender-based violence.
- **Sinéad, Ireland:** A long-time activist, Sinéad became involved in feminist and anti-racist activism at an early age. International solidarity has played an important role in her activism – she has worked in Nicaragua supporting Indigenous communities to resist state oppression and has lived in Chiapas, Mexico, on Zapatista territory. More recently she has been involved in campaigns fighting violence against women, and was a long-term campaigner to decriminalise abortion in Ireland.
- **Ekrem, Turkey:** As an activist, Ekrem has been involved in student movements protesting against the increasing authoritarianism adopted by government forces. He has been particularly active in fighting the xenophobia and anti-Kurdish discrimination which has emerged across Turkish society. He is also active in transnational anti-capitalist networks.
- **Emma, UK:** At sixteen, Emma became active in the peace movement and later joined the *Committee of 100* for which she served time in prison. Although involved in anarchist groups for a number of years, her activism tailed off – partly because the groups didn't seem to be achieving what they had set out to achieve and partly because she had four children and became a lone parent. Emma has recently re-engaged with direct action politics in response to austerity politics and the ecological and environmental emergency.
- **Namazzi, Uganda:** As an activist/researcher Namazzi is currently coordinating and facilitating directly democratic people's assemblies in Uganda as a platform to drive the country's political evolution. She is involved in the cooperative movement and is engaged in transnational activist solidarity networks seeking alternatives to our current capitalist system.
- **Salma, Jordan:** A long-term peace activist in the region, Salma has more recently co-initiated a refugee solidarity group supporting Syrians and Iraqis fleeing conflicts in their own countries. She has a particular interest in trauma work with refugee women and children as they come to terms with the violence they have experienced. She is also involved in transnational activist networks in order to build solidarity and develop new forms of caring practices across movements.
- **Alisha, UK:** Primarily involved with a climate action network in the UK, Alisha was involved in blockading the *Preston New Road* fracking

site. In recent years she has increasingly dedicated her time to an affinity group who have been organising art-based 'spectacles' taking place at government buildings, business headquarters and public spaces, in order to draw attention to the current ecological and climate emergency.

The collective visioning process consisted of an online discussion hub, alongside one-to-one discussions, feeding into a group collective visioning. These three core methods of knowledge co-production allowed for an ongoing process of refinement and collaborative learning to take place, with themes from the discussion hub being further explored through one-to-one discussions, which in turn formed a basis for the group collective visioning – each wave of enquiry feeding back into the next. In a similar way to that of Occupy Manifest, which grew out of the New York Occupy movement in 2011, the process utilised mindful enquiry as a means to provide participants with the space to 'collectively reflect on their deepest values' and to begin embodying/integrating those values more fully.[32] Such practices have become an established resource within social movements in support of collective struggle, with a number of experiments being undertaken at the intersection of mindfulness/subjective change and social change in recent years, including those from the Ecodharma Centre, Ulex Project and Generative Somatics.[33] At the US Social Forum in Detroit in 2010, activists engaged in such enquiry passed a resolution that read: 'We acknowledge that we as agents of change, having been deeply affected by our conditions of oppression, need a deep and abiding commitment to embody the revolutionary change we seek. Revolutionary, systemic change is needed internally, in our relations and in our external conditions'.[34] Paul Gorski, drawing on Steven Hick and Charles Furlotte's conceptual analysis of the relationship between mindfulness and social justice practice,[35] proposed four points of connection between the two: both are concerned with the ways people relate to one another and how we reproduce social conditions; both acknowledge human interconnectedness while rejecting simplistic dualities; both are rooted in consciousness raising, and both rely on self-reflection.[36]

One participant (Alice) described the collective visioning process as being grounded in the principles of 'listening with your heart, sharing from your heart, and being spontaneous'. She added that 'when everyone is given an opportunity to speak, and the range of opinions and perspectives are shared, then there comes a natural conclusion that feels in harmony with the greater good'. The collective visioning process served to rapidly cohere a group of activists with a diversity of ideological, cultural and geographical backgrounds. All of us were surprised, if not moved, by the sense of solidarity formed within the group, and of the collective wisdom which was produced in common – as a sum far greater than its parts. The second part of this book will now bring the voices of these activists into a vibrant dialogue with both classical and contemporary theory, with the fruits of this dialogical process synergised and formulated into an ideological framework of Critique, Utopia and Praxis.

Notes

1 Cited in: Uri Gordon, 'Prefigurative politics between ethical practice and absent promise'. *Political Studies* 66:2 (2017), 521.
2 Graeme Chesters, 'Social movements and the ethics of knowledge production'. *Social Movement Studies* 11:2 (2012), 153.
3 La Revue Socialiste, 'A workers' enquiry', trans. C. Price, 1997, Works of Karl Marx 1880. Available online: www.marxists.org/archive/marx/works/1880/04/20.htm (accessed 4 May 2022).
4 Marta Malo de Molina, 'Common notions, part 1: Workers-inquiry, co-research, consciousness-raising', trans. Maribel Casas-Cortés and Sebastian Cobarrubias, of the Notas Rojas Collective Chapel Hill. *European Institute for Progressive Cultural Policies*, 2004. Available online: http://transform.eipcp.net/transversal/0406/malo/en.html (accessed 13 May 2022).
5 Daniel Guerin, 'Anarchism in the Russian revolution'. *Libcom*, 2005. Available online: https://libcom.org/library/anarchism-daniel-guerin-4 (accessed 23 April 2022).
6 Paulo Freire, *Pedagogy of the oppressed* (Harmondsworth: Penguin, 1996) .
7 Marta Malo de Molina, 'Common notions, part 2: Institutional analysis, participatory action-research, militant research', trans. Maribel Casas-Cortés and Sebastian Cobarrubias, of the Notas Rojas Collective Chapel Hill, August 2005, ed. other members of Notas Rojas, on-line, February 2006. *European Institute for Progressive Cultural Policies*. Available online: http://transform.eipcp.net/transversal/0406/malo/en.html (accessed 13 May 2022).
8 Jamie Woodcock, 'The workers' inquiry from Trotskyism to Operaismo: A political methodology for investigating the workplace'. *Ephemera* 14:3 (2014), 499.
9 Jorge Camacho, 'A tragic note: On Negri and Deleuze in the light of the Argentinazo'. *New Formations* 68 (2010), 59.
10 Mariarosa Dalla Costa and Selma James, *The power of women and the subversion of community* (Brooklyn, NY: Pétroleuse Press, 1971).
11 Chesters, 'Social movements and the ethics of knowledge co-production', p. 154.
12 Boaventura de Sousa Santos, João Arriscado Nunes and Maria Paula Meneses, 'Introduction: Opening up the canon of knowledge and recognition of difference', in B. Santos (ed.) *Another knowledge is possible: Beyond northern epistemologies* (London: Verso, 2008), pp. xlv–xlvii.
13 See: Negri, 'Logic and theory of enquiry: Militant praxis as subject and episteme', in D. Graeber, S. Shukaitis and E. Biddle (eds) *Constituent imagination: Militant investigations, collective theorization* (Oakland, CA: AK Press, 2007), p. 71.

14 Martin Pötz, 'Utopian imagination in activism: Making the case for social dreaming in change from the grassroots'. *Interface* 11:1 (2019), 138.

15 For example, see: Linda Stout, *Collective visioning: How groups can work together for a just and sustainable future* (San Francisco: Berrett-Koehler Publishers, 2011).

16 Stevphen Shukaitis and David Graeber, *Constituent imagination: Militant investigations – Collective theorization* (Oakland, CA: AK Press, 2007), p. 37.

17 Cited in: Judith Brown, 'Ernst Bloch and the utopian imagination'. *Eras Journal* 5 (2003) . Available online: www.monash.edu/arts/philosophical-historical-international-studies/eras/past-editions/edition-five-2003-november/ernst-bloch-and-the-utopian-imagination (accessed 16 May 2022).

18 Ernst Bloch, *The principle of hope (volume 1)*, trans. N. Plaice, S. Plaice and P. Knight (Cambridge, MA: MIT Press, 1986), p. 145.

19 Katarzyna Balug, 'The imagination paradox: Participation or performance of visioning the city'. *Geoforum* 102 (2017), 284.

20 Mika Mannermaa, 'Introduction', in M. Mannermaa, J. Dator and P. Tiihonen (eds) *Democracy and futures* (Helsinki: Committee for the Future, parliament of Finland, 2006), p. 4.

21 Shannon Brincat, 'Reclaiming the utopian imaginary in IR theory'. *Review of International Studies* 35 (2009), 585.

22 Davis, 'Everyone an artist: Art, labour, anarchy, and utopia', in L. Davis and R. Kinna (eds) *Anarchism and utopianism* (Manchester: Manchester University Press, 2009), p. 73.

23 Max Haiven and Alex Khasnabish, *The radical imagination* (London: Zed Books, 2014), p. 63.

24 Ruth Levitas, *Utopia as method: The imaginary reconstitution of society* (London: Palgrave Macmillan, 2013), p. 218.

25 Davis, 'History, politics, and utopia: Toward a synthesis of social theory and practice', in P. Vieira and M. Marder (eds) *Existential utopia: New perspectives on utopian thought* (New York: Continuum, 2012), p. 136.

26 Ibid., p. 127.

27 Friedrich Kümmel, 'Time as succession and the problem of duration', in J. T. Fraser (ed.) *The voices of time* (London: Penguin Press, 1968).

28 Davis, 'History, politics, and utopia', p. 131.

29 Ibid., p. 136.

30 Santos, Nunes and Meneses, 'Introduction: Opening up the canon of knowledge', p. xiv.

31 As a number of participants have requested full anonymity due to a variety of safety and security concerns, the collective visioning group agreed for all members to adopt pseudonyms throughout. Participants who are happy to be identified have been acknowledged and thanked at the start of the book.

32 James K. Rowe, 'Zen and the art of social movement maintenance'. *Waging Nonviolence* (2015). Available online: https://wagingnonviolence.org/feature/mindfulness-and-the-art-of-social-movement-maintenance/ (accessed 10 May 2022).

33 See: www.ecodharma.com; https://ulexproject.org; and https://generativeso matics.org (all accessed 20 May 2022).

34 Rowe, 'Zen and the art of social movement maintenance'.

35 Steven Hick and Charles Furlotte, 'Mindfulness and social justice approaches: Bridging the mind and society in social work practice'. *Canadian Social Work Review* 26:1 (2009), 5–24.

36 Paul C. Gorski, 'Relieving burnout and the "Martyr Syndrome" among social justice education activists: The implications and effects of mindfulness'. *Urban Review* 47 (2015), 703.

Part II

A collective vision

3

The dystopian present

'The root of the prevailing lack of imagination cannot be grasped unless one is able to imagine what is lacking, that is, what is missing, hidden, forbidden, and yet possible, in modern life.'

– Situationist International[1]

'DID YOU HEAR?
It is the sound of your world collapsing.
It is that of ours re-emerging.'

– Subcommander Marcos[2]

Introduction

Any contemporary theory of radical social transformation must begin with a recognition that the processes through which we co-imagine our world(s) are not currently in the hands of those who seek such transformations. Rather, as John P. Clark points out: 'They are dominated above all by economic power and the economistic culture, which, in alliance with the state, aim to train workers, employees, and managers to serve the existing system of production, and to produce a mass of consumers for the dominant system of consumption'.[3] A central theme running throughout the collective visioning process has been an awareness of these dystopian conditions in which we currently find ourselves immersed. These past decades of neoliberal globalisation have seen the rampant commercialisation of planet Earth and its inhabitants (human and more-than-human) in a quest to transform the entire global ecosystem into a 'planetary apparatus of production'[4] – and has thus reframed life itself as a mere commodity to be traded for profit. Most worrying of all has been our apparent wholehearted compliance in the belief that the imperative of the market and the imperative of life are one and the same thing. As Braidotti suggests, our current conditions as engendered by global capital might well take the motto: 'I shop therefore I am!'[5] And so this apparent pinnacle of societal organisation – that of liberal 'democracy' in the service of capitalism – continues to be almost universally reified as the form of governance that will transport us towards collective happiness and prosperity: 'Work hard now, defer joy, consume as much as you can, obey your rulers and all shall be well'.[6] It seems incredible that in spite of all overwhelming evidence to the contrary, the 'high priests of global capitalist ideology'[7] continue to propagate these fantastical dreams.

Furthermore, the temporal conditions produced by this race to the bottom make a meaningful engagement with the present moment almost impossible. For as Braidotti also points out, the centrality of consumption and accumulation in capitalist societies, and the speed in which new commodities appear, induces a state of 'temporal disjunction' as we propel ourselves ever forward in the promise of fulfilment and pleasure.[8] Yet fulfilment and pleasure cannot be found in the future, only in the present, and so we find ourselves unwittingly locked into a perpetual state of dissatisfaction – with our desires subverted and realigned to facilitate further production and consumption. In fact, the central genius of the neoliberal project has been this ability to manipulate conformity and obedience from its citizens not simply through repressive laws and state violence, but through the implanting of a core desire to (at some point in an ever-receding future) finally inhabit this 'imaginary consumptionist utopia'.[9] As Clark explains: 'We live in the shadow of a terrifying utopia … of endless material progress, based on a fundamental utopian fantasy of infinite powers of production and infinite possibilities for consumption'.[10] And thus, the market state has increasingly imposed a global homogeneity in the spheres of thought, activity and what we value as human beings – propagating a materialistic value system that is preoccupied with possessions and the social image they project.

Any critique of the capitalist system must therefore take very seriously not only the dissatisfaction it perpetuates, but the powerful gratifications it also offers, as its expertise in 'hooking' consumers on immediate gratification becomes ever more sophisticated – as we will explore at depth in the following section. In the meantime, our instinctual drives towards joy and pleasure will continue to be channelled through these fabricated needs and desires: solidarity subverted into xenophobic nationalisms, sexual energy commercialised via pornography, and our desire for communion with(in) nature redirected through 'day trips to the zoo'.[11] Even romantic love, claims social theorist Eva Illouz, has become the 'terrain par excellence' to reproduce consumer capitalism.[12] Alisha – a collective visioning participant, describes the situation thus: 'We are immersed in a specific culture whether we like it or not. Even if intellectually we don't want to be involved in a capitalist culture, we still live in it – it's the air that we breathe'. As the forms of oppression adopted by the powerful to subdue their subjects have become increasingly affective, domination has in turn become a participatory process in which the subjects of oppression become willing and active partners in sustaining the conditions necessary for their own subjugation. And while this manipulation of our tendency towards voluntary servitude may well have reached its apex in our contemporary capitalist society, it is by no means a recent phenomenon. In 1577, Étienne de La Boétie in his classic *Discours de la servitude volontaire* made a very similar (and prophetic) observation:

> Men will grow accustomed to the idea that they have always been in subjection, that their fathers lived in the same way; they will think they are obliged to suffer this evil, and will persuade themselves by example and imitation of others, finally investing those who order them around with proprietary rights, based on the idea that it has always been that way.[13]

Thus, tactics of affective domination succeed in suffusing our emotions, relationships and desires, leading to individual and collective feelings of shame, impotence, fear and dependence.[14] As a result, forms of living which perpetuate the controls and exploitations necessary for capitalist relations are reframed, no longer to be experienced as the imposition of external control but as individual choice – as inherent personal desire.

In what follows, we will explore some of the underlying causes and effects of this dystopian present and begin to bring the voices of the activists involved in the collective visioning into dialogue with contemporary theory. This chapter will first look at Big Data Capitalism and the algorithmic conditions within which we find ourselves increasingly immersed, and the subsequent assault on free will, imagination and agency that we now collectively face. We will then examine the causes of our current ecological and climate emergency, exploring the relationship between this bewildering act of ecocide, the rampant materialism that is reified in contemporary society, and the consequent mental health epidemic gripping the planet. And as we draw closer to a wider discussion and analysis of (r)evolutionary love in the following chapters, we will first revisit the theme of love as domination and the exploitative abusive relations, xenophobic nationalisms and patriotisms that it can be observed to manifest as. Finally, we will discuss how, if at all, we might begin to turn this tide in pursuit of free society.

Algorithmic governance and the war on imagination

> 'The real power of capitalist modernity is not its money or its weapons; its real power lies in its ability to suffocate all utopias.'
>
> – Abdullah Öcalan[15]

'The imagination of the end is being corrupted by the end of the imagination'
— Boaventura de Sousa Santos[16]

A major shared concern for the activists involved in the collective visioning process was the insidious use of algorithmic conditioning and media saturation as methods for domination and control. But such concern has not always been the case – in the embryonic stages of the Internet there were legitimate hopes that it would be a space that supported radical political, economic and social change. Many anarchists and left-libertarian thinkers saw a prefigurative politics emerging in those early Internet communities which were inherently decentralised and non-hierarchical in nature. These emerging global electronic networks were seen as ushering in new forms of collective intelligence potentiating a self-organised, networked and deeply democratic global society.[17] And in a sense some of these early assumptions were correct, in as much as the Internet has undeniably acted as a site for a dramatic and radical reorganisation of our political, economic, social and psychological worlds, but as we will now explore – in ways very far from what these activists initially envisioned. While such a vision had (and still has) valid claims for the potential of the Internet as a site for liberation, what would take shape when this space was captured and operationalised to serve the interests of capitalism and the state was significantly underestimated to say the least. As Alice reflects: 'It feels like we've handed over our power in all the important aspects of our lives: where we spend our money, how we spend our time, what we invest our beliefs in, on all levels'.

In 2018, the average total media consumption (TV, radio, time online, gaming and smartphones) for US adults was eleven hours and six minutes per day, up from nine hours and thirty-two minutes per day in 2014.[18] And yet this human–digital complex in which we currently find ourselves immersed is not merely a reflection of the society it is produced within. It is actively, and by stealth, producing and moulding the very social structures that we then proceed to inhabit.[19] So immersed have we become, that it is now almost impossible to distinguish what is social in our lives from what is technological, and with this inability to differentiate we lose a sense of which is meant to serve the other.[20] As we become increasingly integrated into and unextractable from our digitalised world, is it technology that serves the social, or has society itself been reorganised in order to serve the technical? If it is the latter, which seems indisputable at this point in time, then whoever controls the technical controls the social.

In the midst of this collective immersion, new forms of digital capitalism or Big Data Capitalism[21] are tracking, registering, measuring and evaluating every minute action we take in our day-to-day lives, causing us to lose the freedom to act independently of the 'behavioural and performance expectations' embodied in these systems.[22] And as our public administrations similarly collect vast amounts of data on its citizens they become dependent upon the interventions of private tech companies to process and make sense of this data, leading to a dependence on private business interests. Such 'hybridisation' leads to a 'significant non-independence' of government institutions, and governance practices that are based on considerations 'other than the public interest'.[23] This algorithmic governance has obtained a level of control beyond anything we have previously witnessed. It has become the dominant force behind our multiple environments – public, business and now also private, determining the 'architecture of everyday life'.[24] In fact, Nick Clegg, former UK deputy prime minister and now president for global affairs at Meta Platforms, has been leading a lobbying campaign aimed at the US government that lays out the company's rapid plans for how what they are now calling 'the metaverse' could reshape society. What they envisage this metaverse to be is an online space built by companies, creators and developers in which people literally live their lives through virtual reality technologies – from education, to socialising, to work. Robin Mansell, professor of new media and the Internet at the London School of Economics, argues that the socio-political issues associated with this increased algorithmic immersion will be identical to those on existing social media platforms, but in the world of the metaverse they will be on a far larger scale. She concludes: 'it is simply another step in the monetisation of data to the benefit of Facebook and other large platforms sold to people as fun, exciting, helpful for productivity at work and so on'.[25] Surely, asks Emma, 'Mark Zuckerberg can't seriously ask us to believe that he's benevolently connecting the world in order to transform society?'

Far from being merely benign facilitators of these algorithmic conditions, our new masters have become 'choice architects' who by manipulating the choices we have, and the conditions of choosing, develop 'nudging strategies' designed to encourage individuals to make predefined choices – thus rearranging and recreating our personal realities.[26] Ramsay Brown, the co-founder of Dopamine Labs, a tech firm that uses artificial intelligence and neuroscience to help app writers attract and retain users, makes clear the ease with which such invasive reconfigurations are performed: 'We have the ability to twiddle some nobs in a machine learning dashboard we build, and around the world hundreds of thousands of people are going to quietly change their behaviour in ways that, unbeknownst to them, feel second-nature but are really by design'.[27] Within the conditions of this algorithmic enslavement, free will and agency become an illusory construct – with our hopes, desires, dreams and aspirations provided for us, and implanted into our increasingly receptive minds. When asked if it is not then our own personal responsibility to exert self-control when it comes to such digital usage, Tristan Harris, a reformed product philosopher at Google responded: 'but that's not acknowledging that there's a thousand people on the other side of the screen whose job is to break down whatever responsibility I can maintain'.[28] He argues that this 'attention economy' has led to a 'race to the bottom of the brain stem' and warns us not to underestimate the influence and reach of those who control this technology:

> Our generation relies on our phones for our moment-to-moment choices about who we're hanging out with, what we should be thinking about, who we owe a response to, and what's important in our lives ... and if that's the thing that you'll outsource your thoughts to, forget the brain implant. That is the brain implant. You refer to it all the time.[29]

Furthermore, as Rob Hopkins points out: 'our attention and imagination are inextricably linked. One does not exist without the other'.[30] And as our attention is increasingly drawn and redirected in such ways, our ability to imagine anything at all – let alone alternative social and political systems, is eroded in direct correlation. As one activist Maria admits: 'it's hard because I've always lived inside this system, and sometimes my head doesn't have the space to think outside of it'.

It is therefore clear that the entangled nature of our new human–digital complexity is being ruthlessly manipulated by the forces of capital – with our thoughts, desires and even imaginations all being limited and shaped by algorithmic conditioning. But as we have already seen through our earlier exploration of the posthuman, it is not this entanglement itself that imprisons us, for this is simply the way things are – the underlying condition of being human (or more-than-human). It is the seizure and control of these entangled systems and flows within which we continuously reproduce ourselves and society that we must confront. It is here where our freedom can be won or lost. As we have examined, the algorithmic conditioning administered by this corporate-state-technological complex is enjoying extraordinary success in reshaping our subjectivities and intersubjectivities en masse, but for now at least, there also remain uncaptured free spaces in which experiments in horizontal organisation, solidarity and mutual aid are taking place right now. The threat posed to these forces of domination by organising in such spaces has not gone unnoticed, however, and has certainly not been underestimated, as Tom points out: 'You can see the response when people who blog during uprisings are targeted by the state, and are imprisoned, killed or forced to flee. We also see them shutting off the internet when an uprising happens because of the threat it poses'. And so, protecting and expanding these spaces online, in support of the material relations of non-domination which exist offline, will be of major importance for social and ecological activism going forward.

To free ourselves from these systems of domination, as Ken Knabb rightly points out – we have no choice but to begin from where we are now.[31]

The current entangled nature of humans and technology would make an abrupt discontinuity of current technological conditions not only difficult, but extremely dangerous – potentially causing global chaos effecting billions of people. A reappraisal of our relationship with technology will need to be undertaken collectively and with care as we co-constitute a new society – rejecting technologies which cause harm and perpetuate domination, while adapting others to serve the common good. Blueprints for future arrangements are therefore of no use here. Such deliberations must be made dialectically and in responsiveness to conditions as they arise in that moment. But as one way of rebooting these systems of reproduction, and with great congruence to this enquiry, Ignas Kalpokas proposes that we write a new code based on love – a 'love code'. He suggests rewriting the code that underpins the algorithmic conditions we have been exploring in order for love rather than extractive capitalist logics to be at its core – to make love 'the central architectural feature'.[32] But in the meantime, while such struggles continue against our increasing algorithmic enslavement in the digital world, it is essential that we also (with whatever attention and agency we are able to reclaim) remain vigilant in our response towards an even greater existential threat currently facing the material world, and to life itself – to which we now turn.

Powaqqatsi: hurtling towards the cliff edge

'Nature, too, awaits the revolution!'

– Herbert Marcuse[33]

By far the most dangerous and concerning issue for activists that emerged through the collective visioning was that of the current ecological crisis. Many environmental scientists are now describing our current era as the sixth mass extinction event in the history of planet earth, and one caused directly by human activity.[34] The scientific evidence could not be clearer – we are in a state of 'planetary emergency' that presents an 'existential threat to civilisation'.[35] And as Sethness-Castro reminds us, 'the very survival of humanity is imperilled'.[36] The warming of the Arctic has destabilised the jet stream and northern polar vortex – causing extreme movements of warm air north and cold air south. At one point in 2018, temperatures recorded in the Arctic were twenty degrees Celsius above average for that time of year.[37] As a consequence Arctic Sea ice is now declining at a rate of 13.1 per cent each decade,[38] which in turn has led to a dramatic acceleration in the rate of rising sea levels from around 2013 onwards. Current models predict that the acceleration will continue,[39] with the World Bank warning us to prepare for over 100 million people internally displaced and millions more climate refugees forced into migration in the very near future.[40]

The rate, manner and ferocity with which human beings are consuming resources and food is literally destroying our web of life, constructed over billions of years, upon which all of us, human and more-than-human, depend for survival – a phenomenon the Hopi people of North America call *Powaqqatsi*: 'an entity or way of life that consumes the life force of other beings in order to further its own'.[41] As a consequence of this *Powaqqatsi*, we can see that biodiversity – the diversity within species, between species and of ecosystems, is declining faster than at any time in human history.[42] In the last fifty years alone, humanity has wiped out sixty per cent of mammals, birds, fish and reptiles.[43] At present, twenty-five per cent of the remaining animal and plant life on this planet is under direct threat of extinction, suggesting that around one million species could go extinct, many within decades.[44] If current trends persist we could lose *more than a third or even half of all animal and plant species on earth within the next fifty years*.[45] That is unless radical transformative action is taken right now to reduce the drivers of this biodiversity loss, first and foremost being the capitalistic-extractive values and behaviours driving current production and consumption patterns. And yet, in 2020, the loss of primary old-growth tropical forest actually increased by twelve per cent compared to 2019. And this happened in a year that the global economy contracted by at least three per cent due to the COVID-19 pandemic.[46] It is therefore abundantly clear that in order for us not only to survive this crisis, but to use it as a catalyst for building free ecological society, humanity will need to rapidly transform the ways in which our societies function and interact with(in) natural ecosystems.[47] Human and more-than-human relations are after all profoundly 'symbiotic', argues Kasozi, who warns us to be conscious that the survival of each species, humans included, are inseparable.

The current scientific consensus is that we need to radically decrease CO_2 emissions in order to stay below 1.5 degrees Celsius warming of global ambient temperatures if we are to stand any chance of avoiding a catastrophic tipping point leading to climate change advancing exponentially,[48] with subsequent impacts such as mass starvation, disease, flooding, storm destruction, forced migration and war (many of which are already observable globally).[49] In 2019, however, global CO_2 emissions actually *rose* by 0.6 per cent, having risen steadily over the previous decades – the 2019 emissions being sixty-two per cent higher than the year of the first IPCC report in 1990.[50] And following an unprecedented drop of emissions in 2020, again due to the COVID-19 pandemic, global CO_2 emissions from coal and gas rebounded to once again grow more in 2021 than they fell in the previous year[51] – business as usual. Without doubt, it is fossil fuel companies that have been the main drivers of these CO_2 emissions. From 1988 to 2015, the contribution to global warming by fossil fuel companies doubled, producing in just twenty-eight years the equivalent of their emissions in the prior 237 years since the Industrial Revolution.[52] During that period, just 100 companies produced seventy-one per cent of global greenhouse gas emissions.[53] And by 2015, the fossil fuel industry and its products accounted for ninety-one per cent of global industrial greenhouse emissions and seventy per cent of all human-made emissions.[54]

Another leading driver of climate change and biodiversity loss that is largely overlooked (or perhaps wilfully ignored) is the massive expansion of the oppression of non-human animals as food, with an out-of-control animal industrial complex striving to profitably double the consumption of animal 'products' globally by mid-century.[55] But the evidence is clear, and the difference in emissions between meat and plant production is stark – to produce 1 kg of wheat, 2.5 kg of greenhouse gases are emitted, whereas 1 kg of beef creates a staggering 70 kg of emissions. This use of animals for human consumption, as well as livestock feed, is responsible for fifty-seven per cent of all food production emissions, compared with only twenty-nine per cent coming from the cultivation of plant-based foods.[56] Aside from the clear ethical implications concerning the daily terror, torture, murder and dismemberment of non-human animals in order to satisfy the desire for humans to consume their flesh (which will be discussed at depth in the following chapter), research published in *Nature* confirms that without a rapid switch to plant-based diets, critical environmental limits will rapidly move beyond the point at which humanity will struggle to survive.[57] Marco Springmann at the University of Oxford, who led the research, warns us that 'we are really risking the sustainability of the whole system'.[58] And Johan Rockström at the Potsdam Institute for Climate Impact Research in Germany, also part of the research team, agrees that humanity faces a clear choice: 'Greening the food sector or eating up our planet'.[59]

So, then, what (we might ask) of accountability? At the United Nations building in New York on 22 September 2019, the We Mean Business Coalition (consisting of eighty-seven major companies with a combined market capitalisation of over US$2.3 trillion and annual direct emissions equivalent to seventy-three coal-fired power plants) reassured us that they will 'catalyse business action to drive policy ambition and accelerate the transition to a zero-carbon economy'.[60] And on the face of it, for some at least, this might appear to be good news. Yet while such dramatic declarations of corporate responsibility in relation to this ecological catastrophe can certainly be witnessed on an increasingly regular basis, can we really trust the very institutions that have driven us so close to the proverbial cliff edge to now apply the brakes? Douglas Rushkoff, a professor of digital economics, certainly thought so, at least momentarily. He describes a time he was invited to a super-deluxe private resort to deliver a keynote speech on technological responses to the climate emergency to a group of hedge-fund billionaires. It soon became apparent however that this exclusive audience were not in the slightest bit interested in the material he had prepared, and that they had but one question: how would they maintain authority over their security forces after a catastrophic event such as environmental collapse, mass social unrest or a nuclear explosion? He explains:

> The single question occupied us for the rest of the hour. They knew armed guards would be required to protect their compounds from the angry mobs. But how would they pay the guards once money was worthless? What would stop the guards from choosing their own leader? The billionaires considered using special combination locks on the food supply that only they knew. Or making guards wear disciplinary collars of some kind in return for their survival. Or maybe building robots to serve as guards and workers – if that technology could be developed in time. That's when it hit me: at least as far as these gentlemen were concerned, this was a talk about the future of technology … [T]hey were preparing for a digital future that had a whole lot less to do with making the world a better place than it did with transcending the human condition altogether and insulating themselves from the very real and present danger of climate change, rising sea levels, mass migrations, global pandemics, nativist panic and resource depletion. For them, the future of technology is really about one thing: escape.[61]

And so, rather than evolving into the embodiment of corporate responsibility as they would have us believe, as the scientific evidence alerting us to this anthropocentric ecocide has stacked up, fossil fuel and transportation corporations, the meat industry and affiliated trade associations have simultaneously rolled out massive public disinformation and government lobbying campaigns to prevent any meaningful response to these threats, while thwarting the adoption of any binding emissions commitments. Between 2000 and 2016, more than $2 billion was spent on lobbying climate change legislation in the United States alone.[62] Unfortunately, as a 2019 report by the UN Special Rapporteur on Extreme Poverty and Human Rights notes, in the US (the main historical driver of the crisis) this was 'depressingly effective' – the Kyoto Protocol was not ratified as a result, and there has been a dramatic decrease in public understanding of climate change.[63] And in a concerted effort to literally reshape climate science data, in 2017 the US president's office posted its own official, Dr Indur M. Goklany, into the Interior Department in order to, among other duties, insert new text into established scientific findings.[64] The wording, known internally as 'Gok's uncertainty language', inaccurately claimed that there is a lack of consensus in the scientific community that the earth is warming and included a debunked claim that increased carbon dioxide in the atmosphere is actually beneficial. And even as the Biden administration re-joined the Paris agreement, their continued promotion of the oxymoronic 'green capitalism' meant that their newfound environmentalism remains at best a fantasy. As the Indigenous activist Ta'Kaiya Blaney of the Tla A'min Nation told the COP26 meeting in Glasgow – the process is nothing more than 'a performance ... an illusion constructed to save the capitalist economy rooted in resource extraction and colonialism', and that accordingly: 'I didn't come here to fix the agenda – I came here to disrupt it'.[65] In fact, after all the rhetoric of COP26, the IPCC calculates that currently agreed international pledges and targets will still produce a 3.2-degree Celsius median global temperature increase by 2100[66] (which will result in the previously mentioned catastrophic consequences to our more-than-human commons), and as Climate Action Tracker confirms: 'there remains a substantial gap between what governments have promised to do and the total level of actions they have undertaken to date'.[67] Emma, understandably perplexed by this behaviour asks:

> How is it that they can be so deluded? It gobsmacks me! I really want to ask them what on earth they think they are doing causing so much harm. What society do they envisage? The fossil fuel billionaires, those who are colluding in the climate emergency when all the scientists are so clear about the danger. They have no excuse – no excuse.

For most current victims of climate change around the world there is little hope, and for many only despair. The recognition that our current social arrangements are literally jeopardising the continued survival of humanity (and of so many of our more-than-human neighbours) leads to understandable confusion and disorientation. And so, a very real danger arising from this collective bewilderment is that by reflecting on the absurdity of our current state of affairs, the wider population will conclude that the situation is entirely hopeless with nothing to be done, causing them to further retreat from political engagement in the public sphere and allowing the current system to continue unchallenged. As Ekrem observes: 'Something very strange is happening – lakes are evaporating and turning into salt flats, the ice-caps are melting and sea levels are rising, but still, we humans keep ignoring it'. In unity, Emma laments:

> The world is screaming out and it takes a lot not to hear it. I find it impossible to understand. I think it must be a survival mechanism on some level. Even in the crap newspapers there are reports of mass extinctions occurring. I don't think it's a conscious wilful ignorance, I think it speaks to people's lack of power – of what an individual can do against big corporate lobbyists.

And Alice recalls how at an environmental action in Canterbury, UK, where she was part of a road blockade, one of the drivers started to heckle them. One activist engaged the driver and asked if he knew what was happening to the planet and the limited time we had to solve things? The driver responded, 'I don't give a damn; I've got to get to the cinema with my kids'. Perplexed, Alice enquires: 'Why is there this inability to be present with and directly aware of what's happening? Is it a safety mechanism? Is it too much to hold? All these animals that are now extinct as a result of human activity – forever, forever!' It is of course understandable that potential imminent futures involving societal collapse, ecological catastrophe and ultimately mass extinction may well lead to patterns of hopelessness and denial. But if we are to avoid such future scenarios, or at least find ways of adapting to the first two, then facing reality head on seems to be the only option. And the evidence suggests that by focusing on such potential futures, climate change becomes more proximate psychologically, which in turn increases a person's likelihood to take action in response.[68] Alice argues that in order to develop such psychological proximity to the facts of our current ecological emergency a process of grieving is necessary. And in order to assist this process she facilitates grieving circles for ecological activists. For Alice, grieving allows us to discover an 'intimacy with life' and acts to remind us of 'all that we care for and love'. In her own words:

> It feels like a sane response to the grief that so many of us are experiencing in relation to our world, our brethren, plants, animals, and people. It can feel a little overwhelming to open to that scale of grief, and very often at the core of that is a sense of separation. Coming together as a community can dissolve that sense of separation and create the intimacy which I feel so many of us are lacking – that sense of belonging and holding. We start to see how connected we all are in our struggle – rediscovering empathy, compassion and love.

In his work with student activists exploring these issues, Jem Bendell has observed a similar process:

> I have found that inviting them to consider collapse as inevitable, catastrophe as probable and extinction as possible, has not led to apathy or depression. Instead, in a supportive environment, where we have enjoyed community with each other … something positive happens. I have witnessed the shedding of concern for conforming to the status quo, and a new creativity about what to focus on going forward.[69]

Bendell admits that in facing our climate predicament, he has learned that 'there is no way to escape despair'. But he does envision a way through despair: 'It is to love'.[70] As one example of this move to love, in October 2018, the environmental activist group Extinction Rebellion (XR) was launched in the UK – adopting tactics of non-violent civil disobedience in pursuit of radical change to minimise the risk of mass extinctions and ecological collapse. And in a speech made on an occupied Westminster Bridge on Rebellion Day, 17 November 2018, XR organiser and activist Skeena Rathor articulated the centrality of love as a grounding principle for this new movement: 'If we are honest with ourselves and look into our hearts' deep interior, if we are honest from there – then this isn't just about saving humanity, this is about our courage to love as we have never loved before. Let us live now at the edge of our courage to love'.[71] In April 2019 the group disrupted London with eleven days of protests that have been cast as the biggest act of civil disobedience in recent British history.[72] XR occupied four prominent sites in central London for over a week: Oxford Circus, Marble Arch, Waterloo Bridge and the area around Parliament Square – bringing central London to a standstill and leading to over 1,100 arrests with chants of 'we love you' each time an arrest was made. Iconic locations were blocked, the Shell building defaced, Goldman Sachs targeted and a Day of Love organised with rebels marching from the Eros Statue at Piccadilly Circus to Oxford Circus in a profoundly non-violent direct action. Within two weeks, on 1 May 2019, the reluctant Conservative UK government had been forced to declare an environmental and climate emergency (a key demand of XR) – making them the first in the world to do so. But, as we have enquired earlier in this section, have the UK government – or any other government for that matter – really taken any meaningful action as a result?

It seems clear that the direct action described above was indeed successful in transforming public and political discourse around the environmental crisis at that crucial moment. And furthermore, it has acted to politicise and mobilise a substantial group of people in the UK and many other countries who would likely not have otherwise engaged. However, as the London anarchist paper *Rebel City* has explained, XR has inherited the split nature of many green movements – one half remaining 'class blind' and focusing on one issue without seeing how it is vitally linked to the whole social and economic structure, and the other half learning to 'understand the connections and build links that transcend them'. The critique in *Rebel City* concludes: 'It's a pipe-dream to think we can reverse climate change without the dismantling of capitalism as a world-exploiting system. You can't have some nice democratic non-ecocidal market economy'.[73] And they are correct. As we will explore, any attempted compromise with the state immediately opens a space for counterrevolution and defeat. Thus, for contemporary activists, if truly resolved to imagine, co-constitute and then sustain free ecological society, our revolution must become permanent. It must become (r)evolution – an ongoing process without end. Encouragingly, there are some signs of this now happening in XR. Gail Bradbrook, an XR co-founder, described a clear prefigurative turn in XR organising in the midst of the COVID-19 pandemic, when many local XR groups morphed into mutual aid networks.[74] And in one XR communiqué, acknowledging the futility of appealing to the government to take the necessary actions, they in turn concluded: 'We will bring people together and do it ourselves.

We will occupy spaces to listen and discuss the hard truths: what does crisis mean to you? How is it affecting your community? What can we do about it together?'[75] – questions that will be examined at great depth in the remaining chapters of this book.

For now, it remains clear that this unprecedented planetary emergency is by far the greatest challenge that humanity has faced in its so far brief history. And as we have also discovered, somewhat disastrously, our collective ability to co-imagine creative and transformative responses to this threat is being greatly diminished by the moment-to-moment syphoning and redirection of our attention through the algorithmic conditioning processes of digital capitalism. A number of activists in the collective visioning have therefore reflected on how the subsequent sense of fear, bewilderment, dissociation and collective anxiety we are now experiencing as a result of these conditions are therefore only to be expected, as we will now go on to explore.

Materialism, existential anxiety and contemporary capitalist society

'It would be mad not to be mad today.'

– Srećko Horvat [76]

It is very easy to find a wealth of research showing there to be a direct correlation between materialism and mental health.[77] Across a series of studies, results have confirmed that people's wellbeing improves as they place relatively less importance on materialistic goals and values, whereas orienting towards materialistic goals is associated with a decrease in wellbeing.[78] Consequently, by valuing possessions as 'happiness medicine' or a measure of personal success, consumers face a 'material trap' in which materialism fosters social isolation, which in turn reinforces materialism in a 'bidirectional relationship' over time.[79] Materialism and loneliness then form a self-perpetuating cycle in which materialism 'crowds out' social relationships.[80] And this situation has not occurred by chance. Ajay Singh Chaudhary describes twenty-first-century capitalism as an 'extractive circuit' which literally criss-crosses the world, with every 'node' along this circuit – ecological, political, social and individual – being 'extracted and exhausted' to their fullest extent.[81] This circuit perpetuates itself in a rapidly advancing 'feeding frenzy' in which 'services' such as the one-day delivery, expedited shipping and the integration of business and leisure time become an essential means of facilitating the precarious lives of the downwardly mobile informal worker. In this 'always on' capitalism, every single moment of life thus becomes a part of production – integrated, profitable and ultimately unsustainable. Salma argues that in such precarious, alienating times the majority of people she encounters are living their lives 'in fear' – fear of losing their jobs and fear of not being able to feed their children or send them to school. She describes a growing discontent in her country, particularly around economic and political matters:

> People in Jordan now, they are really fed up, everything is really expensive, and they can't think of anything else, they are not able to live a life of dignity where the basics of life are covered. Young people are unable to find work ... people are going to prison because they can't pay the rent of their house or they can't repay a loan, and they are suffering ... There is a fear of not being able to meet the basic needs of life. So yes, it's becoming more like fear than love – unfortunately.

And so, if we really are going to develop a theory and praxis of (r)evolutionary love, argues Dembe, we must first acknowledge that 'our old paradigm has been mostly influenced by greed' and an 'unending desire for power and control', and informed by 'ignorance and a lack of understanding of our true essence as human beings'. From his perspective there are reasons why we segregate into different tribes, into different political factions and different religious affiliations:

> It's because human beings have become fearful of each other – they are worried that there is not going to be enough for themselves. So, under the delusion that they can guarantee enough for themselves and their families only – they create a division of the in-group and the out-group, and this has been the story of humanity for such a long time. But we can't continue on this self-destructive path, we must act in a new and revolutionary way, and I think the framework for this revolution can be love, because love doesn't discriminate, it's all-encompassing, it's inherent within us.

Dembe therefore contends that there are two main forces that influence society today – 'one is love and the other is fear'. Unfortunately, he laments, 'the predominant force across the world right now is fear', and this fear is operationalised strategically by both 'governments and terrorists'. And thus, he concludes 'the government and the terrorist hold a monopoly of violence – maintaining order by keeping people in fear'. And as we have discussed, compounding these experiences at an increasing rate is the additional psychological and existential distress caused by the environmental changes we are currently living through. The American Psychological Association has termed this condition *Solastalgia* – leading to feelings of alienation, a diminished sense of self and an increased vulnerability to stress.[82] Fundamentally, argues Alice, 'the media, advertising companies and people in power survive on our rejection of ourselves, our sense of lack, not being good enough and feeling disempowered'. And thus, in spite of the robust evidence that links capitalism to poor mental health outcomes, there remains little political will to acknowledge it – let alone address it. Instead, governments and pharmaceutical companies direct funding to studies looking at genetics and physical biomarkers as opposed to the environmental causes of distress, perpetuating the present crisis in which the contradictions between capitalism's relentless pursuit of profit and fundamental human needs become increasingly unsustainable. As a result, the most basic conditions required for positive mental health and wellbeing are being severely undermined, and contemporary capitalist societies are consequently 'plagued by neuroses'.[83] One of the activists proposed that symptoms of such psychological maladies include 'aspiring to power, the ideology of growth and competition, and consumerism', adding that 'people are never fundamentally evil, but many have been made insane by capitalism'. And in pursuit of an anti-psychotic praxis to overcome such capitalist induced lunacy, Rosie prescribes love:

> We can get the sense of the boundlessness of love, of the abundance of love available. It's not as if there's a limited quantity of love, but I think our society and our culture says there is. But that lack can be met by love. And maybe a lot of people haven't experienced that, and so maybe we need ways for people to have that sense that it's even a possibility. The possibility of seeing what it's like to connect – with others, with nature, with the world, with something bigger than ourselves – and what that can bring to us.

Echoing Rosie, bell hooks believes that the most powerful antidote to this cycle of anxious consumerism inherent in our capitalist societies are political praxes grounded in love. 'Dominator thinking and practice', she argues, relies for its maintenance on the 'constant production of a feeling of lack, of the need to grasp', and it is by 'giving love' that we will find a way to end this suffering.[84] But before we turn to a deeper exploration of the liberatory potential of such loving praxis in the remaining chapters, it is important to first revisit what else might be enacted politically *in the name of love*.

Partitioned love: sexisms, racisms, patriotisms and creating *the other*

'One would have to be extremely naïve to be unaware of the fact that the catechisms of citizenship preach the love of homeland in order to serve all the interests and privileges of the ruling class, and that for the benefit of this class they promote hatred between the weak and disinherited of various countries.'
Élisée Reclus, 1898.[85]

'Our movement is a movement built on love. Its love for fellow citizens. Its love for struggling Americans who've been left behind, and love for every American child who deserves a chance to have all of their dreams come true.'
– Donald J. Trump, 2017.[86]

For a post-capitalist, post-patriarchal, postcolonial, free ecological society to become anything more than an abstract dream, the conditions through which it will emerge must be prefigured in the here-and-now by those who claim to seek it. Sadly however, a number of activists described how there are still many cases of sexism, racism, misogyny and violence that are 'embedded in a lot of organising'.[87] Sinéad described how activist circles in Ireland had reproduced such patterns of domination:

> There are the snide remarks and put downs – things are said to undermine women's confidence. I think a lot of it is unconscious much of the time, it's the masculine conditioning and they just don't realise they are doing it ... I've been involved in loads of different movements and if something comes along where you're going to be in the limelight, you're going to be in the media, it's a bit of a sexy issue, then the women can make the cups of tea, the women can make the banners, the women can do all the invisible bits of the work that need to be done, and the men can take control and dominate. And the minute that women rise up and challenge this the person leaves, because if it's not going to be beneficial to them personally, to promote them in some way, then they will leave. Many men in movements, I'm not saying all men, but many men cannot take direction from women – they just can't do it. They have to be in a senior role. So, it can be very difficult.

And of even greater concern, Tom was aware of actual incidents of sexual assault and violent attacks that had taken place within organising groups in Canada – a betrayal of principles and ideals that he found difficult to comprehend. Similarly, back in Ireland, while organising alongside the male-dominated trade union movement on larger campaigns, Sinéad recalls how sexual harassment was a constant threat:

> [The union officials] work with women and they talk about gender equality in the movement and blah blah blah, and then they get drunk and start feeling everybody up. And they just can't see how that's not cool. And this really undermines any trust, friendship, kindness and caring within a movement. And if you are a woman from a minority ethnic group it can be even worse because weirdly there are perceptions that they are more open to being sexually harassed.

The activists reflected how such harassment often goes unacknowledged, and how very often nobody says anything for fear of retribution. Even worse, in some groups the person who is the victim is thrust out of the group due to the aggressor being more popular or being able to rally people behind them. As Tom explains: 'the group attempts to maintain cohesion through exclusion'. And Sinéad further reflects on how the current configuration of capitalist patriarchal society reduces the agency of women to engage in activism in the first place, with competing caring roles and economic precarity limiting the ability of female activists to meaningfully participate in struggle even further:

> For women, literally every area of life has limitations, things are constantly pressing down on you. We are expected to hold so much. Society expects so much more from women. A lot of the women I know who are politically active also tend to be the ones who don't have children. A lot of them are also from privileged backgrounds and don't have to worry so much about making ends meet.

Somewhat reassuringly, it also remains possible to find examples of more equitable, respectful, and non-dominating organisational practices in contemporary struggles globally. In Brazil for instance, the Movement of Landless Workers (MST) consciously work to prefigure the kind of society they aim to build, based on mutual aid and responsibility, and in which machismo, racism and oppressive power relations are constantly challenged and delegitimised. For instance, when discussing arrangements for the care of children and the elderly within the activist collectives, the MST decided that such caring relations should be framed as a social issue, not just a familial one. And so they have started building kindergartens as spaces for socialisation, care, affection and education – with the entire collective involved in the work, previously located within the family, and specifically undertaken by women – and thus allowing the kinds of misogyny described by Sinéad and Tom no stable ground on which to establish/reproduce itself.[88] Such initiatives, if nurtured and multiplied, potentiate the development of what Silvia Federici calls 'self-reproducing movements' – in which movements reorganise social relations within their own communities in ways that prefigure and transform the forms of caring labour dominant in wider society.[89] An affective struggle explored in greater depth in the next chapter.

The collective visioning participants were therefore keen to differentiate between the co-optation and subversion of love as a justification for domination, hatred and division, and the (r)evolutionary love we collectively pursued in this process. Thus the participants resonated with Hardt's earlier rejection of patriotism or love of nation/race as a corrupt identitarian form of love,[90] and similarly Goldman's view of it as a 'menace to liberty' and a 'superstition' created and maintained through a 'network of lies and falsehoods'.[91] For Sinéad, there is an inherent danger in an over-connection with a nation-state – with an 'excessive love of country' leading to racism and xenophobia: 'I definitely think that love can be corrupted in that sense, and lead to divisions'. Similarly for Tom – love 'gets into trouble when it's exclusive'. Any type of movement, ethic or politics that demands exclusivity in creating a transcendent ideal, he argues, whether it is a country or a specific subject or citizen – 'will immediately run into issues of coercion, domination and enforcement'. And also, for Dembe, as long as a concept of love excludes some people, or focuses upon the few, it is limited – 'it is not love in its wholeness'. He thus concludes that 'nationalism isn't really driven by love but by fear':

> This kind of love is a blind love, it is limited, it is not the type of [(r)evolutionary] love that we are talking about. It's actually fear in the name of love. You are telling this group that because you are special, because I love you, and because you hold a special position in the universe, I am trying to protect you from all those other people. So, I don't think we can call that love. I think it's fear disguised as love ... With a wider love you are open minded – you recognise others as your neighbours – as friends – as your community. You don't exclude them. You don't build a wall!

Ekrem too warns that we need to be careful that our love does not create further boundaries – that a new free society is 'borderless'. And here he extends the scope of such a love beyond the human to a more-than-human love which includes 'other humans, our relationship with the environment, and the relationship we have with animals that live alongside us in our societies' – a theme explored at depth in the next chapter. As Ekrem proposes: 'We need a society based on love. And that love will be an extended one, and a sustained one. A love which doesn't create othering – one that doesn't create a small circle of humans to be protected and loved while others are left'. Msizi reflects that in his own Zulu culture such a 'love of the same', far from being a natural state has in fact been a recent development imposed through colonialism and apartheid. He explains how previously, members of his community had practiced Ubuntu: 'we helped each other without wanting something in return. If there was a child-headed household, the community would come together and support it, and every elder would be considered a parent – we were all family'. But Msizi argues that a radical change occurred in his community, as through the imposition of colonial domination they lost their autonomy:

> Somewhere along the line we lost that inner feeling of Ubuntu – of giving love to one another. Our colonial masters and the apartheid government used a system of divide and rule. So, this race was better than that race – whites were obviously at the top, and Indians were below the whites but better than the blacks. And even the blacks were pitted against each other – this tribe is better than that tribe, Xhosa were better than Zulu, Soto were not as good as Zulu. It created a sense of competition that wasn't there before. We lost the Ubuntu – where the tribal communities would support each other, and work together.

Such purposeful divide-and-rule tactics of partitioning love are by no means isolated. Hassan describes how at the start of the Syrian revolution it was possible to observe a radical solidarity emerge in which previously separate groups – educated and uneducated, rich and poor, and Muslim, Christian, Arab and Kurd came together in protest against the regime. And in order to destroy this newfound solidarity, he explains, the regime fabricated problems between the different groups:

> They wanted Kurdish people to hate Arabic people, Muslims to hate Christians. The regime sent men who weren't from our community to attack Christians and tell them 'we don't want you here' and tell them to leave. The regime created an enemy and our revolution was stolen. In the early days the revolution was for all Syrians, for all people, not for one religion over another. But then strangers appeared and used religious words, and made religious demands, and started to fight the local organisers ... Before this I had friends and I didn't know if they were Christian or Muslim – it just didn't matter. So [the regime] worked on destroying the solidarity between people ... and they changed everything.

And so, we see that what is presented as love of country does not necessarily exclude further *othering* of groups within the territory it is aimed at cohering if it is required as a further means of social control. As Sinéad explains: 'there is love of country, but also a love of country in which people behave in a certain way!' She observes this in the way the Traveller community are alienated in Irish society through what amounts to hegemonic discrimination: 'They are indigenous Irish citizens, an integral part of the society, but they are not accepted, they are not part of this love. It's a form of social control. You must conform. Patriotism and conformity are interlinked. Authoritarian leaders can play on this and use it to their advantage'. In terms of such marginalisation, Katie suggests that there is a direct correlation between the ability of a community to ground itself in (r)evolutionary love and that community's prior experience of marginalisation, proposing that such communities become 'multilingual' in oppression and are thus a source of learning:

> The black person in the U.S. is fluent in their own community wherever that is, and also a larger mainstream white community, in order to function and survive. Because of the connectedness with others who are oppressed I think there's probably more possibility for love being something that really matters. So those of us who come from more oppressive communities have more to learn.

As a member of one such oppressed population, Lowanna likens the relationship between the colonial state and her Indigenous Australian community to one of family violence, with the community as 'victims of family violence – tired, scared and exhausted'. And when reflecting how/if such communities can recover and heal when the broader social relationship is based on such violence, her response at once describes the transformational potential of – and simultaneously embodies – the (r)evolutionary love being theorised:

> We had learned violence but we hadn't had the opportunity to learn love. So, we undermine that violence through love. We reset the relationship between brothers and sisters, black fellas and white fellas, to a healthy and functional family type relationship. It's a massive shift. You have to bring everyone with you. You have to be inclusive. If you set boundaries on that love then it's not revolutionary, is it? So, I'm going to love my coloniser and transform them in the process.

Turning the tide

'We live in capitalism, its power seems inescapable – but then, so did the divine right of kings. Any human power can be resisted and changed by human beings.'

– Ursula K. Le Guin[92]

'In 1968, just before he was killed, Martin Luther King Jr. said "Only when it is dark enough, can you see the stars". It is now dark enough.'

– Vijay Prashad[93]

Although expressing a deep concern about the multiple complex challenges we are collectively facing, most activists in the collective visioning process also remained convinced that 'another world is (still) possible' and that our dystopian present is pregnant with potential for radical social transformation – as we will see in the following chapters. Throughout history, we can see that times of global crisis have led to fundamental shifts in the dominant political, economic and social paradigms of the day. Following the Great Depression, Keynesianism replaced the neoclassical orthodoxy that came before it. The crisis of stagnation of the late 1970s then opened the door to neoliberalism which immediately (and with great efficiency) set about deconstructing the Keynesian model and its institutions. In a rapid continuation of this cycle, the 2008 economic crisis and more recently the COVID-19 pandemic have acted to erode the previously unassailable neoliberal consensus, resulting in the current vacuum of ideological uncertainty. But in truth the libertarian left has been slow to respond – less organised and with far fewer resources than the forces of capital who have rushed to prefigure the next paradigmatic evolution. Ground has certainly been lost. In fact, given the current rate of anthropogenic environmental devastation it is becoming increasingly likely that we will simply run out of time to make the radical changes necessary to avert the impending ecological and societal disaster we are currently hurtling towards. With less optimism than many of the collective visioning participants, a number of political philosophers now argue that the long term trajectory that activists should take as their working assumption is the 'protracted, crisis ridden and irreversible decay of industrial civilisation'.[94] From this perspective, activist projects involving mutual aid, cooperation and permaculture techniques remain highly relevant, but not necessarily as prefigurations of the new society within the existing one, but as the building blocks of one to be built in the rubble of the old. But for now, at least, the window of opportunity remains (narrowly) open, and the trajectory towards whatever replaces the current system is open to affect, and directable – towards further domination and an escalation of our current dystopic conditions, or towards non-domination and free society. It would be prudent therefore to establish what factors might be blocking our ability to act, and to locate a suitable ground on which we can then begin the work of reversing this tide.

It probably goes without saying that those who have controlled politics – monarchs, governments, the military and economic powers, have tended to favour theories and models that have legitimised the need for their continued domination. The homogeneity of contemporary political opinion has therefore not been constructed from a 'theoretical line of educated thought' but rather from theorists who happen to have been members of the ruling classes at various points throughout history.[95] Similarly, these very same custodians of our political epistemologies have ensured that proponents of free society, and anarchists in particular, have been almost entirely erased from history as the legitimate popular social and political movements they once were – with even the word 'anarchy' being subverted and propagandised in order to crush left-libertarian discourse. The stereotype of anarchism as a threat to civilised society was firmly established in the nineteenth century in response to its growing popularity as a political ideology and social movement. And this negative characterisation remains deeply rooted in the contemporary public imaginary. Such characterisations of contemporary activists who adopt anarchistic praxes as violent and disordered continues to be a regular go-to trope for politicians and the mainstream media alike.[96] This demonisation of many ecological, anti-capitalist, feminist and anti-racist activists is operationalised in order to prevent the threat of large sections of society identifying with their actions and building a mass movement for change. Thus, by erasing the identity and humanity of the individual activists (who are actually likely to have far more in common with the wider public than those in power), and focusing on their groups through anarchist stereotypes and as thugs, they become associated with the violence and disruption that the media chooses to focus on rather than the message their activism seeks to advance.[97]

Throughout history, those who govern have always been faced with this problem of suppressing our solidarity and taming our passions in order to better protect and serve the requirements of exploitative and hierarchical institutions, but while this might have served the needs of a small ruling class it has certainly not served the collective wellbeing of wider society. So for those of us in pursuit of a free society, the problem is not how to bring our passions under rigid control, but to explore how a fuller, freer and constructive expression of them might contribute to a radical solidarity and the realisation of such a world.[98] As we have discussed, the dizzying array of injustices, oppressions and violence that we find ourselves called on to navigate today may well leave us feeling frozen and without agency – locked into a negation of the present in order to avoid the trauma of the horrors that unfold. And such a response is of course entirely understandable. Yet this frozen state does not merely negate the horrors – it negates transformation, and it separates us from those around us. As Ruth Kinna warns us, there is a notable trend in which certain political praxes align more with a 'dystopian escape' than a 'utopian achievement'.[99] Thus by unpacking the dystopian features of contemporary society (as this chapter has attempted to do) without transforming the feelings of anger and hopelessness this understandably evokes into an impetus for creating alternatives, we run the risk of being trapped in destructive patterns of rage and despair – an aversion to the here-and-now, rather than its liberation. And such a response leaves us powerless, cut off and subject to further domination. In order for us to achieve genuine progress and social change, Jack argues that a positive narrative is required – not just 'we don't want this – we don't want this'. He suggests a new narrative based on the commons and in community: 'We have lived like this in the past, and the commons is where we need to be moving towards again, but maybe not in the same way as before – there are ways of organising ourselves that will be new. But that sense of community just feels absolutely paramount'.

As we have seen, an ontology of separation causes love to manifest as domination – in the service of a separate autonomous self. Conversely, and as we will explore in what follows, an ontology of entanglement and immanence potentiates the (r)evolutionary love this book pursues, manifesting as non-domination and in service of both the *I* and the *WE* – as intimately interrelational. The following chapters will now make the case for (r)evolutionary love as an alternative political response – to turn outwards, to reconnect and in that connection to transform ourselves and the worlds we co-create. Braidotti explains that moving into such an affirmative politics is not about the avoidance of pain, but rather about 'transcending the resignation and passivity that ensue from being hurt, lost and dispossessed',[100] and thus transforming the pain of oppression into positive, creative, powerful praxis. What is important here politically is the agency released in the move from being locked in negation to imagining new worlds – an agency that can then be utilised in co-creating the material relations and networks to realise such worlds, in the here-and-now. A political project to which we now turn.

Notes

1 Situationist International, *Situationist international anthology*, ed. and trans. K. Knabb (Berkeley, CA: Bureau of Public Secrets, 2006), pp. 106–107.

2 Subcomandante Marcos, 'Introduction', in N. Henck (ed.) and H. Gales (trans.) *The Zapatistas' dignified rage: Final public speeches of Subcommander Marcos* (Chico, CA: AK Press, 2014).

3 John P. Clark, *The impossible community: Realizing communitarian anarchism* (New York: Bloomsbury, 2013), p. 265.

4 Braidotti, *The posthuman*, p. 7.

5 Ibid., p. 62.

6 Peter Marshall, 'Preface', in L. Davis and R. Kinna (eds) *Anarchism and utopianism* (Manchester: Manchester University Press, 2009), xiv.

7 Saul Newman, 'Anarchism, utopianism and the politics of emancipation', in L. Davis and R. Kinna (eds) *Anarchism and utopianism* (Manchester: Manchester University Press, 2009), p. 209.

8 Rosi Braidotti, 'Posthuman affirmative politics', in S.E. Wilmer and A. Žukauskaitė (eds) *Resisting biopolitics: Philosophical, political, and performative strategies* (New York: Routledge, 2016), p. 41.

9 John P. Clark (2009) 'Anarchy and the dialectic of utopia', in L. Davis and R. Kinna (eds) *Anarchism and utopianism* (Manchester: Manchester University Press, 2009), p. 19.

10 Clark, *The impossible community*, p. 127.

11 Jack Hipp, 'The Eros Effect and the embodied mind', in J. Del Gandio and A.K. Thompson (eds) *Spontaneous combustion: The Eros Effect and global revolution* (Albany, NY: SUNY Press, 2017), p. 160.

12 Eva Illouz, *The end of love: A sociology of negative relations* (New York: Oxford University Press, 2019), p. 229.

13 Étienne De La Boétie, *The politics of obedience: The discourse of voluntary servitude*, trans. H. Kurz (Auburn, AL: Mises Institute, 2015), p. 60.

14 Nick Montgomery and Carla Bergman, *Joyful militancy: Building thriving resistance in toxic times* (Chico, CA: AK Press, 2017), p. 51.

15 Abdullah Öcalan, *Manifesto for a democratic civilization, vol. 1, Civilization. The age of masked gods and disguised kings* (Porsgrunn, Norway: New Compass Press, 2015), p. 19.

16 Boaventura de Sousa Santos, *The end of the cognitive empire: The coming of age of epistemologies of the South* (Durham, NC: Duke University Press, 2018), p. ix.

17 Sky Croeser, 'Post-industrial and digital society', in C. Levy and M. Adams (eds) *The Palgrave handbook of anarchism* (Cham, Switzerland: Palgrave Macmillan, 2019), p. 626.

18 Rob Hopkins, 'From what is to what if? Unleashing the power of imagination'. *STIR* 28 (2020), 17.

19 José Van Dijck, Thomas Poell and Martijn Waal, *The platform society: Public values in a connective world* (Oxford: Oxford University Press, 2018), p. 2.

20 Murray Bookchin, *The ecology of freedom: The emergence and dissolution of hierarchy* (Stirling: AK Press, 2005), p. 325.

21 See: David Chandler and Christian Fuchs, *Digital objects, digital subjects: Interdisciplinary perspectives on capitalism, labour and politics in the age of Big Data* (London: University of Westminster Press, 2019), pp. 1–20.

22 Steffen Mau, *The metric society: On the quantification of the social* (Cambridge: Polity Press, 2019), p. 4.

23 Ignas Kalpokas, *Algorithmic governance: Politics and law in the post-human era* (Cham, Switzerland: Palgrave Macmillan, 2019), p. 100.

24 Ibid., p. 27.

25 Miranda Bryant, 'Is Facebook leading us on a journey to the metaverse?' *The Guardian*, 26 September 2021.

26 Kalpokas, *Algorithmic governance*, p. 59.

27 Ramsay Brown, cited in: John Brooks, 'Tech insiders call out Facebook for literally manipulating your brain'. *KQED Science*, 2017. Available online: www.kqed.org/futureofyou/379828/tech-insiders-call-out-facebook-for-literally-manipulating-your-brain (accessed 2 May 2022).

28 Tristan Harris, cited in: Bianca Bosker, 'The binge breaker'. *The Atlantic*, 2016. Available online: www.theatlantic.com/magazine/archive/2016/11/the-binge-breaker/501122/ (accessed 23 September 2021).

29 Ibid.

30 Hopkins, 'From what is to what if? Unleashing the power of imagination', p. 19.

31 Ken Knabb, *The joy of revolution* (Berkeley, CA: Bureau of Public Secrets, 1997), p. 136.

32 Kalpokas, *Algorithmic governance*, pp. 114–115.

33 Herbert Marcuse, *Counterrevolution and revolt* (Boston, MA: Beacon Press, 1972), p. 265.

34 Jem Bendell, 'Deep adaption: A map for navigating climate tragedy'. *IFLAS* Occasional Paper 2, 2018.

35 Timothy Lenton et al., 'Climate tipping points – Too risky to bet against'. *Nature 575* (2019), 595.

36 Javier Sethness-Castro, *Imperilled life: Revolution against climate catastrophe* (Oakland, CA: AK Press, 2012), p. 100.

37 Jonathan Watts, 'Arctic warming: scientists alarmed by "crazy" temperature rises'. *The Guardian*, 27 February 2018.

38 NSIDC/NASA, 'Vital signs of the planet: Arctic sea ice minimum'. *NASA global climate change vital signs of the planet*, 2020. Available online: https://climate.nasa.gov/vital-signs/arctic-sea-ice/ (accessed 26 January 2022).

39 David Malmquist, 'Sea-level report cards: 2019 data adds to trend in acceleration'. *Virginia Institute of Marine Science*, 2020. Available online: www.vims.edu/newsandevents/topstories/2020/slrc_2019.php (accessed 8 May 2022).

40 Kanta Kumari Rigaud et al., *Groundswell: Preparing for internal climate migration* (Washington, DC: The World Bank, 2018).

41 Vandana Shiva, 'Foreword', in *This is not a drill: An Extinction Rebellion handbook* (London: Penguin, 2019), p. 5.

42 Sandra Díaz, Josef Settele and Eduardo Brondízio, 'Summary for policymakers of the global assessment report on biodiversity and ecosystem services'. *IPBES*, 2019, p. 2.

43 World Wildlife Fund, *Living planet report – 2018*, M. Grooten and R. Almond (eds) (Gland, Switzerland: WWF, 2018), p. 7.

44 Díaz et al., 'Summary for policymakers of the global assessment report on biodiversity and ecosystem services', p. 3.

45 Cristian Román-Palacios and John J. Wiens, 'Recent responses to climate change reveal the drivers of species extinction and survival'. *Proceedings of the National Academy of Sciences of the United States of America*, 10 February 2020. Available online: www.pnas.org/content/early/2020/02/04/1913007117 (accessed 16 March 2022).

46 Fiona Harvey, 'Destruction of world's forests increased sharply in 2020'. *The Guardian*, 31 March 2021.

47 William J. Ripple et al., 'World scientists' warning of a climate emergency'. *BioScience* 70:1 (2020), 4.

48 IPCC, 'Summary for policymakers', in *Global Warming of 1.5°C: An IPCC Special Report* (World Meteorological Organization: Geneva, Switzerland, 2018).

49 Bendell, 'Deep adaption: A map for navigating climate tragedy'.

50 Pierre Friedlingstein et al., 'Global carbon budget 2019'. *Earth System Science Data* 11:4 (2019), 1783–1838.

51 Friedlingstein et al., 'Global carbon budget 2021'. *Earth System Science Data*, 2021 [Preprint]. Available online: https://essd.copernicus.org/preprints/essd-2021–386/ (accessed 15 May 2022).

52 Paul Griffin, 'The carbon majors database CDP carbon majors report'. *Climate Accountability Institute*, 2017, p. 2.

53 Ibid, p. 8.

54 Ibid.

55 Anthony J. Nocella et al., *Defining critical animal studies: An intersectional social justice approach for liberation* (New York: Peter Lang, 2014), pp. x–xi.

56 Xiaoming Xu et al., 'Global greenhouse gas emissions from animal-based foods are twice those of plant-based foods'. *Nature Food* 2 (2021), 724–732.

57 Marco Springmann et al., 'Options for keeping the food system within environmental limits'. *Nature* 562 (2018), 519–525.

58 Damian Carrington, 'Huge reduction in meat-eating 'essential' to avoid climate breakdown'. *The Guardian*, 10 October 2018.
59 Ibid.
60 We Mean Business Coalition, '87 major companies lead the way towards a 1.5°C future at UN Climate Action Summit'. Press release, 22 September 2019. Available online: www.wemeanbusinesscoalition.org/press-release/87-major-companies-lead-the-way-towards-a-1–5c-future-at-un-climate-action-summit/ (accessed 7 March 2022).
61 Douglas Rushkoff, 'Survival of the richest', in *This is not a drill: An Extinction Rebellion handbook* (London: Penguin, 2019, p. 59).
62 Robert J. Brulle, 'The climate lobby: a sectoral analysis of lobbying spending on climate change in the USA, 2000 to 2016'. *Climatic Change* 149 (2018), 289–303.
63 OHCHR, 'Climate change and poverty: Report of the Special Rapporteur on extreme poverty and human rights', delivered to *the Human Rights Council Forty-first session*, 24 June – 12 July 2019.
64 Hiroko Tabuchi, 'A Trump insider embeds climate denial in scientific research'. *The New York Times*, 2 March 2020.
65 Libby Brooks, 'Hundreds of global civil society representatives walk out of COP26 in protest'. *The Guardian*, 12 November 2021.
66 IPCC, 'Summary for policymakers', in *Climate change 2022: Mitigation of Climate Change. Contribution of Working Group III to the Sixth Assessment Report of the Intergovernmental Panel on Climate Change* (New York: Cambridge University Press, 2022), p. 21.
67 See: Climate Action Tracker, *Temperatures: Addressing global warming*, 2021. Available online: https://climateactiontracker.org/global/temperatures/ (accessed 14 May 2022).
68 Rachel McDonald, Hui Yi Chai and Ben R. Newell, 'Personal experience and the "psychological distance" of climate change: An integrative review'. *Journal of Environmental Psychology* 44 (2015), 109–118.
69 Bendell, 'Deep adaption: A map for navigating climate tragedy'.
70 Jem Bendell, 'Doom and bloom: Adapting to collapse', in *This is not a drill: An Extinction Rebellion handbook* (London: Penguin, 2019, p. 80).
71 From a speech made by activist Skeena Rathor, Westminster Bridge, 17 November 2018.
72 Guy Faulconbridge and Andrew Marshall, 'Extinction Rebellion has a message for the world – We've only just begun'. *Reuters World News*, 1 May 2019.
73 Rebel City, 'Climate change is not a single issue'. *Rebel City* 12 (2019), 4.
74 Quoted in: Damien Gayle and Damian Carrington, 'Extinction Rebellion eyes shift in tactics as police crackdown on protests'. *The Guardian*, 3 September 2021.
75 Extinction Rebellion, 'Extinction Rebellion launch plans for UK rebellion'. *Popular Resistance*, 2021. Available online: https://popularresistance.org/extinction-rebellion-launch-plans-for-uk-rebellion/ (accessed 23 April 2022).
76 Horvat, *The radicality of love*, p. 124.

77 See: David Matthews, 'Capitalism and mental health'. *Monthly Review* 70:8 (2019), 49–62; and Tim Kasser et al., 'Changes in materialism, changes in psychological well-being: Evidence from three longitudinal studies and an intervention experiment'. *Motivation and Emotion* 38 (2014), 1–22.

78 Ibid., p. 2.

79 Rik Pieters, 'Bidirectional dynamics of materialism and loneliness: not just a vicious cycle'. *Journal of Consumer Research* 40:4 (2014), 615.

80 Ibid., p. 616.

81 Ajay Singh Chaudhary, 'The extractive circuit: An exhausted planet at the end of growth'. *The Baffler* 60 (2021). Available online: https://thebaffler.com/salvos/the-extractive-circuit-singh-chaudhary (accessed 12 March 2022).

82 American Psychological Association, *Mental health and our changing climate: Impacts, implications and guidance* (San Francisco, CA: ecoAmerica, 2017), pp. 25–27.

83 Matthews, 'Capitalism and mental health', p. 51.

84 bell hooks, 'Toward a worldwide culture of love'. *Lion's Roar*, 2018. Available online: www.lionsroar.com/toward-a-worldwide-culture-of-love/ (accessed 10 May 2022).

85 Élisée Reclus, 'Evolution, revolution, and the anarchist ideal', in J. Clark and C. Martin (eds) *Anarchy, geography, modernity: Selected writings of Élisée Reclus* (Oakland, CA: PM Press, 2013), p. 143.

86 Cited in: Grant J Silva, 'Racism as self-love'. *Radical Philosophy Review* 22:1 (2019), 85.

87 Tom, collective visioning participant.

88 Janaina Stronzake, 'People make the occupation and the occupation makes the people', in K. Khatib, M. Killjoy, and M. McGuire (eds) *We are many: Reflections on movement strategy from occupation to liberation* (Oakland, CA: AK Press, 2012), p. 119.

89 Silvia Federici, *Revolution at point zero: Housework, reproduction, and feminist struggle* (Oakland, CA: PM Press, 2020).

90 Hardt and Negri, *Commonwealth*, p. 182.

91 Goldman, 'Patriotism: A menace to liberty', p. 49.

92 Ursula K. Le Guin, Speech made at the *65th National Book Awards*, New York, 2014.

93 Vijay Prashad, 'This concerns everyone', in K. Khatib, M. Killjoy and M. McGuire (eds) *We are many: Reflections on movement strategy from occupation to liberation* (Oakland, CA: AK Press, 2012), p. 15.

94 Uri Gordon, 'Utopia in contemporary anarchism', in L. Davis and R. Kinna (eds) *Anarchism and utopianism* (Manchester: Manchester University Press, 2009), p. 272.

95 Eva Fabrizio, 'Social movements are political movements: What's geopolitics?' *Geopolitics* 9:2 (2010), 479.

96 Benjamin Franks and Ruth Kinna, 'Contemporary British anarchism'. *La Revue LISA* 7:8 (2014), 355.

97 Fiona Donson et al., 'Rebels with a cause, folk devils without a panic: Press jingoism, policing tactics and anti-capitalist protest in London and Prague'. *Internet Journal of Criminology*, 2004, p. 26. Available online: http://orca. cf.ac.uk/60834/1/Rebel%20with%20a%20cause%20 (accessed 8 May 2022).

98 Clark, 'Anarchy and the dialectic of utopia', p. 17.

99 Ruth Kinna, 'Utopianism and prefiguration', in S. Chrostowska and J. Ingram (eds) *Political uses of utopia: New Marxist, anarchist, and radical democratic perspectives* (New York: Columbia University Press, 2016), p. 208.

100 Rosi Braidotti, 'Generative futures: On affirmative ethics', in A. Radman and H. Sohn (eds) *Critical and clinical cartographies: Architecture, robotics, medicine, philosophy* (Edinburgh: Edinburgh University Press, 2017), p. 301.

4

The deep commons

'The first man who, having enclosed a piece of ground, bethought himself of saying "this is mine", and found people simple enough to believe him, was the real founder of civil society. From how many crimes, wars and murders, from how many horrors and misfortunes might not any one have saved mankind, by pulling up the stakes, or filling up the ditch, and crying to his fellows "Beware of listening to this impostor; you are undone if you once forget that the fruits of the earth belong to us all, and the earth itself to nobody."'

– Jean-Jacques Rousseau[1]

Introduction

In *Down to Earth*, Bruno Latour identifies three core utopias which underpin contemporary political and social imaginaries: (1) the *local* – a desire to return to the imagined security of national, regional, ethnic or identitary boundaries; (2) the *global* – a perpetual advance towards an infinite horizon with limitless growth; and (3) the *out-of-this-world* – an increasing propensity towards post-truth, and the pursuit of security through outright denial and sheer fantasy.[2] And of course all three of these utopian desires have been expertly manipulated by those in power throughout history, and never more so than in our current algorithmic conditions as explored in the previous chapter. Of central importance to our enquiry, however, is the nature of these current political utopias – that they are transcendent rather than grounded, or, put another way, rather than here-and-now they are nowhere, in an ever-receding future/past, or otherwise in an alternate reality altogether. They are impossible. It is here that Latour asks an important question: Do we continue to nourish dreams of escaping or do we start seeking a territory that we and our children can inhabit?[3]

It is clear that in the face of our current overlapping social and ecological crises, the overwhelming response has been to flee, to escape. The super-wealthy who hold the most capital create luxurious fortresses to shield them from those they have betrayed, others cling for dear life to the illusory security of a nation or people by building walls, closing borders and protecting *me* and *mine*, while the growing numbers of dispossessed find themselves in imposed exodus and placeless/groundless. And so, in alignment with Latour, this book concurs that in response we should become 'terrestrials' once more[4] – to re-orient ourselves as human in relation to the multitude of other terrestrials with whom we find ourselves entangled and to start our political project from this ground. And in unity also with David Abram's assertion that at some point (and it will have to be very soon) technological civilisation has no alternative other than to 'accept the invitation of gravity and settle back into the land'.[5] But further than that – if we are to move beyond our current states of bewilderment, disorientation and denial, we will need to establish new (and learn from existing) grounded utopias which, rather than being *not-now* and *nowhere*, are co-imagined and lived both *here* and *now* – a politics of immanence. What if, as we find ourselves frozen in the space between these impossible utopias – bereft of agency and dissociated from the material present – the home we have been dreaming of, striving for and extending towards is right here and right now, and always has been?

Continuing to be grounded in themes emerging from the collective visioning process, this chapter will first explore the conditions of empathic entanglement that act as the basis for societal formation and the radical loving-caring praxes which underpin many contemporary struggles. Next, by extending popular conceptions of the commons to include these more-than-human psycho-socio-material relations, the deep commons will be proposed as a ground through which this (r)evolutionary love might circulate in order for new political (inter)subjectivities to manifest. The apparent binary tension between personal autonomy and social solidarity that exists in much of contemporary political/philosophical thought will then be re-examined in light of these more-than-human loving entanglements, and Indigenous concepts of the deep commons will be considered as alternatives to our current colonial, capitalist and anthropocentric political imaginaries. And finally, the concept of degrowth will be examined in pursuit of the temporal shift to a slower pace of life required to avert our impending ecological disaster.

(R)evolutionary love: rediscovering the Agapeic web

'The problem that confronts us today, and which the nearest future is to solve, is how to be one's self and yet in oneness with others, to deeply feel with all human beings and still retain one's characteristic qualities.'

– Emma Goldman[6]

A free society can only emerge from the conditions which precede it. And thus, it is essential for us to ascertain whether or not our present conditions contain the potential for such societal formations. Dembe questions Hobbes' view that 'the natural state of men, before they entered into society, was a mere war ... of all men against all men',[7] and proposes that we critically evaluate how these views have influenced our core conceptions of government and political organisation. From Dembe's perspective, 'love has its own history ... its own story' – and it is love that has 'literally held our societies together'. The question for him then is 'how do we create society on a foundation of love, and not fear?' There is now a growing tendency within contemporary left-libertarian thinking to critique the notion of us ever arriving at any point of revolutionary closure[8] – a point demonstrated (somewhat ironically) by Fukuyama's proclamation of 'The end of history' in 1989![9] What is posited instead is a long-term open-ended process of social change, beginning at the level of 'the individual spirit'[10] – a process of (r)evolution to be explored at depth in the next chapter. Furthermore, from our new-found perspective as entangled beings attempting to navigate this more than human psycho-socio-material commons, it becomes impossible to abstract a mode of political praxis which exists anywhere other than the here-and-now. Whether consciously or not, struggles are conceived, co-created and actualised in the flow of this radical interconnectedness and commonality, and thus, as Stevphen Shukaitis points out, the *effectiveness* of political organising and its *affectiveness* are 'inherently and inevitably intertwined'.[11] For (r)evolutionary love to achieve its transformative potential we must ground ourselves in this reality – that free society will not be built elsewhere or at another time – it will be here-and-now or nowhere-and-never:

> Gestures of kindness and care, random acts of beautiful anti-capitalism, exist and support life in many more places than just where black flags are flown and revolutionary statements issued. Rather than considering interpersonal and ethical concerns as an adjunct and supplement to radical politics, affective resistance is about working from these intensities of care and connection.[12]

Ultimately, as Nina Power points out, moments of apparently spontaneous uprising in which our common love for humanity can be seen to manifest are in fact only able to appear because they already exist – in the countless acts of care, emotional labour and love which co-constitute the social totality.[13] And therefore as Simon Springer reminds us, another world is not only possible, but 'already exists in this very space, in this exact time'.[14] So rather than a new world being a distant utopian dream, argues Reclus, it already 'manifests itself in a thousand different forms'. He claims one would have to 'be blind not to notice it'. For him, the free society already 'springs up all around us, like new flora sprouting up from the refuse of the ages'.[15]

And as Katie explains – far from being an abstract concept, this (r)evolutionary love is observable right in front of our eyes:

> I help at a day-care in Harlem for babies and infants from very poor households, and the women who work there are not even making a living wage. These women aren't being paid enough to live and yet they are so loving. They will come in on one of their few days off and use some of the little money they have to buy gifts for a child's birthday. That's love. There it is, right in front of me.

In contemporary capitalist society such loving-caring practices are only considered to be legitimate forms of production when carried out within the market and commodified/bureaucratised. For instance, childcare is only considered to be valuable (and therefore rewardable) if provided by a private facility, often at the expense of alternative forms of childcare based on love, non-domination, communal participation and the flourishing of the person. And it is this question of what and how we value our human biophysical interchanges that is central. Rather than measuring the value of such practices through a narrow economic lens, ecofeminist Ariel Salleh suggests that their value is simply observable, as 'children dance by, as trees bear down with fruit', and 'as corn shoots up from the soil'.[16] And ultimately, as Ruth Levitas points out, the simple fact is that 'the economy' around which our society is currently structured is a conscious fabrication – it quite literally 'does not exist'. It is merely an 'abstraction of social practices looked at from their economic point of view'.[17] This means therefore that a radical restructuring of society, consciously grounded in such loving-caring practices is entirely conceivable and desirable. As Gustav Landauer famously proclaimed, the state can be understood as 'a social relationship', and therefore one that could be 'destroyed by creating new social relationships' – by 'relating to one another differently'.[18] In response to critics who argued that the elimination of the state and hierarchical political institutions would inevitably lead to chaos and the breakdown of society, the anarcho-feminists of the late nineteenth century, Goldman included, offered *motherhood* as a metaphor for the anarchist society they envisioned – proposing that love, creation, sexual egalitarianism and affective relations might co-constitute a non-dominating form of social control.[19] Reflecting on the nature of such anarcho-feminist politics, Martha Hewitt argues that it calls on us to 'rethink the nature of revolution as process, as transformative praxis of thought, feeling, and collective social activity'.[20] And similarly Jennifer C. Nash describes such a love as a 'labour of the self' that cultivates a ground for 'political communities rooted in a radical ethic of care'.[21] From this perspective then, domestic life is no longer outside the political sphere but the very ground from which it springs.

But how might new social relations grounded in this (r)evolutionary love be formed, nurtured and maintained? In response to this question Rosie argues that there is already an inherent 'longing for connection, for relating to others, and for building community' that we all share as humans. Furthermore, she proposes that a diversity of prefigurative praxes can be explored and developed that 'keep tapping into this longing and desire at a group level' – and thus maintaining an interest and curiosity into how we might recreate and extend such ways of being with each other over time. Massimo De Angelis in his book *Omnia Sunt Communia* envisions a 'new commons renaissance' grounded in such day-to-day activities that serve the purpose of reproducing life, both of human beings and of nature. De Angelis describes how these 'commons of reproduction' are already being set up spontaneously around the world in order to access healthy food, housing, water, social care and education.[22] It follows that the further development and interconnection of these commons will enable us to respond with greater capacity to the impending social and ecological crises in ways which amplify 'commons autonomy' rather than reverting to the capitalistic and top-down logic of states, as we will further explore in the following section. Clark reflects on this tragically neglected history of communal solidarity, arguing that it might provide us with a 'true ethical substantiality' and act as our 'primary material base' – an ethical resource available in the present moment, upon which we can build a 'free, non-dominating society'.[23] And Alice argues that rather than needing to be created anew, a free society is already within our grasp – it is simply a matter of remembering and reconnecting to that which was always present:

> It's like there has been a river that has been flowing underground that we need to tap back into. It's remembering that there is already the wisdom to make the changes we need to make. There will of course be a need for creativity and imagination in order to add more flavours to it – but the base of it all is in the remembering that we are literally all connected – that very simple truth.

This is the rediscovery of the *Agapeic web* – the conditions of entangled interrelationality through which (r)evolutionary love circulates and manifests. A mode of being that opens to the all, the entirety of being, rather than manifesting as an attachment to an abstract *us*, or to *me* or *mine*. And far from such a reframing of our fundamental state being a naïveté – such a conception is in fact legitimised by current scientific thought. One example has been the discovery of mirror neurons by biologists in the 1990s, which has placed empathy firmly at the centre of our evolutionary and social development.[24] The research shows us something that perhaps we are all aware of to some extent – that we mirror the emotions and behaviours of those around us – that we feel *with* others. As Maria explains: 'When I see people hurting, it hurts me too. It feels wrong in my heart to leave someone who needs help and not do anything. For the animals that can't speak or do anything [about their plight] – my heart hurts and I have to do something – I can't help it'. The fact that these mirror neurons have been discovered and observed in action confirm the affective entanglement we have been exploring to be an inherent, material function of being human, hardwired to the brain. As primatologist Frans De Waal puts it, these mirror neurons 'erase the line between self and other'.[25] The research shows that this empathic matrix is not something we choose to participate in, it is something we automatically inhabit – it is our natural home. Furthermore, these findings challenge the belief that empathy is a uniquely human trait, as the observations were initially on chimpanzees – leading to the conclusion that empathy has a long evolutionary heritage beyond that of the human. And on a material level, the human brain itself relies on other brains for its very existence and growth. In a very fundamental way, argues neuroscientist David Eagleman, the experience of 'me' is dependent on the existence of 'we':

> We are a single vast superorganism, a neural network embedded in a far larger web of neural networks. Our brains are so fundamentally wired to interact that it's not even clear where each of us begins and ends. Who you are has everything to do with who we are. There's no avoiding the truth that's etched into our neural circuitry: we need each other.[26]

Consequently, through our multiple social interactions we impact each other's internal biological states and quite literally influence the long-term construction of each other's brains. And it is through this process, argues another neuroscientist, Louis Cozolino, that we finally observe how 'love becomes flesh'.[27] In unity, Dembe discusses this evolutionary nature of (r)evolutionary love:

> We can see that in periods where we try to supress our true nature, it keeps coming out – it keeps coming out. In small daily actions, human beings act with love. Towards each other, towards strangers, towards people we know, towards family. There are of course actions in society that are violent, but on a grand scale overall we act with love, otherwise we would have chaotic societies. It is these small loving actions that hold society together – not because of governments, not because of coercive forces, but because on the whole this side of our nature outpaces the more negative sides. At a societal level we are all connected, we might not be aware of it on a conscious level but we are connected.

These findings validate the work of the nineteenth-century anarchist philosopher Peter Kropotkin and his assertion that mutual aid has been our core evolutionary drive, outperforming competition in both human and non-human societies in terms of evolutionary success – a position long contested by Social Darwinists. This book would also contend that such findings extend and build on Kropotkin's work by challenging the duality inherent in his theory whereby individual humans (or animals) cooperate with other separate individuals in order to survive and thrive in community. Kropotkin's '*perception* of oneness [emphasis added]'[28] that he considers to be resultant of this evolutionary drive now takes on material form in an entangled plurality, and love (which Kropotkin views as always personal) is in fact free to circulate in a contagious manner via this matrix of mirror neurons – as perhaps our next (r)evolutionary step.

The deep commons: a world where many worlds fit

'Coat yourself in love – like a bee coating itself in nectar. We can fly into that flower every day and realise – we are all coated in the same nectar! That level of relating totally changes your perception in beautiful ways. It creates a completely different universe.'

– Alisha

The Commons emerged as a central concept throughout the collective visioning process – perhaps unsurprisingly given its increasing popularity for linking ecological, anti-capitalist, feminist and anti-racist struggles across the world and their attempts to reclaim shared access and decision making over collective resources, spaces and knowledge. Yet this proliferation of commoning practices has seen a parallel and increasing tendency for capitalist institutions to co-opt the language, tools and guiding principles of the commons to justify projects that in reality lead to further commodification, accumulation, and dispossession.[29] In East Africa, for instance, the World Bank has promoted the widespread appropriation of communal lands by private companies under the pretext of preserving the commons for future use.[30] And so, as Indian conservationist Suprabha Seshan reminds us: 'while salesmen bombard zombie shoppers with organic, green and climate-friendly solutions, the reality on the ground is burning, burying, conversion, clearance and pollution'.[31] De Angelis describes how contemporary commons are dominated by such 'capital loops' – circuits of capitalist enclosure that seek to maximise profit regardless of the destitution they cause in their wake.[32] And so great care must be taken when developing social and political projects of the commons, for if they are carried out within such capitalistic contexts there is great danger of eventual co-optation. For such projects to truly open and extend a free commons they must remain explicitly and consciously anti-capitalist. The very notion of property, even when owned in common, and especially private property that has been accumulated to benefit the few at the expense of others, through charging rents or expropriating value from the labour of others – such property becomes a nonsense from the perspective of our more-than-human plurality. In the deeply entangled interrelationality we have explored, notions of mine/yours and ours/theirs become destabilised and difficult to locate or define. As Proudhon reminds us – property is dependent upon both the sovereignty of man and inequality of conditions,[33] and thus in our new posthuman condition the displacement of human sovereignty and the interrelationality of conditions illuminates the absurdity of continuing with property relations in their current form. Moreover, it is entirely likely that subsequent actions born from such a re-evaluation of this property/ownership paradigm would result in a profound decrease in conflict and war – for what would we then be fighting to gain dominion over, or to protect from others?

But given the embeddedness of private property relations in our collective psyche, how might we best ensure that such a co-optation of the commons does not continue ad infinitum? Rebecca Hollender proposes that we distinguish between a 'politics of the commons' and 'commoning the political'. A *politics of the commons*, she explains, builds collective forms for sharing resources, spaces and knowledge, but is non-transformative as it does not confront the structural, long-term, systemic causes of enclosure and expropriation (one example being affluent communities in advanced capitalist societies creating communal land trusts). *Commoning the political* on the other hand, holds in common the anti-capitalist political process itself (an example being the Zapatistas). This second approach of commoning more effectively frustrates capitalist enclosure and co-optation because 'it goes beyond traditional state-based, Euro-centric, or universalistic leftist models to allow for a pluriversal and long-term transformation by combining radical political practices with antagonistic strategies for confronting capitalist domination'.[34] From this perspective the commons are extended and seen as an 'auto-institution of society'[35] – as multiple practices of commoning proliferating autonomously from the state, while in parallel transforming it. In this sense the commons extends far beyond a mere way of framing our commonly shared resources and can be seen as a process of 'counter-sovereignty' – which aims to decolonise spaces (geographical and social) once occupied by 'empire, capitalism and land-right power'.[36] Guido Ruivenkamp and Andy Hilton have further extend this reconceptualisation, arguing that the commons can be perceived as 'the creation of new forms of sociality', as new collective practices of 'living, working, thinking, feeling and imagining' that act against the contemporary capitalist forms of producing and consuming the common wealth.[37] Furthermore, this co-creation of the commons, by virtue of it taking place within a profoundly patriarchal system, remains a deeply feminist struggle. As Federici has discussed so thoroughly across her body of writing, women's subsistence work continues to provide the main source of food security to enable billions of people to survive across the planet. And these efforts remain extremely important, not only because of the survival of so many of us being dependent on this work, but also due to the transformative potential it offers those of us interested in building free ecological society.[38] As she explains: 'reproductive work, insofar as it is the material basis of our life and the first terrain on which we can practice our capacity for self-government, is the "ground zero for revolution" '.[39]

From an ecological perspective, a similar leap can be observed – from viewing nature as a common resource to be managed, to that of a set of eco-systems towards which we (humans) have a duty of care. As David Bollier explains: 'unlike markets, commoners do not treat the environment as an object or commodity, but as a dynamic living system that enframes their lives'.[40] However, although far preferable to the current capitalistic view of nature as a resource to be consumed, a mere shift towards nature as an abstracted set of ecosystems (and therefore still inherently *other* – to be protected by/from humans) retains an implicit anthropocentric dualism and does not go anywhere near far enough in reframing what the commons might be(come). Neera Singh works to further erode this duality by reframing commons as spaces for 'affective encounters between humans and more-than-humans'. Such commoning practices, she argues, enable us to 'think, feel, and act as a commoner' and help us to think about the commons 'not just as lived-in landscapes but as living landscapes that are alive with dynamic social and ecological relations'[41] – and thus radically reimagining the relationship between human and nature, or indeed human nature, with(in) this more-than-human matrix.

There has long been a conceptualisation within anarchist thought of humanity being nature made self-conscious.[42] Thus the anarchists of the late nineteenth/early twentieth century theorised what they felt to be an essential human nature through the systematic study of the natural world, upon which they based their theories of social justice and the possibility of a free society[43] – Kropotkin being a famous example. More recently, Bookchin's social ecology challenged the nature/human duality implicit in this approach by collapsing human nature into just one overarching nature with two inter-twined aspects: *First nature*, or biotic nature, and *Second* or social nature.[44] And although this concept of first/second nature is far closer to reflecting the entangled conditions we are exploring in this book, the reification of second nature still contains an inherent anthropocentrism which fails to extend the enquiry quite far enough. While aware of the potential for inviting accusations of peddling 'eco-la-la' – as Bookchin accused Deep Ecologists of doing in the 1990s,[45] the entangled interconnectivity this book takes as its onto-logical basis perhaps shares more in common with the eco-centric 'total field image' of deep ecology theory, which offers a more interrelational view of nature and our place in it.[46] However, although Arne Naess' foundational work on deep ecology is indeed grounded in complexity and symbiosis – at least biologically/materially – subsequent strands of the deep ecology movement have often reduced this to becoming *one* with nature, contradicting such plurality.[47] This enquiry therefore adopts the same philosophical starting point as both of these green anarchisms, that is 'to rethink human society's sense of itself and its place in the wider ecology',[48] while taking great care to navigate a path that avoids both the potential anthropocentric bias of social ecology and the holism of deep ecology. And it is here where perhaps a more fully liberatory frame for the commons might be found – by locating our struggle for a free society in the entangled plurality that has emerged as a theme in this collective visioning process, through contemporary posthumanist enquiry, through anarchist theory and praxis before it, and over millennia through multiple Indigenous ontologies, in our more-than-human psycho-socio-material relations – in the deep commons.

And thus, we discover that the concrete objective reality in which we have sensed ourselves to inhabit, that has seemed so obviously stable and solid, and so unquestionably substantial, begins to discohere upon closer examination. At this point we are no longer standing apart from a world of separate noumenal beings. We find ourselves to be radically contingent. What we begin to distinguish is an entangled matrix of sensations and perceptions – a pulsing, quivering, energetic field of collective experience in which our shared phenomenal worlds are repeatedly co-produced moment by moment. This discovery might well be accompanied by a sense of anxiety as the relative stability and certainty offered by our previous conceptual framework is displaced. Yet it is exactly here, in this intimate entanglement, that we are able to recover the freedom to reconfigure ourselves (individually and collectively) in order to intentionally plot a course through the fluid, constantly shifting conditions of life. For if this entangled, fluid nature of things were not the way things are, then how would anything happen at all? How would life evolve? How could the dynamic world we experience ourselves as part of manifest in the first place? It is here that we might discover that freedom has in fact always been a latent (yet frequently obscured) feature of the here-and-now. And if, as we are discovering, an essential prerequisite for the manifestation of life is that of freedom, then it follows that any state of unfreedom is unnatural and anti-life, and can only be imposed as an artifice through domination – as a way of attempting to solidify that which is fluid, and of taming that which is inherently free. Such a paradigmatic shift might then act to destabilise the conceptual frameworks that have seemed to legitimise our voluntary servitude for so long. And as De La Boétie argued more than four centuries ago – tyranny is defeated when the consent to be enslaved is removed: 'Resolve to serve no more, and you are at once freed'.[49]

Such a reformulation of what it is to be human thus brings into question the historical onto-epistemologies that have shaped our shared understanding of how the political subject manifests and how the political subject might realise freedom. Braidotti notes how the categorical distinctions that previously separated the human subject from her *others* has shifted considerably, sending what were universally defined humanist assumptions as to what constitutes the basic unit of reference for a human being 'into a spin'.[50] Similarly, anarcho-feminist philosopher Chiara Bottici argues that the very notion of a self-enclosed individual – a Cartesian ego – does not make any sense from such a perspective. We are rather, she concludes, 'processes' and 'webs of affective and imaginal relations, which are never given once and for all'.[51] Building on Paul B. Preciado's call to construct a 'communism of (all) living bodies within and together with the earth',[52] Bottici develops a philosophy of transindividuality which outlines a form of 'somatic communism' in which bodies come to exist only through other bodies in a 'constant process of individuation that involves the *inter*- the *supra* but also the *infra*-individual level'.[53] But Bottici is quick to point out that such a process does not mean abandoning individualities and distinctions, it rather involves conceiving every individuality as transindividuality, as the result of a process of 'affecting and being affected' that takes place at multiple levels:

> An ontology of transindividuality enables us to both retain and distinguish between different individualities, while according none of them any type of ontological superiority: stones, as well as pets or any other candidate for our animal chauvinism, are to some extent animate. Along with hierarchies, all rigid boundaries between 'man' and 'woman', 'human' and 'animal', 'animals' and 'plants', 'life' and 'non-life' are also questioned.[54]

From a left-libertarian perspective this invites us to reimagine our struggles in order to accommodate such post-unitary concepts of the human subject within this new entangled complexity. And while cultures of resistance against domination remain essential, the reframing of freedom as an inherent feature of the present moment presents us with the opportunity of building new cultures of affirmative politics, allowing what we have now framed as (r)evolutionary love to circulate in a contagious manner – and suffusing individual subjectivities through an entangled (intersubjective) matrix in the here-and-now. So, for Tom, the struggle is about much more than merely changing people's minds – it is about 'bringing people into a common world and a common understanding' – to have them 'not just see it but feel it'. Entangling ourselves relationally in this deep commons, he argues, will allow us to develop 'a profound amount of affinity and caring – reaching out to a broader number of beings'. Ultimately, argues Salma, we all 'come from the same source', and Alice similarly describes a 'collective unconscious' or a 'collective energy of love' which becomes clearer through collective struggle. She articulates the importance of recognising this shared commonality: 'We all come from and return to the earth, so we can develop a love and care for that which we come from. And all other life on this planet similarly comes from and returns to the earth, so we can recognise our family, our connection with all other species in this respect...' Consequently, Alice argues that a 'complete appreciation for all life – as brethren, brothers and sisters' can be discovered. And it is to this radically more expansive sense of family that we now turn.

Becoming *fēmina implexa*: more-than-human loving entanglements

'Let us look forward to the time when the deer emerges from the forest and, looking at us with its dark eyes, comes before us to be petted, and the bird, aware its own beauty, triumphantly perches on the shoulder of a beloved human companion, asking her for its share of love'.

– Élisée Reclus[55]

At the same time as we might observe such (r)evolutions in the way in which we perceive our place as humans with(in) the deep commons, there often remains a bizarre disconnect between the increasing calls for action to protect 'the environment' and 'nature' made by so many of us and the daily terror, torture, murder and dismemberment of non-human animals in order to satisfy the insatiable desire for humans to consume their flesh – depersonalised and reimagined as meat. And such a widespread cognitive dissonance clearly aims to protect those who consume the flesh of other living beings from the horrific reality of such butchery. Reclus recalls witnessing the slaughter of a pig as a child, an experience that resulted in him becoming a lifelong vegetarian: 'One of them bled the animal slowly, so that the blood fell drop by drop ... [S]he let out a continuous cry, punctuated with childlike moans and desperate, almost human pleas. It seemed as though one were listening to a child'.[56] And a number of collective visioning participants expressed a parallel desire for humans to evolve towards a vegan diet. Love and non-violence are synonymous, argues Katie, which is why she chose to become a vegan at an early age: 'My veganism is about my commitment to non-violence, and I want to enact it in everything I do. To eat meat would be an act of killing and violence for me. I see veganism as an act of love'. Alice laments how we have elevated ourselves above other species and placed ourselves apart. And for her this mode of relation has become 'increasingly ridiculous', and thus it is time for us to 'undo this unconscious hierarchy we are operating within'.

Global capitalism has overseen the rapid spread of transnational industrial models of intensive animal agriculture. In 2003 the United States became the first country to raise over one billion farmed animals in a single year. Today, sixty billion animals are used on an annual basis to provide humans with meat and dairy products. On this current trajectory the figure could reach 120 billion by 2050.[57] As long as this mass murder of non-human animals for flesh-consumption persists, and as long as it remains shrouded in denial even within the most self-declared radical of circles, then any talk of environmental protection, love of the world or even free society will remain mere self-delusory contradictions – a perverse nonsense. Simon Springer, equally perplexed, invites us to think for a moment how appalling this scenario would be if the category of the 'Other' was shifted from non-human animal to another marginalised group, for example, women, children, the LGBTQ+ community or an ethnic minority:

> Who among us would post a picture to Facebook of yourself smiling beside the decapitated corpse of a Muslim child? If you're horrified by the analogy, responding by shaking your head and consoling yourself by saying 'It's just a turkey, it's completely different', that is your prejudice speaking. You've just identified the problem. This is the face of anthroparchy and you've just acknowledged your own adherence to human supremacist thinking. Tarry with it for a moment. Don't allow yourself to rationalize the violence of your eating habits, as such post hoc thinking is the exact same thought process that white supremacists have engaged in when making 'sense' of their own bigotry and loathing. Look the negative in the face. A radical dialectic demands more of us. It requires that we break with conventional thinking, and insofar as political ecology is concerned, it means that we must move from liberation to total liberation, so that the animal other is brought permanently into view.[58]

How then might such a profound level of cognitive dissonance be challenged and overcome? Especially when the vast majority of us remain largely wedded to human-centred and human-defined concepts of the political. For Dembe, (r)evolutionary love involves first and foremost the recognition that 'we are all sentient beings'. It involves being concerned, being empathetic, and considering conditions from the perspective of the other (human and non-human). And thus, Alisha suggests that: 'We need to move into a level where we are not always looking through the lens of my own superiority as a human – where I experience myself as an animal – as a part of this lively, moving system'. But such a transition will be no easy task. The (what had seemed to be self-evident) belief in a human nature divisible from a separate non-human nature has been central in the construction of political theory and practice since the enlightenment. And unfortunately, while social constructivism has been successful in explaining how social inequality is man-made and socially constructed, it has also unwittingly led to the understandable conclusion that there is a clear binary opposition between nature and culture (the ground and the constructed). For Jack this profound separation has led to an 'awful relationship' with nature: 'it's us AND that which we call nature … and we have to re-vision that, and give ourselves a different story and narrative as human beings'. He argues that a reframing of our position with(in) nature will produce a transformative effect: 'how we act – what we do – the choices we make', and therefore changing this story of 'inside/outside nature' is paramount. And once again love may well hold the key – this time in the guise of *biophilia*. The term biophilia, or the 'love of life and living systems', describes our biologically rooted psychological orientation towards connection with other life forms and nature as a whole – with such nature connections resulting in strong emotional and psychological benefits.[59] In the free society Alice envisioned as part of the collective visioning process, she described such a sense of being 'woven back into nature', and a greatly enhanced feeling of connection:

> Usually when I see a city environment people are walking on the pavement in a park – they don't ever interact with a tree. It's all very separate. But this time there weren't linear paths. They weren't linear and with straight lines, it was all just mixed in. And there was a sense of wanting to be in nature with other people … It felt like we were re-wilded, like there had been in our soul or our spirit essence a coming back to that untethered part of ourselves that hasn't been bound by fear and trapped in boxes and labels. It was like we'd reclaimed this part of ourselves that is wild and free and spontaneous and creative. And that felt good. I can feel my heart rippling just saying it!

And similarly, Paul Chatterton explains how, on a material level, biophilia is being utilised right now in multiple urban design approaches in order to replicate the experience of nature in cities through ways that reinforce such connections.[60] Practical applications of this approach are being experimented with through hybrid natural/built urban design projects such as living walls, sky gardens and breathing buildings, all attempting to create a deep reconnection and love for nature and non-human animals at the heart of our communities. Importantly, as Richard White and Hannah Gunderman have pointed out, human indifference, neglect and violence towards our more-than-human family is in no way 'natural' or intrinsic to the human condition. Rather, and crucially, such 'anthroprivilege' is a learned behaviour. And this is vitally important, because it 'allows a vista of hope and new possibilities to emerge. *If* this is learned behaviour, then we can still unlearn, re-educate, and liberate ourselves in progressive ways'.[61] As previously discussed, we are currently witnessing a paradigmatic change, scientifically led, in which commonly held core beliefs in the separation of humans and nature are being displaced in favour of a non-dualistic understanding of becoming – a nature–culture continuum in which what is engendered and that which is engendering are ultimately inseparable.[62] And so for a free society to manifest, it will be essential for the self-interested, calculating and competitive *homo economicus* (economic man) upon which our current failing models have been based, to take the (r)evolutionary leap to *fēmina implexa* (entangled wo/man) – and to rediscover our profound interconnection with(in) the deep commons. And thus, the current version of reality that so many political realists assert dominion over will need to be reconsidered and learned anew – and rapidly. Springer concludes that by attuning ourselves to 'the affective lives of the animal other', and with this 'current that flows through all life on this planet', we will arrive at the realisation that love and life are ultimately indivisible:

> Love is the preeminent condition, temporarily shattered only through the falsity of separation. The reflexivity that both veganism and anarchism imply is an attempt to reconnect with this vital frequency and realize the 'Other' of nature as 'Self'. When we establish our politics as a total liberation ecology, the human/nature binary breaks down allowing everything to transform from the assumed fixity of partition to an inherently shared processes of symbiosis and mutual becoming.[63]

It is therefore entirely feasible that our newfound entangled nature might additionally work to relax much of the political and philosophical tension that has existed between individualist and communalist conceptions of societal formation, which has led to a misleading either/or dichotomy between the two ideals. Rather, from a posthuman perspective this apparent binary between individual and community, or between personal autonomy and social solidarity, might be considered as little more than a political abstraction which acts to obscure the immanent potential for free society in the here-and-now. Resonating with Latour's impossible utopias located in an ever-receding future/past, Clark suggests that the entire history of civilisation could be encapsulated in this fabricated opposition between universality and singularity, and that this imperial project of 'dualistic polarization' is now reaching its perfection through global capitalism: 'The ensuing world historical project has progressively reduced society to a polarity between a realm of abstract universality and a realm of abstract singularity, the multitude of increasingly atomized individuals'.[64] As an alternative to such atomisation and the resultant experiences of alienation we explored in the previous chapter, the empowerment of both individuality *and* community as seen in anarchist and libertarian-left praxes allows for a dynamic and creative tension to exist between the two. In fact, Katsiaficas defines freedom itself as the 'dialectical unity' of these apparent opposites.[65] And such a dialectical relationship in turn potentiates the conditions required for a plurality of what Davis has called 'communal individualities'[66] to co-exist in our more-than-human entangled complexity. As Salma explains:

> There is still an 'I' but in a much bigger way, in a much more global sense. We are still individuals, but as love removes the barriers, we look past the

'I' and look past the 'you' and act as 'we'. So, we become a new entity, right? We develop empathy and compassion for all of us, and for all animals. And then we become like a mirror and reflect what we have inside onto the outside.

Jason Del Gandio speaks to this radical entanglement when he describes how as individuals we are uniquely constituted by our situational conditions, and society is therefore perpetually involved in the unfolding of a diversity of realities. These individual realities are intensely interrelational and are thus not as ultimately separate from one another as might first appear but are 'intertwined in an intricate web of world-becoming'.[67] Tom underlines the importance of embedding activism in this sense of the deep commons:

> This WE in organising is an important thing to ground yourself in, because it is in these assemblages that insurrection or revolution or movements form. It's not in our disparate selves that these things are cemented. That's too alienating, and that's what neoliberalism and capitalism thrive on – the abstraction of the person into atomised individuals, as opposed to thinking of oneself as a dividual – and always already relational and embedded in these entangled relations. So, the joy is experienced by the WE in and through our endeavours.

Consequently, there is no need to reify me and mine over the other, nor to negate the self in order to reify the communal. The simultaneous flourishing of both modalities ceases to be a contradiction. And while it is neither likely nor desirable for the often creative, productive tensions which exist between individuality and community to ever disappear, a rediscovery of this sense of entanglement will in turn increase harmony between the two, and thus make more feasible a liberation of life to its fullest expression – the constitution of free society. And in order to ensure this sense of radical community is extended to include our more-than-human plurality, modes of praxis that reflect this must also be established. Rosie thus describes how she facilitates nature connection work with activists in order to produce a sense of connection with 'that which is bigger than us', while at the same time 'intertwined with and part of us'. The feeling of interdependence most activists experience as a result, she claims, becomes an important motivation for their activism, and the recognition of their place in nature produces a newfound humility:

> It's another way of looking – another way of seeing the world – a different lens for how you might relate to the world. Our current society makes us see the world in a particular way, like we are separate from it – we're above it, we control it. And these exercises show us it's not like that – we are part of it and subject to it. We are part of these systems. We are embedded in them.

Grounding ourselves in this deep commons will, argues Salma, make absolutely clear how 'nature is not apart from us'. And then when we act, we act from love because 'we know that we come from nature, we come from the soil'. Implicit in this formulation of a world of radical interconnection is the freedom to reconfigure our individual and collective subjectivities, and therefore the agency with which to animate social and political transformation in the here-and-now. For Alisha, the fruits of this more interconnected and communal way of looking at/being in the world changes the very fabric of how we live, and thus 'if we can understand the malleability of perception then we can make beauty arise, and make meaning arise, and make a world arise that you want to live in'. Clark explains that such a radical dialectic sees the social world, the natural world and the world of ideas, as a site of constant change and transformation – a perpetual 'state of becoming'.[68] And when considering how to construct a politics that might successfully navigate such perplexing conditions of entangled plurality, especially given the culture of extreme political polarisation we currently find ourselves in, it is of note that the anarchist tradition has already demonstrated a long history of actively embracing many seemingly irreconcilable extremes. Davis describes this remarkable ability for unity in diversity:

> Anarchism is both traditional and innovative, scholarly and popular, reflective and action-oriented, libertarian and egalitarian, critical and constructive, confrontational and compassionate, destructive and creative, organised and spontaneous, rational and romantic, sensual and spiritual, natural and social, feminine and masculine, rooted and cosmopolitan, evolutionary and revolutionary, pragmatic and utopian, personal and political, individualistic and communitarian.[69]

And furthermore, rather than a recent (and exclusively European) mode of political praxis, Maia Ramnath reminds us that it is possible to trace a long global tradition of such anti-authoritarian, egalitarian thought/praxis orientated towards a 'nurturance of individuality and diversity' within a 'matrix of interconnectivity'.[70] Tom therefore warns against any Eurocentric negation of the diversity of anarchistic praxes observable today by limiting its genealogy to one particular social movement. He explains how most of the activists he organises alongside are people who do not have a European heritage and so their praxes are based in their own local traditions of egalitarianism, emancipatory politics, anti-authoritarianism and decentralised networks. And it is to these Indigenous perspectives we now turn.

Thinking from the Earth's heart

Indigenous concepts of the deep commons

Boaventura de Sousa Santos reminds us that any process of constructing a free society must be grounded in a plurality of knowledges not only (or even mainly) from the Global North but from the Global South. And moreover, through knowledges anchored in the experiences of resistance of all the social groups who have systematically suffered injustice and oppression by capitalism, colonialism and patriarchy – a collective endeavour of changing the world while 'constantly reinterpreting it'.[71] Many of the entangled posthuman perspectives explored so far can already be seen to mirror commonly shared Indigenous peoples' conceptions of what it is to be human: an inextricable interrelationality with the non-human world, a refusal of anthropocentrism, an acknowledgement of interactive ecologies shared by human and non-human beings, and a deeply process oriented ontology.[72] The Huuy-ay-aht people of Vancouver Island, for instance, consider themselves to be governed by the principle of *Hishuk Tsa'walk*, meaning 'everything is one' and denoting the interdependent, entangled and reciprocal relationship between human beings, non-human beings and the land.[73] And the Maori principle of *Whakapapa* describes a similarly interrelational conception of the world, seeing everything – the rocks, rivers, plants, mountains, animals and humans – as connected through shared networks of creative becoming.[74] Or as one Nasa Indigenous leader from Southwest Colombia neatly summarises: *somos la continuidad de la tierra, miremos desde el corazón de la tierra* ('we are the extension of the earth, let us think from the earth's heart').[75] Thus we must first acknowledge that rather than (or to be more generous – as well as) the posthumanities being a new academic field of enquiry, this method for framing the world can find a deep affinity with multiple Indigenous epistemologies over millennia. And with this acceptance of such Indigenous knowledge(s) significantly predating the Western academy, it is therefore also clear that at this point we should not claim to discover them. We might rather allow them to rediscover us – allowing them to permeate and infuse the co-creation of new knowledge(s) as we proceed.

When, as we will explore at depth in Chapter 6, in 1983 the Marxist founders of the Zapatista Army of National Liberation (*Ejército Zapatista de Liberación Nacional* – EZLN) ventured into the mountains of Chiapas in Mexico to form a guerrilla nucleus, they came into contact with a *campesino* movement with deep roots in the Indigenous Mayan culture. And it was the willingness of the EZLN to learn from the local culture, blending Indigenous philosophy with revolutionary theory and praxis that transformed the Zapatista philosophy into the more anarchistic form that we are familiar with today – with a commitment to horizontality and participatory decision making, cooperative forms of working and a critique of the state that emphasises social transformation rather than seizure of state power.[76] One local member of the EZLN reflected on this reclamation of their Indigenous values:

> Our ancestors lived and worked collectively. Whenever they organised some community project, they included everybody. This way of working together,

of living collectively, had been lost. People [now do their work] individually, every person for themselves ... So, we began to think about whether there was another way to do things. We began to see that many solutions are possible if people work together.[77]

Similarly, Maria describes how she has always lived very close to Mayan ruins and has often dreamt of occupying their beautiful cities again, reminding us that 'Mayans didn't disappear – we are still here! We were just dragged into the current system'. She reflects upon how in Mexico previous generations would have been far more connected to nature – following the lunar cycles and the natural cycles, and with a greater sense of 'everything as being related'. She claims that this conception of the world worked for a long time, but that 'something got corrupted': 'Success was being healthy, being happy, and now success is measured by your wealth, and by what things you have. It was corrupted by putting personal success above the success of your community'. Another related concept – *Buen Vivir* has in recent years become a popular theoretical go-to for describing forms of ecologism or post-development related to Indigenous peoples. However, its abstract nature is often in danger of obscuring its own grounding in Indigenous political struggle. *Buen Vivir* is itself a translation of the Ecuadorian Kichwa's *Sumak Kawsay* which describes both the everyday praxis of *living well*, and the utopian *good life* to be reached through such praxis.[78] Capitalism has long-since subverted any such shared sense of living well by fostering a collective phobia of material scarcity as a self-evident common sense. And so, by equating living well with living affluently, capitalism has convinced us that freedom is more closely identified with affluence than with personal autonomy, and with empowerment over things rather than empowerment over life.[79] Conversely, *Sumak Kawsay* can be understood as a decolonial concept embedded in the discourse and politics of the Ecuadorian Indigenous movements, with a central (anarchistic) critique of Eurocentric visions of the state and society. Firmly grounded in the entangled more-than-human ontology of the deep commons, the concept is at its heart anti-statist and anti-capitalist and calls for radical, communitarian autonomy within a pluralistic society – heavily critiquing the unifying, homogenising and alienating effects of modern capitalism.[80] In alignment, Tom describes how the concept *Aanikobijiganag* – an Anishinabeg word which refers to 'all our relations' (foremost spatially, but also temporally seven generations back and seven generations forward) has embedded non-domination as central to the Indigenous struggle in Canada:

It's a more expansive concept of personhood – how we are entangled, how we are embedded with persons who are close to us and distant to us. When you engage with that kind of onto-epistemological practice in an ethical way and it becomes tangibly connected to politics you can't think of domination as justifiable anymore. It becomes alien.

A further expression of the deep commons can be found in the South African isiZulu phrase '*Umuntu ngumuntu ngabantu*' which asserts that 'I am because we are'. Msizi explains how 'deep down all of us know this, and every now and then something reminds us – we are connected to each other, and we need each other'. This phrase is associated with the Ubuntu concept indigenous to what is now southern, central and eastern Africa. It is a living philosophy of radical interconnectedness and interdependence, and an ethic of care arising from that understanding. In South Africa, for instance, the commons movement has developed struggles to resist urban water privatisation that are grounded in existing Ubuntu-based communal practices for sharing water resources.[81] Msizi continues:

> These practices of supporting each other that we call Ubuntu are actually what we are also calling (r)evolutionary love. Ubuntu means to give love without expecting anything in return, which takes a bit of practice! When you act with Ubuntu, you don't need to know the particular person, it's just because they are a human being, and in fact it also applies to animals and nature at large.

Another example of Ubuntu-based community praxis is *Ilima* – in which the community works together in order to meet the need of an individual member. Msizi explains:

> If my house was falling apart, and I told the community that on Friday I would like Ilima, then on that day the community would come together and visit me and help to re-pitch my house without expecting anything in return, and then eat and drink together – it was fun! The community would celebrate their achievement together. There was no expectation for payment. It's very different to the new system – now people expect to be paid if they help.

And similarly, from a Ugandan perspective, Dembe describes how an understanding of the profound interrelationality inherent in the Ubuntu philosophy engenders a more communitarian model of social formation which subverts the usual hegemonic capitalist logic: 'I am because we are, and I exist through the rest of the community, and without the rest I cease to exist. That is our concept of love ... Because of this grand idea we are led to organise communities at local and grassroots levels that work together to solve our problems – to view each other as collaborators rather than competitors'. Moreover, this (r)evolutionary love, circulating via the deep commons, can also be seen to manifest as a form of postcolonial praxis. From an Indigenous Australian perspective, Lowanna describes how love has allowed her and her comrades to give kinship to their wider communities and allowed them to say, 'hello brother, hello sister, hello aunty, hello cousin', thus providing previously alienated individuals and communities with a sense of belonging to 'more than we are told as colonised peoples in colonised countries'. She contends that colonisation is not just about her and her community as Indigenous people – it's about all of us:

> As genocide peoples we are going through deep cultural recovery. We wanted to find a way that we could have a discussion that wasn't guilt driven, that wasn't of anger. To love is to give away taking things personally. I didn't want to carry that weight any more. I didn't want to be that person who had been created as a colonist's vision of what indigeneity is about. There is a sense in Australia that we need to narrow down who is indigenous. But we wanted to expand it out so that everyone has a place – with kinship. We're all black then! Let's do it. Let's love each other.

Lowanna argues that the cultural strengths and values of Indigenous peoples can build reciprocal relationships that are generative in nature – a mutual 'opening up' to respecting other people's views. She explains how this approach has helped to raise the level of social debate across their communities. A constructive agonism based in love: 'We broke down the fear the white fellas had of how to develop relationships with indigenous peoples. We broke down that fear. We don't want a sad-fest of guilt. We want people to have fun with this. Love seems to be a less traumatic pathway of resetting this relationship of white and black together'.

We are therefore able to isolate a distinct lineage of praxis, grounded in Indigenous struggle, which in a diversity of ways prefigures the free society this book pursues. But as Tom reminds us: 'not every indigenous society was non-hierarchical' and 'not every indigenous society was participatory'. And so, it is important that there is an honest and critical engagement with such practices in order to decide which offer value to this shared political project. And Alice too is careful not to romanticise imagined Indigenous, tribal ways of living from 'ages past' – but argues that there remain many global aspects of Indigenous social structures and belief systems that are worth protecting and reclaiming. And so, beyond a mere collection of practices and beliefs belonging to other cultures to be admired from afar, those of us who find ourselves to be profoundly alienated from this deep commons, if we are willing, and with some humility, might utilise them as a means for rediscovering liberatory aspects of our own long-forgotten Indigenous wisdom traditions. The *Unist' ot' en* clan of British Columbia, Canada, who have been resisting the construction of gas pipelines across their ancestral land for over a decade, run an annual training camp in order to assist settler allies who come to support the struggle. One purpose of the camp is to assist these allies in understanding the clan's distinct epistemologies – their way of being with(in) nature. Environmental scientists James Rowe and Mike Thompson describe the experience:

During the exercise, we were blindfolded, spun around and then guided by a partner to a tree of their choosing. 'Be with the tree, make a connection' were the simple instructions. After our partners returned us to our starting points, we removed our blindfolds and went searching for our newfound ever-green friend. Every single participant found their tree. [The facilitator] then explained that the land is living and breathing. We are always in relationship to it, but our relations to the land can be intentionally deepened, so that we come to experience trees, water and animals as friends, even kin.[82]

Rosie reflects on how from a Western/Global North perspective Indigenous culture and knowledge(s) are often seen as relating only to so-called *less developed* societies in the Global South. But such a framing of indigeneity fails to recognise the eco-centric and communitarian Indigenous cultures and epistemologies of the North which have been purposefully obscured and replaced with capitalist, colonial and patriarchal imaginaries. As Rosie explains:

For me it's about reclaiming something that would have been very present within our cultures hundreds and thousands of years ago – a connection with the earth far more intimate than we have right now. It's a part of who we are that we've chosen to forget. There's no need to appropriate other people's cultures – go back and look at your own. Something has been lost in our cultural knowledge. We [in the West/Global North] appropriate other cultures because our own are so far back in our knowing.

As Silvia Federici explains in *Witches, Witch-Hunting and Women*, it remains widely unacknowledged that alongside the slave trade and the extermination of Indigenous peoples globally, the witch hunts stood at 'a crossroad of a cluster of social processes that paved the way for the rise of the modern capitalist world'.[83] The burning alive of tens of thousands of women as witches during the sixteenth and seventeenth centuries in Europe served to almost completely sever the lineage of traditions and overarch-ing worldview rooted in a wider entangled sense of the position of humans with(in) nature – grounded in a participatory experience with plants, ani-mal and the elements. This atrocity cleared the way for the domination of so-called enlightened reason over an externalised natural world – now reframed as a passive and mechanical set of objects.[84] But Alice proposes that if we can re-access this innate wisdom there will be a 'natural bubbling up of love', suggesting that rather than having to start anew, we simply need to 'uncap what's being capped by the powers that be'. The deep commons might then be illuminated once more by a reclamation of the knowledge(s) stolen through this genocide of Indigenous groups and cultures:

From the witch hunts of Europe to the annihilation of the indigenous Americans – the voices that spoke of all life as connected and all life as sacred were fundamentally banished, corrupted, and retold in ways that were disempowering and disconnected. And now our work is to undo all that, and reclaim our indigenous wisdom which knows these things. For me that feels a lot more accessible than needing to dream up completely new ways of organising.

We can thus discern a broad spectrum of epistemic doorways across a diversity of Indigenous cultures which act to reconnect us with the deep commons. And these Indigenous concepts resonate deeply with the post-anthropocentric, interrelational and process-oriented posthuman ontologies emergent in the contemporary academy. The following chapters will therefore propose that this deep commons might enable the conditions for free society to finally emerge via a politics of immanence and a global community of communities. But before we can proceed, a change of pace will be required.

Slowing down and degrowth

'Marx says that revolutions are the locomotive of world history. But perhaps it is quite otherwise. Perhaps revolutions are an attempt by the passengers on this train – namely, the human race – to activate the emergency brake.'
– Walter Benjamin[85]

The collective visioning participants were united in their rejection of the current dominant ideology of exponential growth and called for a radical deceleration of the disorienting velocity with which modern society has been synchronised. As previously discussed, ecological ideals of sustainability, biodiversity and the commons have been subverted by capitalist institutions in order to mask their economic liberalisation and state deregulation projects, reframing them as 'sustainable development'. This discourse of sustainability which emerged from the 1992 Earth Summit has essentially depoliticised the conflict between development and growth – allowing negotiations between government, business lobbyists and environmental NGOs to be framed by the erroneous idea that new markets and technologies can boost economic growth and protect natural systems simultaneously.[86] This ideology of growth (or indeed its fetishisation) bolstered by the neoliberal TINA (There Is No Alternative) mantra, is now almost entirely accepted as a natural and self-evident truth by both capitalists and socialists alike, making the arguments for alternative models increasingly challenging to make. Ekrem describes how 'we keep on developing – developing, but that development has become a major threat to humanity'. He argues that a paradigmatic shift towards degrowth is required immediately to avert further ecological devastation. Such proponents of degrowth do not merely call for alternative forms *of* development, but for alternatives *to* development – targeting not just capitalism but productivism itself, acknowledging that 'the essence of capitalism is accumulation and expansion'.[87]

The current hegemonic narrative of a perpetually rising GDP as indicative of a nation's success may well make continued growth seem desirable. Yet the evidence suggests otherwise: the wellbeing of individuals and communities in wealthy nations in fact decreases at a much faster rate than the wealth (measured by GDP) increases, indicating that it is redistribution, not growth, that improves wellbeing.[88] Giorgos Kallis argues that how civilisations allocate their surplus unproductive expenditure (above and beyond what is necessary to meet basic human needs) gives them their collective character.[89] Of course, decisions as to how this surplus might be spent have generally been made by a small ruling class and not society at large, but, nevertheless, distinctive characteristics are plain to see – the Egyptians, for example, devoted their surplus to pyramids, the Tibetans to monasteries and the Europeans of the Middle Ages to churches and cathedrals. However, in contemporary capitalist civilisation this surplus is accumulated and invested to produce *yet more growth*, and channelled to 'privatised acts of exuberant consumption'.[90] Degrowth thus turns this model on its head – envisioning both a radical reduction in surplus to begin with, and then a creative and democratic utilisation of what surplus remains to collectively establish a free ecological society.[91]

Cultivating a path to degrowth is further complicated however by the relationship between time and our current algorithmic conditions. Our deep immersion in technological platforms mediates subjective reality to such an extent that our experience of time accelerates exponentially. The subsequent time deficit has a direct correlation with our ability to act – and to evaluate and respond to the crisis situations in which we currently find ourselves. As Peter Doran explains: 'The gap between action and reaction seems to be closing, and news cycles defy historical horizons as we become enclosed in captivating circuits of spectacles that undo and destabilise narrative and our capacity for narrative itself'.[92] Thus, a substantial and purposeful degrowth in the digital attention economy will also be essential in order to rescue human agency and time, which are intimately connected. Without such a reclamation of our autonomy over time, radical social change will be unthinkable – literally. And so, our very survival depends on it. Emma agrees that the speed and velocity with which contemporary society proceeds makes the formation and maintenance of the meaningful, respectful, compassionate community relations necessary for prefiguring a free society increasingly challenging, and thus the practice of slowing down and becoming present for others becomes a political act:

> It's practically impossible to be slow and offer respect and to be really be with people in the way that we're structured now. It's practically impossible. So, you have to make it a special practice. I encounter it with fellow activists – their carefulness with each other – their willingness to accept that difference is difference and not something to become defensive over.

Alice similarly finds herself yearning for a simpler way of life in which we are more aligned with the more-than-human world and more 'in tune' with its rhythms – which she calls 'nature-time' – a sense of our connection with these rhythmic cycles. And consequently, the free society she imagines sees a significant temporal shift to a slower pace of life: 'The pace of the people has completely slowed down. No one is rushing'. María too imagines a life that 'goes slowly'. And for Alisha, slowing down is key for a re-engagement with our sensory world:

> Even if it's just for five minutes of the day in which you actually stop moving and open to what you are seeing, hearing and feeling in that moment. That would be revolutionary because people would begin to relate more fully and directly with the world around them. Just one small act of engagement. This kind of engagement with the earth is delicious, and I think once a person feels it, they want more. I can't imagine anyone getting to the end of even ten days of doing that without feeling that their heart has been opened in some way.

But Rosie asks another important question: 'how might we balance the slowing down that's needed for connection and community building with the urgency presented by our current crises-ridden external conditions?' And of course, as political subjects in the midst of an ecological catastrophe, and located precariously between localism and globalism, between an insular security and an expansive growth, the urgency with which we need to get *there/elsewhere* does indeed appear to present a problem for proponents of degrowth. But as we have discovered, by shifting our perspective to the here-and-now we are no longer locked into a desperate race towards such imagined futures or pasts. The next chapter will therefore argue that through a politics of immanence, loving-caring-community building *is* the concrete action that co-constitutes free society. And so, the removal of the imagined distance between the here/now and our projected destination releases a surplus of time and agency with which to conduct our common political project.

Notes

1 Jean-Jacques Rousseau, *On the Origin of the Inequality of Mankind*, 1754. Available online: www.marxists.org/reference/subject/economics/rousseau/ine quality/ch02.htm (accessed 14 May 2022).
2 Bruno Latour, *Down to earth: Politics in the new climate regime* (Cambridge: Polity Press, 2018), p. 52.
3 Ibid., p. 5.
4 Ibid., pp. 91–99.
5 David Abram, *The spell of the sensuous: Perception and language in a more-than-human world* (New York: Vintage Books, 2017), p. 272.

6 Emma Goldman, 'The tragedy of women's emancipation', in A. K. Shulman (ed.) *Red Emma speaks: An Emma Goldman reader* (Amherst, MA: Humanity Books, 1998), p. 158.

7 Thomas Hobbes, *Man and citizen: 'De Homine' and 'De Cive'*, ed. Bernard Gert. (Indianapolis, IN: Hackett Publishing, 1991), p. 118.

8 See: Laurence Davis, 'Social anarchism or lifestyle anarchism: An unhelpful dichotomy'. *Anarchist Studies* 18:1 (2010), 62–82; and Uri Gordon, *Anarchy alive!* (London: Pluto Press, 2008), pp. 40–46.

9 Francis Fukuyama, 'The end of history?' *The National Interest* 16:3 (1989), 1–18.

10 Davis, 'Social anarchism or lifestyle anarchism', 78.

11 Stevphen Shukaitis, 'Nobody knows what an insurgent body can do: Questions for affective resistance', in J. Heckert and R. Cleminson (eds) *Anarchism and sexuality: Ethics, relationships and power* (Abingdon, UK: Routledge, 2011), p. 46.

12 Ibid., p. 62.

13 Nina Power, 'Feminism and the Eros Effect', in J. Del Gandio and A.K. Thompson (eds) *Spontaneous combustion: The Eros Effect and global revolution* (Albany, NY: SUNY Press, 2017), 238.

14 Simon Springer, 'Space, time, and the politics of immanence'. *Global Discourse* 4:2–3 (2014), 162.

15 Élisée Reclus, 'Anarchy', in J. Clark and C. Martin (eds) *Anarchy, geography, modernity: Selected writings of Élisée Reclus* (Oakland, CA: PM Press, 2013), 130.

16 Ariel Salleh, 'Re-worlding – With a pluriversal new deal'. *Arena*, 2020, p. 6. Available online: https://arena.org.au/re-worlding-with-a-pluriversal-new-deal/ (accessed 12 January 2022).

17 Levitas, *Utopia as method: The imaginary reconstitution of society*, p. 205.

18 Landauer, 'Weak statesmen, weaker people!', in *Revolution and other writings: A political reader*, p. 214.

19 Brigitte Koenig, 'Visions of the future: reproduction, revolution, and regeneration in American anarchist utopian fiction', in L. Davis and R. Kinna (eds) *Anarchism and utopianism* (Manchester: Manchester University Press, 2009), 179.

20 Marsha Hewitt, 'Emma Goldman: The case for anarcho-feminism', in D. Roussopoulos (ed.) *The anarchist papers* (Montreal: Black Rose Books, 1986), p. 169.

21 Nash, 'Practicing love: Black feminism, love-politics, and post-intersectionality', 14.

22 Massimo De Angelis, *Omnia sunt communia: On the commons and the transformation to postcapitalism* (London: Zed Books, 2017), p. 13.

23 Clark, *The impossible community*, p. 78.

24 Frans De Waal, *The age of empathy: Nature's lessons for a kinder society* (London: Souvenir Press, 2019), p. 79.

25 Ibid.

26 David Eagleman, cited in: Rod Tweedy, 'A mad world: capitalism and the rise of mental illness'. *Red Pepper*, 2017. Available online: www.redpepper.org.uk/a-mad-world-capitalism-and-the-rise-of-mental-illness/ (accessed 17 March 2022).

27 Louis Cozolino, *The neuroscience of human relationships: Attachment and the developing social brain* (New York: W. W. Norton & Company, 2014), p. xv.

28 Peter Kropotkin, *Mutual aid: A factor in evolution*, ed. W. Jonson (Marston Gate, UK: Amazon, 2018), p. 191.

29 Rebecca Hollender, 'A politics of the commons or commoning the political? Distinct possibilities for post-capitalist transformation'. *SPECTRA* 5:1 (2016), 4.

30 See: Silvia Federici, 'Women, land struggles, and the reconstruction of the commons'. *WorkingUSA* 14:1 (2011), 41–56.

31 Suprabha Seshan, 'From this wounded forest: A dispatch'. *Counter Currents*, 2019. Available online: https://countercurrents.org/2019/04/from-this-wounded-forest-a-dispatch (accessed 5 March 2022).

32 De Angelis, *Omnia sunt communia*, p. 107.

33 Pierre-Joseph Proudhon, *What is property?* 1876, p. 37. Available online: https://libcom.org/files/Proudhon%20-%20What%20is%20Property.pdf (accessed 29 October 2021).

34 Hollender, 'A politics of the commons or commoning the political?', p. 3.

35 Pierre Dardot and Christian Laval, *Common: On revolution in the 21st century,* trans. M. MacLellan (London: Bloomsbury, 2019), p. 575.

36 Lauren Berlant, 'The commons: Infrastructure for troubling times'. *Environment and planning D: Society and space* 34:3 (2016), 397.

37 Guido Ruivenkamp and Andy Hilton, *Perspectives on commoning: Autonomist principles and practices* (London: Zed Books, 2017), p. 7.

38 For a good overview of Federici's work in this area see: *Revolution at point zero.*

39 Silvia Federici, *Re-enchanting the world: Feminism and the politics of the commons* (Oakland, CA: PM Press, 2019), p. 196.

40 David Bollier, 'Commoning as a transformative social paradigm'. *The next system project*, 2016, p. 18. Available online: https://thenextsystem.org/node/187 (accessed 16 May 2022).

41 Neera Singh, 'Becoming a commoner: The commons as sites for affective socionature encounters and co-becomings'. *Ephemera* 17:4 (2017), 767.

42 The statement '*L'Homme est la nature prenant conscience d'elle-même*' ('Humanity is nature becoming self-conscious') first appeared in Reclus' best-known work: *L'homme et la terre*. This sentiment was revived by Bookchin's declaration of humanity being 'nature rendered self-conscious' in *Post-scarcity anarchism* (Berkeley, CA: Ramparts press, 1971), p. 124, and became a central theoretical underpinning of the contemporary social ecology movement.

43 Price, 'Green anarchism', p. 281.

44 Murray Bookchin, *Social ecology and communalism*, ed. Firik Eiglad (Edinburgh: AK Press, 2007), p. 29.

45 This was Bookchin's accusation of Deep Ecology theory in the 1990s, see: Murray Bookchin, 'Deep ecology, anarchosyndicalism and the future of anarchist thought', in M. Bookchin et al. (eds) *Deep ecology and anarchism* (London: Freedom Press, 1997), p. 47.

46 Arne Naess, 'The shallow and the deep, long-range ecology movement: A summary'. *Inquiry* 16 (1973), 95.

47 See for example: Finn Janning, 'Deep ecology movement: Love and care in the present moment – The philosophy of Arne Næss'. *The Mindful Word*, 2017. Available online: www.themindfulword.org/2017/deep-ecology-movement-naess (accessed 15 March 2022).

48 Price, 'Green anarchism', p. 287.

49 De La Boétie, *The politics of obedience: The discourse of voluntary servitude*, pp. 46–48.

50 Rosi Braidotti, 'Posthuman relational subjectivity and the politics of affirmation', in P. Rawes (ed.) *Relational architectural ecologies: Architecture, nature and subjectivity* (London: Routledge, 2013), p. 26.

51 Chiara Bottici, 'Imagination, imaginary, imaginal: Towards a new social ontology?' *Social Epistemology* 33:5 (2019), 439.

52 Paul B. Preciado, *Counter-sexual manifesto* (New York: Columbia University Press, 2018), p. 13.

53 Chiara Bottici, *Anarchafeminism* (London: Bloomsbury Academic, 2021), p. 153.

54 Ibid., p. 282.

55 Élisée Reclus, 'The extended family', in J. Clark and C. Martin (eds) *Anarchy, geography, modernity: Selected writings of Élisée Reclus* (Oakland, CA: PM Press, 2013), p. 137.

56 Élisée Reclus, 'On vegetarianism', in J. Clark and C. Martin (eds) *Anarchy, geography, modernity: Selected writings of Élisée Reclus* (Oakland, CA: PM Press, 2013), p. 157.

57 Erika Cudworth, 'Farming and food', in C. Levy and M. Adams (eds) *The Palgrave handbook of anarchism* (Cham, Switzerland: Palgrave Macmillan, 2019), pp. 642–643.

58 Simon Springer, 'Total liberation ecology: Integral anarchism, anthroparchy, and the violence of indifference', in S. Springer, J. Mateer, M. Locret-Collet and M. Acke (eds) *Undoing human supremacy: Anarchist political ecology in the face of anthroparchy* (New York: Rowman and Littlefield, 2021), p. 282.

59 Edward O. Wilson, *Biophilia* (Cambridge, MA: Harvard University Press, 1984).

60 Paul Chatterton, 'The zero-carbon city', in *This is not a drill: An Extinction Rebellion handbook* (London: Penguin, 2019), p. 167.

61 Richard J. White and Hannah C. Gunderman, 'Kindness and compassion for mutual flourishing in post-human worlds: Re-imagining our relationships with insects'. *EuropeNow* 45, 2021. Available online: www.europenowjournal.org/2021/11/07/kindness-and-compassion-for-mutual-flourishing-in-post-human-worlds-re-imagining-our-relationships-with-insects/ (accessed 22 April 2022).

62 See: Braidotti, *The posthuman*, and particularly the chapter 'Post-anthropocentrism: Life beyond the species', pp. 55–104.

63 Simon Springer, 'Abandoning our humanity'. *DOPE Magazine*, 2021. Available online: https://dogsection.org/abandoning-our-humanity/ (accessed 18 December 2021).

64 Clark, *The impossible community*, pp. 13–14.

65 George Katsiaficas, 'From Marcuse's "political eros" to the Eros Effect', in J. Del Gandio and A.K. Thompson (eds) *Spontaneous combustion: The Eros Effect and global revolution* (New York: SUNY Press, 2017), p. 55.

66 Laurence Davis, 'Individual and community', in C. Levy and M. Adams (eds) *The Palgrave handbook of anarchism* (Cham, Switzerland: Palgrave Macmillan, 2019), p. 63.

67 Jason Del Gandio, 'Rethinking the Eros Effect', in J. Del Gandio and A.K. Thompson (eds) *Spontaneous combustion: The Eros Effect and global revolution* (Albany, NY: SUNY Press, 2017), p. 105.

68 Clark, *The impossible community*, p. 21.

69 Davis, 'Individual and community', p. 65.

70 Maia Ramnath, *Decolonising anarchism: An antiauthoritarian history of India's liberation struggle* (Oakland, CA: AK Press, 2016), p. 7.

71 Santos, *The end of the cognitive empire*, p. ix.

72 Bignall and Rigney, 'Indigeneity, posthumanism and nomad thought', p. 160.

73 Ibid., p. 161.

74 Ibid.

75 Cited in: Arturo Escobar, 'Thinking-feeling with the Earth: Territorial struggles and the ontological dimension of the epistemologies of the South'. *Revista de Antropología Iberoamericana* 11:1 (2016), 27.

76 Hilary Klein, 'The Zapatista Movement: Blending indigenous traditions with revolutionary praxis', in B. Maxwell and R. Craib (eds) *No gods, no masters, no peripheries: Global anarchisms* (Oakland, CA: PM Press, 2015), p. 22.

77 Ibid., p. 41.

78 Philip Altmann, '*Sumak Kawsay* as an element of local decolonisation in Ecuador'. *Latin American Research Review* 52:5 (2018), 749–759.

79 Bookchin, *The ecology of freedom*, p. 348.

80 Altmann, '*Sumak Kawsay* as an element of local decolonisation in Ecuador'.

81 See: Patrick Bond, 'The right to the city and the eco-social commoning of water: Discursive and political lessons from South Africa', in F. Sultana and A. Loftus (eds) *The right to water: Politics, governance and social struggles* (New York: Earthscan, 2012).

82 James K. Rowe and Mike Simpson, 'Lessons from the front lines of anti-colonial pipeline resistance'. *Waging Nonviolence*, 2017. Available online: https://wagingnonviolence.org/2017/10/lessons-front-lines-anti-colonial-unistoten-pipeline-resistance/ (accessed 19 March 2022).

83 Silvia Federici , *Witches, witch-hunting and women* (Oakland, CA: PM Press, 2018), p. 12.

84 Abram, *The spell of the sensuous*, p. 199.

85 Walter Benjamin, *Selected writings, vol. 4, 1938–1940*, eds H. Eiland and M. W. Jennings (Cambridge, MA: Harvard University Press, 2003), p. 402.

86 Giorgos Kallis, 'The degrowth alternative'. *The Great Transition Initiative*, 2015. Available online: https://greattransition.org/images/GTI_publications/Kallis-The-Degrowth-Alternative.pdf (accessed 27 January 2022).

87 Ibid., p. 4.

88 See: Herman Daly, *Beyond growth: The economics of sustainable development* (Boston, MA: Beacon Press, 1997).

89 Kallis, 'The degrowth alternative', p. 2.

90 Ibid.

91 It is worth noting, however, that in the short term the transition to such a society may well require a counterintuitive *massive growth* in energy efficiency and clean renewable energies which would for accounting purposes register as an increased GDP for that period. See: Robert Pollin, 'De-growth vs a green new deal'. *New Left Review* 112 (2018), 22.

92 Peter Doran, 'Climate change and the attention economy'. *Open Democracy*, 2019, p. 4. Available online: www.opendemocracy.net/en/transformation/climate-change-and-attention-economy/ (accessed 13 February 2022).

5

Activating the Agapeic web

'Ultimately it is in the streets that power must be dissolved: For the streets where daily life is endured, suffered and eroded, and where power is confronted and fought, must be turned into the domain where daily life is enjoyed, created and nourished.'

— Reclaim the Streets[1]

Introduction

Rather than focusing merely on a rejection of capitalism and the state, the collective visioning participants took as their starting point a more expansive view of the interdependent and entangled nature of their own and others multiple struggles. And there exists a long political lineage of such theory and praxis within the anarchist tradition, encompassing a wide range of issues linking anti-capitalist, feminist, anti-racist and ecological politics intersectionally, and expanding our understanding of what constitutes social transformation – from merely abolishing hierarchical institutions alone, to a far more comprehensive redefinition of social ecologies across all spheres of life. Reclus, for instance, argued that the free society would only be realised through a complete analysis and transformation of the entire panorama of the forms in which domination manifests: capitalism and class domination, statism, nationalism, patriarchy, racism, ethnic oppression, speciesism and the domination of nature itself.[2] He invited us to 'expand our love' in order to realise our place within '*la grande famille*' or 'extended family'.[3] Landauer similarly envisaged a radically expansive 'complete community' – a community encompassing 'not only all of humanity but the entire universe'.[4] As we saw previously, Goldman too was convinced that the new social order she had spent her life fighting for could only be brought about through 'the consideration of every phase of life'.[5] And in 1891 Malatesta had also reflected on this move towards a deeper understanding of such entanglement:

In the present condition of society, the vast solidarity which unites all men is in a great degree unconscious, since it arises spontaneously from the friction of particular interests ... On the other hand, the oppressed masses, never wholly resigned to oppression and misery, who today more than ever show themselves ardent for justice, liberty, and well-being, are beginning to understand that they cannot emancipate themselves except by uniting, through solidarity with all the oppressed and exploited over the whole world.[6]

Consequently, when a resurgence of anarchist (and anarchistic) praxes occurred in the late 1960s, we saw single issue movements rediscover this wider solidarity through a move towards a collective rejection of all forms of domination.[7] In 1977, the Black feminist Combahee River Collective stated the centrality of such a politics in their own struggle:

We are actively committed to struggling against racial, sexual, heterosexual, and class oppression, and see as our particular task the development of integrated analysis and practice based upon the fact that the major systems of oppression are interlocking. The synthesis of these oppressions creates the conditions of our lives.[8]

And as a further expression of this cross-pollination of activism, the 1990s saw the emergence of another movement frame clearly resonating with Landauer's 'complete community' – that of 'Total Liberation'.[9] A communiqué from the Earth Liberation Front, an environmental direct-action group founded in the UK in the early 1990s, articulates this broadening of struggle: 'We want to be clear that all oppression is linked, just as we are all linked, and we believe in a diversity of tactics to stop earth rape and end all domination. Together we can destroy this patriarchal nightmare, which is currently in the form of techno-industrial global capitalism'.[10] bell hooks argues that it is essential for us as political activists to critically examine our 'blind spots' concerning these multiple manifestations of domination, noting how many of us are motivated to act against domination only when we feel our self-interest to be directly threatened, rather than a collective transformation of society and an end to the politics of domination in its entirety.[11] She concludes that an 'ethic of love' is required in order to expand our capacity to care about the oppression and exploitation of others, and warns: 'Until we are all able to accept the interlocking, interdependent nature of systems of domination and recognise specific ways each system is maintained, we will continue to act in ways that undermine our individual quest for freedom and collective struggle'.[12]

But while the deep commons might offer a new lens though which to better understand both the nature of these intertwined systems of oppression and their alternative as free ecological society, the question remains – what forms of praxis will take us there? In what follows, we will first explore (r)evolutionary love as a radical solidarity – producing spontaneous mutual aid at times of rapid social change and acting to establish affinity both in and across movement organisations. Next, we will examine how throughout history mass movements have been co-opted by political parties in order to gain power for their own self-interest rather than completing the task of dismantling the institutions of state domination. The perceived antinomy of revolutionary and evolutionary theories of social change will then be questioned and *(r)evolution* proposed as an alternative model for radical social transformation. The temporal gap between current struggles and imagined futures is problematised, prefigurative praxes critiqued, and a politics of immanence explored in remedy. And finally, the question of how a free society might respond to the potential of violence and ongoing political contestation will be examined, and an agonistic pluralism that complements consensus-based approaches considered in response.

Love as affinity: building a radical solidarity

'Love allows me to be amongst the grief and the despair and the frustration and the stress of direct action. It keeps me grounded – reminds me why I'm here. This has to be the basis for me. And when this is in place, so much is possible.'

– Anna

'I would love to see us all connected. It would be a revolution for real ... Imagine the power – if through love we all came together.'

– Maria

A key question pursued throughout the collective visioning process was how we might build the scale of movement necessary to both avert the impending ecological catastrophe and co-produce free society? A clue, this book will argue, can be found in the Agapeic web, as explored in the previous chapter, and through the radical solidarity inherent in its entangled contingency – a (r)evolutionary love which Tom argues 'strengthens relationships within movements' and also 'across them'. Such a radical solidarity is perhaps most evident at times of abrupt societal change. For instance, when a natural disaster such as an earthquake or flood destroys the physical infrastructure of a locality it can simultaneously cause the rapid disintegration of the dominant social hierarchies and associated market relations. But as Olli Tammilehto explains: 'social chaos or general panic does not usually ensue', and 'new egalitarian social structures arise in a moment'.[13] In fact it is more likely to be the ruling elite who panic most as they witness the precarity of their hold on power. Meanwhile, the majority of the population immediately set about organising themselves horizontally to provide support for fellow survivors such as grassroots rescue teams, food aid and shelter. Reclus similarly reflects that such practices arise naturally in 'everyday life' among those who, in order to collectively manage conditions of precariousness and lack, engage in 'spontaneous mutual aid' – putting aside division and self-interest.[14]

But this is not to say that love and mutual aid are to be considered one and the same. In fact, many anarchist theorists who have thought deeply on this subject have been keen not to conflate the two concepts. In his seminal work *Mutual Aid*, Kropotkin makes just this point: 'It is not love to my neighbour – whom I often do not know at all – which induces me to seize a pail of water and to rush towards his house when I see it on fire; it is a far wider, even though more vague feeling or instinct of human solidarity and sociability that moves me'.[15] From an evolutionary perspective therefore, for Kropotkin it is 'not love … upon which society is based in mankind'.[16] It is rather, as Iain McKay explains in his anthology of Kropotkin's work: 'a more hard-nosed recognition that it is in [our] own interests for survival to do so'.[17] For him, *mutual aid, justice* and *morality* are thus 'ascending steps of an ascending series' and mutual aid must therefore precede what he calls the 'more refined relations' as a foundation for any ethics.[18] However, as we have learned from De Waal in the previous chapter, there is now a growing body of evidence that confirms the affective entanglement we have been exploring thus far to be an inherent, material function of being human, hardwired to the brain. And in considering Kropotkin's views in light of this paradigmatic shift which places empathy firmly at the centre of our evolutionary and social development, it might be useful to briefly revisit these assumptions regarding the relationship between love and mutual aid.

From the perspective of our historical patriarchal imaginaries, love makes us vulnerable and is therefore dangerous and irrational, making it an unstable ground on which to construct a legitimate ethical relationality. Pamela Sue Anderson discusses how this association of vulnerability with only negative affects such as fear and shame causes it to become 'a label that discriminates' – and a label which has been fixed to women, gays, lesbians and other disadvantaged identity groups.[19] In the patriarchal (re)telling of these myths, she argues, love is therefore portrayed to either liberate or to constrain relationality according to gender differentiation.[20] The subsequent binaries and hierarchies which result from such a schism have been termed the 'love laws' by Arundhati Roy – rigid rules that lay down 'who should be loved, and how. And how much'.[21] And in order for these myths to continue, argues Carol Gilligan, adherence to these rules requiring *a masculine rejection of love* and *a feminine sacrifice of will and desire* is reinforced for fear of love crossing these imagined boundaries and upsetting this patriarchal order. This gender binary thus leads to a 'betrayal of love' that forces dissociation, splitting and the shattering of the ability to live in connection with others.[22] A growing number of feminist writers and philosophers are therefore calling for a new philosophical imaginary which reframes vulnerability as a positive mode of relationality, one in which Anderson proposes the term be reconceived as 'a capability for an openness to mutual affection'[23] – a call that resonates deeply with this enquiry.

The question therefore presents itself: to what extent have these love laws constrained classical political thought, and indeed to what extent do they continue to constrain contemporary political theory and praxis? And at what cost? For as self-evident as it was for Kropotkin that free society cannot be founded on 'such noble passions',[24] for many of his female contemporaries such as Goldman there was no such inhibition. For her – as we have already discovered – love was no less than the 'creative, inspiring, elevating basis for a new race, a new world'.[25] And so in light of the current feminist-posthumanist reappraisal of the human sciences, is it now possible to reunite reason and emotion in order to develop a new embodied rationality – and to risk love beyond the confines of our gendered positionalities? Can we find the courage to meet the *other* anew in a radical openness and to break these laws that maintain our alienation? Can we finally imagine such intimacy – such community? From this perspective, the 'far wider' experience of solidarity as described by Kropotkin might now be read as an intuition of our underlying interrelationality within the deep commons. In turn, the empathic entanglement borne of this experience might thus be seen to evoke the compassionate responsiveness necessary for the formation of mutual aid relations in the first place – it simply no longer makes sense to be concerned for merely *me* and *mine* and not the (entangled) *other*. Therefore, rather than arguing for one or other series of causal relations, love and mutual aid might be considered in a more nuanced way – as interlinked, and often co-emergent. For if, as this book argues, mutual aid is the form of social relation most congruent with the deep commons, then love is its signifier. And so, it is by no means an uncommon experience for the practice of mutual aid to produce love, or for love to activate mutual aid. During the course of writing this book for instance the COVID-19 pandemic swept the globe, and, as a response, mutual aid groups were spontaneously organised in my own community and in communities around the world in order to ensure that those most at risk were able to access food and medicine and know they were not alone. And of course, no one was surprised, for this is simply what we do at such times – the Agapeic web for all to observe.

Mirroring this phenomenon, mutual aid processes have been evident at times of abrupt revolutionary political and social change throughout history. As former structures of domination have been dismantled, the spontaneous and rapid emergence of self-organised forms of direct democracy have been evident in the form of councils, factory committees and assemblies, among many others. That is of course until new forms of domination are configured and used to crush them – a pattern we will explore at depth later in this chapter. During the French Revolution, for instance, the period of 1790–93 saw around 44,000 autonomous local authorities blanketing France, many in the form of citizen assemblies or sections. This network of communes and sections formed the basis for a radical popular municipal democracy prior to being reined in by the state.[26] Other notable examples include the factory committees, village assemblies, and city and district councils that flourished in 1917 Russia until the Bolsheviks consolidated their power and authoritarian rule was imposed; the 2,100 councils established during the Hungarian Revolution of 1956 prior to their destruction during the Soviet invasion; the *Shoras* (workers' councils) during the Iranian Revolution of 1978–79; the neighbourhood and workplace assemblies that emerged following the Argentinian economic crisis in 2001; and the network of communes and councils which persist to this day in Rojava, northern Syria.[27] And activists involved in the collective visioning similarly recalled many such examples of spontaneous self-organisation, grounded in (r)evolutionary love and producing such radical solidarity. Hassan remembers how when the Arab Spring spread across Tunisia, Egypt and Libya, these initial successes acted as a catalyst for the Syrian people to similarly proceed to organise themselves. At first, they began to gather together in squares at certain times of the day, and then activists across Syria started to go onto the streets. He explains how it didn't matter who was Arab, Kurdish, Muslim or Christian – 'we were all the same'. Hassan describes a sense of profound interconnectedness which enabled a spontaneous self-organisation which he refers to as *alllawieiu aljamaeiu* (الجمعي اللاشعور) or collective unconscious:

> We felt that there was something new happening which joined us together – something common. When we went into the streets we were scared and we knew that we might have received a bullet. You could die. But we were happy inside. The first times we went into the streets I cried. I liked this new way of being together. I liked this solidarity and working together to try and make a difference. I was very happy. It was like I'd been holding a mountain on my shoulders, and I had put it down. I felt free. All of us were the same. When it started in my town we didn't sit down and set rules, but as we rose up, we acted in the same way – we were the same. We acted together without thinking. We didn't discuss things before acting – we organised naturally. There was something common between the people that appeared in this moment. This is how we act in moments of revolution. In the streets we were one.

In unity, Lesley Ballau, an Anishinaabe woman who was an activist in the Indigenous-led Idle No More wave of protest across Canada in 2012–13, described their movement with the Anishinabek word *Pauwauwaein* meaning 'a revelation' and 'an awakening'. She described how what happened through this movement wave resulted in a 'great collective voice' and a 'new and possible hope that was only seen in fragments and small and scattered pieces before this'.[28] Jack similarly describes a 'radical fearlessness' that can be found in such movements. He recalls how it feels: 'like there's nothing that can go wrong', and that there is a 'trust' and a 'love' – providing a 'powerful backbone' to assist in sustaining struggle. (R)evolutionary love can thus be seen to act as a framework of plurality, as Jack explains: 'I might be with another person [in struggle] and we're both looking at things very differently, but there is a radical love that is connecting us – that's burning, that's alive, and it's all good'. And Tom similarly describes such a radical solidarity occurring at the G20 protests in Toronto:

> With the G20 protests a lot of people came together. We had anti-war folks there, we had anarchists, feminists, we had all sorts of different people from all sorts of different backgrounds coming together and being sustained by this joy. Even though a lot of people were arrested and a lot of people got tear gassed and the police were violent, there was this upwelling of love, because people you wouldn't expect to come onto the streets came out.

Such affinity is very important politically because it allows a plurality of actors to work on common projects while maintaining and honouring diversity, as can be seen today in multiple contexts among communities of anarchist, Indigenous, anti-racist, anti-colonial, feminist, ecological and queer activists, and many others – working together around shared values while respecting each other's autonomy[29]. And furthermore, the sense of radical solidarity experienced in such moments when (r)evolutionary love manifests in common can have a transformative effect upon individual political subjectivities and their consequent sense of agency. The 2011 occupation of Zuccotti Park in New York, for instance, was described by David Graeber as a 'simple, unauthorised act of love' and an exercise in the politics of mutual aid, solidarity and caring that 'changed people's conceptions of what politics could be about'[30]. Jack describes such a moment of transformation while at an anti-mining camp in Germany:

> I was at Ende Gelände and it just blew my heart open. Seeing the collaboration of thousands of these really good people and the ideas that were flowing around. I just thought yeh – this is exactly what I want to be doing. So, it all just sparked, and I thought this is it! There was an openness in my being – a brightness, a clarity, an energy, a burning fire. It was such a different experience of being whenever I was engaging in that way.

As we have established, these movements are grounded in forms of anarchistic organisation that are not new in and of themselves – horizontal, self-organising and relationally caring and supportive. But what is new are the sheer numbers and diversity of those choosing to organise in this way.[31] Anna describes an affective turn that she has observed in contemporary activism. She recalls her involvement in radical left-wing groups in Germany as a young activist, and how 'it was all very rational, very pragmatic, and very logical', concluding that 'the heart wasn't there ... this heart quality seemed to be missing in political movements'. She reflects with enthusiasm, however, that the majority of actions she has been involved in recently are far more open to this aspect of organising:

> There is love, there is care, there is compassion, there is grief, there is power-lessness, there is joy, there is inspiration – we just don't shy away from it – it's absolutely essential. And when I was sixteen in my first activist group – to con-nect with our heart, and connect with the earth – to really act from this place was unthinkable. But now this colours our activism.

Also reflective of this affective turn has been the notable resurgence of the affinity group model of organising evident across contemporary anarchist, ecological, anti-capitalist, feminist and anti-racist activism in recent years. Such affinity groups are generally small, autonomous communities of activists who form strong personal bonds in order to undertake specific political actions as a self-sufficient collective unit, either as an independent group or in coordination with other affinity groups who share similar aims. The name originates from the Spanish *Grupos de Afinidad*, who co-constituted the Iberian Anarchist Federation during the Spanish civil war, and which was then revived by the anti-nuclear movements of the 1960s and 1970s.[32] Rosie describes how her affinity group had been nurtured and sustained by the kind of loving-caring practices we are discussing here, with a great deal of care being taken to 'create community' and 'deepen relationships'. And Dembe similarly describes his involvement with an affinity group in Kampala, explaining how grounding their activities in such an ethic of care has produced a profound effect on the culture of the group. He describes how over time a unique culture has been developed: 'We are truthful, we are honest, and we treat each other well. And this is easier to achieve when you are in a group of people who collectively respect these kinds of values. There is a very strong feeling of brotherhood and sisterhood among the group members. We are moved to work for a higher ideal – that is for the common good'. And so, it is possible, argues Jack, to observe an encourag-ing maturity and evolution across many contemporary activist circles where on an interpersonal level there is a 'real energy' being put into inclusive, anti-oppressive and anti-colonial ways of organising, and in developing ways for skilfully navigating difficult dynamics as they arise in a group. He suggests this might be part of a wider process of realising our interrela-tionality with each other and with the world, and a realignment of how we struggle: 'adopting (r)evolutionary love as the fuel that powers the motor as we move forward'.

Yet in spite of such encouraging developments, free society can often seem further away than ever. Recent years have witnessed an active backlash of authoritarian politics in which there has been a resurgence of xenophobic nationalisms, racism, anti-feminist movements and the purposeful undermining of existing democratic systems. The Arab Spring was quickly followed by a countermovement towards authoritarian regimes. The radical left governments of Latin America have either adopted authoritarian tactics themselves or been overthrown and replaced by right-wing authoritarian strong men, and a similar wave of reactionary right-wing actors can be seen across Asia. We can also see a rebound towards authoritarianism in countries across Africa south of the equator. And the continued dominance of the US and electoral successes of right-wing parties across Europe have completed this picture of a globalised network of authoritarian capitalism that is far less concerned with adhering to the image of a progressive neoliberalism, often openly aligning to far-right politics, and – perhaps most worrying of all – is increasingly accepted and tolerated as a legitimate form of governance by many of those who are oppressed. In the UK, for instance, a 2019 survey found that an increasing public disenchantment with politics has been accompanied by a willingness to accept authoritarian leaders – with a majority (54 per cent) of participants believing that the country needed 'a strong ruler willing to break the rules'.[33] And as extraordinary legal measures have been introduced by governments around the world in response to the COVID-19 pandemic, the crisis has offered a convenient opportunity for such governments to expand the surveillance state, silence critics and consolidate power.[34] For many, the revolutionary social change being demanded by anarchist, ecological, anti-capitalist, feminist and anti-racist activists might seem naïve or even absurd, but as Ken Knabb points out: 'all the alternatives assume the continuation of the present system, which is even more absurd'.[35] So where have we been going wrong? And how might we reimagine contemporary struggle in order to succeed?

Beyond the revolutionary moment: love as the means and the end

'It cannot be sufficiently emphasized that revolution is in vain unless inspired by its ultimate ideal. Revolutionary methods must be in tune with revolutionary aims. The means used to further the revolution must harmonize with its purposes ... Revolution is the mirror of the coming day; it is the child that is to be the man of tomorrow.'

– Emma Goldman[36]

'It is beautiful to see how much we can – with our actions and our intentions in the here and now – cultivate these (r)evolutionary seeds and their flowering.'

– Alice

For over three centuries, efforts to animate radical social change have been largely focused on the state, with the main debates concerning how to win state power, whether by parliamentary or by extra-parliamentary means.[37] Throughout this period it has been possible to observe how one-by-one the mass movements of the time have been co-opted by political parties in order to gain power for their own self-interest rather than completing the task of dismantling the institutions of domination. And as a result, all such parties have grown to resemble the very state systems they have claimed to oppose, both in their organisational structures and in the limitation of their imagination. Ekrem describes his sense of disappointment and missed opportunity in relation to the authoritarian counterrevolutions that have occurred in recent years across the Arab world:

> This is not why we spent so many hours and days in Tahrir Square. It is history repeating itself – there was military rule, [Mubarak] went, and now there is military rule again! And this has happened right across the Arab spring. It's a concrete living example – people came together, social movements came together, and it ends up all the same. People come together to face a challenge as a community, as a society, and then later on when they have attained their goals the revolution is stolen from them.

Thus, the new 'revolutionary' party arises in the name of free society, but actually causes its demise. As new state institutions are created there might well be a newfound sense of hope and optimism among the newly liberated populace. But in most cases the very tyrants who the revolutionaries sought to replace rapidly return to power, or they are replaced by new and often more refined systems of domination as the hierarchies inevitably re-emerge within the stasis of the institution. In 1898, almost twenty years prior to the October Revolution, Reclus prophetically warned his 'revolutionary friends' in Russia of the dangers of conquering state power and in turn adopting the very tools of domination that their revolution was seeking to displace:

> If the socialists become our masters, they will certainly proceed in the same manner as their predecessors, the republicans. The laws of history will not bend in their favor. Once they have power, they will not fail to use it, if only under the illusion or pretense that this force will be rendered useless as all obstacles are swept away and all hostile elements destroyed. The world is full of such ambitious and naïve persons who live with the illusory hope of transforming society through their exceptional capacity to command.[38]

These words of Reclus are as pertinent now as they were then, perhaps even more so. For as Bookchin similarly reminded us: 'political parties are *products* of the nation-state itself, whether they profess to be revolutionary, liberal, or reactionary'.[39] Thus the fundamental difference that distinguishes one party from another is merely the kind of nation-state it wishes to establish. Yet in spite of this, conventional political histories examining revolutions have focused exclusively on the rivalries between liberal, radical and revolutionary parties for control of the state, ignoring this far more important political battle which takes place between the state-centric revolutionary party and the new, usually directly democratic institutions co-created by the people on the ground. In fact, it has been possible to observe such a pattern in most, if not all, modern classical revolutions. The English Revolution saw the communalism of the Levellers and Diggers subverted by Cromwell's state-centric parliamentarians resulting in the mass enclosure of common land and greatly assisting the eventual rise of industrial capitalism.[40] Similarly in the French Revolution, when the previously centrist Jacobins were locked in a power struggle with their rival Girondins, a revolutionary rhetoric was adopted as an attempt to gain mass support. And in Russia, the Bolsheviks, who were highly authoritarian, adopted an almost anarchist rhetoric in their own power struggles with the Mensheviks, the Socialist Revolutionaries and their liberal rivals. Of course, once power was in their hands, the Jacobins decimated the sections, and the Bolsheviks the soviets, transforming France and Russia into increasingly authoritarian nation-states and effectively ending their revolutionary processes.[41]

The Spanish Revolution again followed a similar path. In January 1933, following a wave of uprisings across Barcelona, Madrid and Valencia, the residents of the small Andalusian town of Casas Viejas took to the streets and declared *comunismo libertario* (libertarian communism). In order to supress the uprising, the local civil guards set fire to a building shielding some of the revolutionaries, killing eight women and men. They then rounded up and shot a further twelve men in the town square. The tragedy reverberated throughout the country, energising resistance to the state, and becoming one of the catalysts leading to the social revolution in the subsequent years.[42] In fact by 1936, millions of ordinary Spanish people applying the organisational forms of the Confederación Nacional del Trabajo – Confederation of Anarcho-Syndicalist Labour Unions (CNT) and the Federación Anarquista Ibérica – Iberian Anarchist Federation (FAI) had taken large sections of the economy into their own hands. These new free areas, cooperatives and village communes were collectivised and self-administered, with the efficiency of their collective enterprises far exceeding that of comparable ones in the nationalised or private sectors.[43] As an example, in Barcelona all healthcare was organised via the Medical Syndicate which managed 18 hospitals (six of which were created anew in this period), 17 sanatoria, 22 clinics, six psychiatric establishments, three nurseries and one maternity hospital – an incredible achievement given the wartime context.[44] In his *Homage to Catalonia*, George Orwell describes the 'special atmosphere' of liberation and hope he witnessed on arriving in Barcelona in 1936: 'There was a belief in the revolution and the future, a feeling of having suddenly emerged into an era of equality and freedom. Human beings were trying to behave as human beings and not as cogs in the capitalist machine'.[45]

From mid-1936, however, a broad alliance of parties was formed aiming to reconstruct the state, including the Marxist Unión General de Trabajadores (UGT), the Communist Party, Republicans and Catalan nationalists. Subsequently a new national government was declared and the UGT leader Fransisco Largo Cabellero was made prime minister. In a much-criticised move, senior figures of the CNT then began negotiations to enter this government claiming to do so in the 'spirit of anti-fascist unity'.[46] Alarmed, the FAI argued that this was not only a violation of their core principles but also a strategically poor decision that essentially 'disarmed the movement'.[47] And in a combined policy document between the CNT and UGT the scale of compromise was made starkly apparent. Relinquishing its central anti-statist position, the CNT objected only to 'a totalitarian form of government', instead opting for a 'true social democracy' – a 'Social Democratic and Federalist Republic'.[48] They then further agreed to open a 'new constitutional period' during which they would go so far as to participate in the state elections. The Peninsular Committee of the FAI were astonished by this reversal of ideological position and immediately responded to the declaration: 'There is no doubt that the proposal is consonant with the desires long harboured by the current government to render void whatever revolutionary transformation has been made in Spain'.[49] However, these concerns were quickly dismissed in a circular from the National Committee of the CNT: '[W]e shut the mouths of the defeatists, pessimists, those who will not listen to reason and those who take advantage of the circumstances to speak of revolutionary losses, cave-ins, treasons and liquidations'.[50] Tragically, yet unsurprisingly, in the following months the Republican army proceeded to dismantle hundreds of collectives and dissolve the regional council, arresting hundreds and with many being tortured and killed. By the summer of 1937 most urban and rural collectives had been legalised and brought under state control, and the CNT-FAI members of the national government and Generalitat removed from their positions. The social revolution was effectively over. The CNT-FAI, although retaining a considerable membership, had little power to act as republican Spain collapsed, with Nationalist troops finally entering Barcelona in January 1939.[51] Vernon Richards argued that the CNT were guilty of falling victim to the very illusions they had so frequently criticised in the socialists – believing that power was only a danger when in the 'wrong hands' and for a 'wrong cause'.[52]

If we are to judge the results of the decisions made by the CNT in the Spanish Civil War, he reflected, we can draw only one conclusion: 'Where the means are authoritarian, the ends, the real or dreamed of future society, is authoritarian and never results in the free society ... [G]overnment – even with the collaboration of socialists and anarchists – breeds more government'.[53]

As we have seen, this pattern has continued into our present era, leading Hannah Arendt to conclude that rather than making a gradual progress towards free society, hopes for a further transformation of the state towards participatory democracy in fact rapidly diminished – 'buried in the disasters of twentieth-century revolutions'.[54] And as Ekrem previously mentioned, a striking contemporary example of this phenomena can be observed in the *Arab Spring* wave of revolutions. On 4 January 2011, 26-year-old Tunisian street vendor Mohamed Bouazizi died from self-immolation in response to ongoing police harassment – leading to massive protests across the country. By 14 January, Tunisian dictator Ben Ali had been forced from power and had fled the country.[55] Inspired by this spontaneous uprising, and similarly animated by the death of a young man, Khaled Said, who had been beaten to death by police just weeks previously, Egyptian protestors occupied Tahrir Square in Cairo on January 25, and they once again ousted the dictator (this time Mubarak), just 18 days later.[56] Over the course of the following months a wave of leaderless, horizontal, decentralised and anti-hierarchical uprisings spread throughout the region to countries including Libya, Syria, Yemen, Kuwait, Sudan, Oman and Morocco.[57] Across the world, we held our breath as this seemingly unstoppable series of movements emerged as a multiplicity in accordance with local conditions. Not all of the revolutions succeeded in overthrowing their governments, but for the ones who managed to displace the old regime a familiar and tragic pattern could then be observed as one by one the power of these mass movements was once again co-opted by political parties and the revolutions effectively stolen. The Muslim Brotherhood and Nour parties in Egypt, An-Nahda in Tunisia and the Parti du Justice et Développement in Morocco all effectively ended the revolutionary process. In a similar way, the so-called Second Spring of 2019 in Sudan and Algeria that adopted similar organising strategies successfully brought down the long-term dictators Omar al Bashir and Bouteflika respectively.[58] Unfortunately the second spring has followed much the same pattern as the first, with the new governing parties maintaining a continuity of core state policies. But there is of course one important and striking exception to this list – the ongoing (r)evolution in the Autonomous Administration of North and East Syria, and we will examine this remaining beacon of hope at more depth in the next chapter.

This is not to say that change does not occur, for how else would we account for such momentous events as the fall of feudalism, the abolition

of slavery, or the end of the divine right of kings? Without doubt, significant social and economic societal progress has been achieved by this movement of movements throughout history. It is rather to say that the actually
existing free society constituted in the revolutionary moment is rapidly
dismantled and replaced by default forms of social organisation, and thus
the full potential of the moment is lost. And so, this repeated pattern of
stolen revolutions has left us all – every one of us – living a poor imitation
of what might have been. Rather than revolution becoming a 'permanent
condition of life',[59] these struggles have been abstracted as historical foot-
notes and their truth subverted by state powers. As each of these revolutions
attempted compromise with the state, a space was immediately opened for
counterrevolution and defeat. This principle, argues Bookchin, can be taken
as absolutely fixed: 'The vacuum that an unfinished revolution leaves behind
is quickly filled by its enemies, who, sometimes presenting themselves as
"compromisers", "realists", and "reasonable men" try to harness the revolution and steer the energy it has churned up towards its own destruction'.[60]
For the parties, the direct action that drives the revolution is seen as transi-
tory, a means to an end – no more no less. And thus the party system must
eventually supress this power from below in order to sustain itself, squan-
dering the promise of 'government of the people by the people' by imposing
a 'government of the people by *an elite sprung from the people*'.[61] It was witnessing at first hand the French Revolution of 1848 being subverted in this
way by the provisional government that confirmed for Proudhon that 'all
parties, without exception, as they affect power, are varieties of absolutism',
leading him to conclude: 'the political revolution, the abolition of authority
among men is the goal; the social revolution is the means'.[62] Proudhon thus
called for a 'permanent revolution', which unlike the Marxist-Trotskyist
use of the term, which maintained the need for a vanguard party seizing
state control,[63] involved 'the people alone, acting upon themselves without
intermediary' in order to break this cycle of partial revolution.[64] And so for
contemporary activists, if truly resolved to imagine, co-constitute and then
sustain free society, our revolution must become similarly permanent. It
must become (r)evolution – an ongoing process without end.

For anarchists such as Reclus, Landauer and Kropotkin, revolution and
evolution were two sides of the same coin – contingent parts of a slow march
of progress, each leading to the other in a perpetual cycle of alternation. As
Kropotkin describes: 'If we represent the slow progress of a period of evolution by a line drawn on paper, we shall see this line gradually though slowly,
rising. Then there comes a revolution, and the line makes a sudden leap
upwards'.[65] He concludes however that once this height has been achieved
'progress cannot be maintained'. As can be witnessed through history,
the line sharply drops, and 'reaction follows'.[66] After this point, although

the line of progress is often at a permanently higher level than before, it remains only a partial revolution, and the next stage of evolution proceeds from there. In line with the argument made in this book, Kropotkin argues that these moments of revolution, where a sudden leap towards freedom is achieved, are arrived at through a 'wave of brotherly love' that acts to 'wash the earth clean ... [and] sweep away the shards of refuse accumulated by centuries of slavery and oppression'.[67] But he then very quickly (and perhaps prematurely) concludes that 'we cannot hope that our daily life will be continuously inspired by such exalted enthusiasms', nor (as noted at the start of this chapter) the free society be founded on 'such noble passions'.[68] If we follow Kropotkin's logic – that it is in fact a wave of love that results in the moment of revolution – then would not the extension of such a wave in turn extend this free society as a process of (r)evolution? Surely it is exactly such 'noble passions' that a free society *must* be founded on? Landauer appeared to believe so, arguing that the ultimate destiny of revolution – to awaken *'le contr'État*: the state that is no state' – will be arrived at through one connecting quality: 'love as force'.[69] And as established in the previous chapter, social reproduction is already firmly grounded in such loving-caring relations, and therefore these relations offer a stream of continuation from the old to the new – and might then work to avert the usual post-revolutionary vacuum in which the counterrevolution occurs.

If, however, a free society is to be founded on (r)evolutionary love and without 'assistance' from a vanguard revolutionary party, then what of a manifesto? What of strategy and planning? In a famous attack on the revolutionary ideas of Marx, Mikhail Bakunin addressed this question by setting himself in opposition to what he saw as the foolishness of rigidly aligning to a preconceived idea of how revolutionary change should occur: 'We do not, therefore, intend to draw up a blueprint for the future revolutionary campaign; we leave this childish task to those who believe in the possibility of the efficacy of achieving the emancipation of humanity through personal dictatorship'.[70] From this perspective then, and without a clear map to guide us, the question of how to get from the *here* of struggle to the *there* of free society continues to present us with a perplexing dilemma, because as Paul Raekstad and Sofa Saio Gradin explain in their book *Prefigurative Politics*, it is not a question of whether political means and ends *should* be linked, because 'they *already are*'.[71] Namazzi argues that the reason why so many revolutionary movements have failed is because 'the people were clear about what they wanted to move from, but they were not clear on where they were heading', and thus those in power have been able to 'take advantage of this gap in strategy'. But this very sense of trajectory from here to there/ somewhere else, as expressed by Namazzi perhaps illuminates a more central problem – that as long as freedom is deferred while in transit between a past we aim to escape and an imagined utopian future, there indeed remains such a gap to be enclosed and colonised by oppressive forces. But as we are now beginning to discern, it is this very sense of trajectory from here to there, and the resultant gap between the two temporalities which obscures what might be the ground upon which free society can finally be constituted – in the immanence and accessibility of the now.

Thus, we see that the deep commons also contains an important temporal aspect, in as much as the designations of past, present and future are found to be intricately entangled with(in) it. As discussed previously, in his work on grounded utopias Davis builds on Kümmel's idea of time as a temporal coexistence between past, future and present, with the relation of these temporal components not merely conceived as one of succession but also as one of conjoint existence – with both past and future intertwined with the present.[72] From a movement perspective this state of profound contingency calls on us to open many more spaces for radical imaginaries focused on building political projects in the here-and-now, grounded in historical praxis and extending towards an ever changing yet hopeful future. But this relocation to the present is by no means a rejection of utopian thinking – far from it – for visions of future worlds animate struggle in the present. The real danger lies in clinging to and concretising any one fixed vision of the future (or indeed the past) as it will implicitly trap us within what Abram calls 'the oblivion of linear time'.[73] It will trap us, that is, within the same 'illusory dimension' that has already enabled us to lose connection with and fragment apart from the natural world. Jernej Kaluža similarly concurs that we must overcome traditional conceptions of revolution as 'the gap between the sad world of today and the better, joyful world of tomorrow'.[74] And as an antidote he reimagines (what we have now framed as) (r)evolution as a process of multiple ongoing experimentations with a 'fluidity of aims and structure' as they constantly defer to the process of transformation. And such a pluralism, he claims, requires an 'immanent substance' in which each specific praxis can unfold and participate.[75] Of course, this book rejects the monism required for Kaluža's essential immanent substance, choosing instead the entangled plurality of the deep commons, but agrees that such a ground offers an intrinsic cohesive force (theorised here as (r)evolutionary love) through which disparate forms of praxis can coexist and interact.

Temporally speaking then, the most strategic and efficacious location for constructing free society is in this moment, and then the next, and the next – in perpetuity. And so, as Anna explains: 'Acting from the here and now is revolutionary ... Rather than having a fixed vision that the future will look like xyz – it is rather left open – really trusting in where we are coming from and what our intentions and motivations are. More humane, more relational, more caring'. From this perspective any truly inhabitable utopia can therefore only be arrived at, or lived, as a dynamic process in the here-and-now. Kurdish (r)evolutionary Bager Nûjiyan described his own struggle in Rojava as such a grounded utopia firmly rooted in the present. For him and his comrades free society was not just an abstract idea, but their 'concrete way of living' and 'way of connecting with struggle and utopia on a daily basis'.[76] Thus from Nûjiyan's perspective the temporal gap between that which we struggle to escape and our imagined destination had been closed, and the free society relocated to the immanence of the here-and-now where it can finally be reclaimed and occupied.

There are of course a number of well-argued critiques of such a politics of immanence which deserve further engagement. In her classic *Political Protest and Cultural Revolution*, Barbara Epstein contends that the US non-violent direct-action movements of the 1970s and 1980s were weakened by an emphasis on prefigurative politics and community building.[77] By conceiving of community building as politics, she argues, the movements undermined their strategy. She believes very strongly in the efficacy of utopian politics and that it must 'hold out a vision of a non-violent and egalitarian society' which must then 'build the new society in the shell of the old by creating a space within which these values can be realised as far as possible'.[78] Ultimately however she concludes that for a movement to achieve real political impact it must be willing to 'sacrifice community'.[79] Raising related concerns, Uri Gordon has argued that a politics of the here-and-now leads to our struggles becoming trapped in a 'recursive prefiguration' similar to that which can be found in Christianity, in which a future 'radiates backwards on its past'[80] – an 'absorption of the revolutionary/utopian horizon into the present tense'.[81] Such a temporal framing, he argues, works to 'undermine a generative disposition towards the future', allowing a collective denial of both the 'absent promise' of revolutionary transformation in the near future, and the very real prospect of imminent ecological and societal collapse.[82] Prefiguration from this perspective is little more than a way of modelling an imagined future in the present moment as a way of dissociating from the very real and immediate ecological and social crises that cascade around us – 'fiddling while Rome burns' so to speak. Gordon thus argues that adherents to such 'presentism' sidestep these crises by 'avoiding any disposition towards the future altogether'.[83]

Darren Webb similarly critiques what he describes as attempts to 'reconfigure utopia' and to 'rid it of its totalistic and prescriptive dimensions' in order to avoid the risk of 'closure and control', claiming that such an approach merely succeeds in nullifying its utopian potential.[84] He believes that much of the 'vitality, power and direction' that a utopian approach might offer is lost when attempting to circumvent its perceived 'bad' connotations. He repeatedly rejects what he refers to as 'the standard liberal critique' of blueprint utopianism,[85] one assumes in order to ridicule similar arguments made by those on the left, without acknowledging that such critique has a long and established history in anarchist thought. Moreover, the many anarchist revolutionaries and theorists of the late nineteenth and early twentieth centuries who were clear in their opposition to such vanguardist concretised visions of a future society were making their observations within living memory (and often through direct experience) of the devastating consequences of such an approach. He is right, however, in his assertion that without visions of the future, utopian praxis risks becoming 'an empty and endless project that romanticises the process while losing sight of the goal'.[86] And in his critical case study of Occupy Wall Street he makes a similar argument: 'Movements heralding themselves as cracks in capitalist space-time through which transformed social relations are emerging here-and-now might just end up becoming dead spaces in which the inchoate utopian desires that originally gave them life wither away through neglect'.[87]

And of course, he is once again correct – they 'might'. But must they? Are a politics of immanence and a generative praxis, as these scholars claim, really so mutually exclusive? The dangers are certainly real and must be taken seriously – a politics of immanence could well be (and at times is) subverted to provide reassurance and denial in the face of ecological and social systemic collapse. But such an impatience with our collective lack of revolutionary progress in the present, while entirely understandable, might just as easily lead us yet again into a blinkered march towards a frozen future-image conceived of in the past, the abandonment of the now, and the repetition of previous mistakes. Any future utopia we might imagine through the limitations of our current conceptual frameworks will inevitably at some point be found lacking as our capacity to imagine better worlds evolves beyond our original starting point, condemning us to a future 'caught within the paradigms of the present'.[88] For as Braidotti points out: '[w]e cannot even begin to guess what post-anthropocentric embodied brains will actually be able to think up'.[89] And so although it might be possible to identify the impacts and successes of previous struggles with the benefit of hindsight, it is never possible to envisage the whole process in advance.[90] Katie explains:

> I think it's often hard to know what the best course of action is – or at least it's hard to know five years in advance! I think the best one can tell is often just in that moment. To the extent that the impact of one's actions in the world can be unclear, I think a commitment to having those actions be loving – that the intention is that they be loving – is a powerful thing. So, for me that's the place I want to start from. It's about the large choices but also about the tiny choices right in front of us – two inches from our own nose – those choices as well.

Franks therefore asserts that locating our struggles in a prefigurative political praxis will act to 'collapse the problematic distinction between means
and ends' which we have seen as leading to tragic consequences for multiple
failed revolutionary movements.[91] And Landauer goes so far as to claim that
there is ultimately no separation between cause and effect. He conceives of
cause and effect flowing from one to another in an 'eternal' process that
he terms 'reciprocal effect'.[92] He even proceeds to suggest getting rid of
the word 'cause' entirely, exclaiming: 'The cause is dead, long live the living effect!' Inverting Schopenhauer's claim that all reality is effectiveness,
Landauer instead asserts that 'effectiveness is reality' – and therefore all
that can be actual and existing is 'also present and in the moment'.[93] But a
politics of immanence need not (indeed must not) displace the future, on the
contrary it should recognise it as an entangled aspect of what we term the
present. Thus, what is generative must also be processual – with imagined
future(s) and an ever-changing present in a constant dialogical process. And
so rather than prefiguration, perhaps a more useful frame might be that of
an imagined future being constantly *reconfigured* in a process of entangled
relationality with the continually shifting present, which in turn reconfig-
ures itself in relation to this new trajectory, and so on and so forth. Such
a reframing might then ensure that the 'anxious and catastrophic forms of
hope'[94] that Gordon rightly argues will be necessary to create the urgently
needed radical alternatives to our current dystopia remain firmly grounded
in the possible, while generative of the (what for some might seem) impossible. From this perspective then, we might reframe the sequencing of means
and ends from a linear to a non-linear temporal form. And so rather than
prefiguring a path which leads to a particular goal, we frame the path *as
the goal*. Therefore, if our goal is freedom, then praxes must be established
that realise freedom in the present moment, not as a distant promise, but as
the liberation of the now. And so, it is in this space between the *no longer*
and the *not yet* that we must locate our shared political project and the free
society it pursues.

Utopia as process (2): the politics of immanence

'We do not have to sketch in advance the picture of the future society: It is
the spontaneous action of all free men that is to create it and give it its shape,
moreover incessantly changing like all the phenomena of life.'

– Élisée Reclus[95]

'Nothing pre-exists the relations that constitute it.'

– Arturo Escobar[96]

As unfashionable as it remains across academia in general, and as unrealistic as it might be framed within mainstream politics, a growing call can be heard from both the activists who engaged in this collective visioning and from contemporary left-libertarian activism more generally for more 'visionary power' and 'prophetic energy'[97] to be harnessed in order to construct new political praxes which creatively imagine alternatives to our current state of affairs. And thus, for Bookchin, the real issue for activists in modern times was no longer a question of 'reason, power, or technê', but this 'function of imagination' in giving us direction, hope and a sense of place in nature and society.[98] But of course as we have just established – we must simultaneously resist the temptation of then freeze-framing this radical imagination into one (impossible) future. And as Tom makes clear: 'any utopia that we are going to have is going to be built grounded in what we already know'. A free society must be (can only be) co-constituted right here and right now, in a multiplicity of practices and forms, and from the ground up. And somewhat encouragingly, this open, responsive, unfolding of utopia as a process in the here-and-now has played an increasingly central role in movement strategy over previous decades. On the praxis of the alterglobalisation movement, for instance, Marianne Maeckelbergh reflected: 'What makes the alterglobalisation movement different from previous movements is that the "alternative" world is not predetermined; it is developed through practice and it is different everywhere'.[99] And a similar reclamation of the present could be observed in the US Student Occupation Movement that began in New York in 2008 and peaked in California in 2009 – which can be traced as one of the factors that led to the emergence of the Occupy movement in 2011. The pamphlet *Communiqué from an Absent Future* articulated how the student activists saw their tactic of occupation as potentiating a radical imagination which moved the struggle way beyond simply making demands to those in power towards a complete reimagining of the current system: 'The point of occupation [is] the creation of a momentary opening in capitalist time and space, a rearrangement that sketches the contours of a new society...'.[100] And the sheer range and diversity of such praxes that are observable today, rather than indicating a 'confusion or incoherence', provide clear evidence that such an approach offers a unique flexibility and applicability across multiple diverging contexts.[101]

Such anarchistic approaches are not aimed at 'vertical transcendence' but are rather brought back down to earth in a grounding exercise of 'radical immanence' – an act of 'unfolding the self onto the world, while enfolding the world within'.[102] And it is through the co-creation of such living, vibrant, material alternatives that we can tangibly express the utopian potentiality always within grasp – as an immanent feature of the present moment.

Such approaches are of central importance, Springer asserts, because they remind us of the latent agency present in the here-and-now: 'all we have is immanence, this precise moment of space-time in which we live and breathe, and because we are *it*, we can change, reshape, and ultimately transform *it*'.[103] And therefore as Jack explains: 'if love is what we are bringing into perception in this moment, then that is the world we are living in, and that is the relationship'. And so, for him also the idea of an abstracted yet concrete utopia is clearly 'a bit silly'. Our struggles must remain dynamic or else they end up being 'in opposition to life and the dynamism of who we are'. He continues: 'We are infinite beings with infinite dimensions. It needs to be in movement. It needs to be an ongoing dance – grounded in the moment ... How we embody the world can be different for everyone – a multiplicity of connecting fantasies that we keep re-visioning'. A politics of immanence thus bridges the gap between theory and practice, between utopia and the now. For the deep commons to truly act as the foundation for free society it cannot remain but an idea – it must become a lived experience. For Alisha, this requires us to 'fashion new eyes', and this cannot be achieved by merely reading (or indeed writing) a book. For even if a book did enlighten us, she argues, new ways of seeing must be consolidated through practice. She describes such practice as *alchemy*:

> I decided to go out into nature and purposefully try to engage in some way. And what happened over time was the immersion allowed me to start to see the world as animate – everything animate – stones and mountains – looking at it as a kaleidoscope of changing sensations. And then there was more love for the natural world, and more grief ... And now my commitment is towards the birds and the animals, and to the earth itself – to keep engaging. And the activism is like an alchemy – somehow through the reflection and the artistry in it something is formed in my soul, and that to me is (r)evolutionary love. And what drives me on is threading that into my life on a daily basis.

It is in this dynamism that we can see examples of political praxes which are far less constrained by the ideological purity that existed in many previous historical movements. Saul Newman describes these contemporary movements as founded in 'contingency, open-endedness, and freedom of thought and action'. Without a requisite adherence to a concretised ideological 'shape', Newman argues that such activism has more freedom and flexibility to think and act autonomously, to work on multiple fronts and in different contexts and settings.[104] And this fluid, responsive nature makes them difficult to enclose in the usual theoretical classifications. As Marina Sitrin enquires: 'What is the name of this revolutionary process: Horizontalidad? Autogestion? Socialism? Anarchism? Autonomy? None of these? All of them? It is a process that does not have one name. It is a process of continuous creation, constant growth and development of new relations, with ideas flowing from these changing practices'.[105] Thus, an engagement with the world which frames it as 'solid and confined', argues Alisha, will cause your activism to 'get shut down pretty quick'. In remedy, she recommends forms of activism that are 'relational to others, to ideas, to the sensual world, to everything' – containing an energy which can act to 'propel you forward' into further action and further creation. More often than not, direct-action tactics are framed as preventative or disruptive, aiming to stop or hinder a project we might be in struggle against – and this is of course an effective and necessary use of direct action. But an alternative and complementary way of framing direct action can also be as a constructive tactic – as the creation of alternative social spaces and relations beyond hierarchy and domination.[106] Thus our struggles can be seen as communal processes through which 'subjects emerge' – with the apparent dichotomy between individual and community destabilised.[107] Such an approach can therefore be politically transformative both subjectively and intersubjectively. As Maria explains:

> We are trying out better forms of living right now here in my community in Mexico by aligning to permaculture values – by not damaging our planet, by taking care of the water, taking care of the plants, taking care of the animals. And it's not only me, there are a lot of other people too – trying better forms of living together. We just need to connect. We need to connect our love. And then we need to act as a model for the people who aren't with us yet but might want to be. People are afraid of changing – they don't know how. If they can see that something else works, then they might believe.

And so, to build the scale of movement required, Angelo reassures us: 'we don't need everyone to become anarchists, but if the masses are exposed to "real freedom", then they will like it and it will be revolutionary'. If people discover new ways in which to practice freedom, their lives will naturally align to it. This can allow for 'spaces of solidarity in which new projects can grow'. Such spaces of solidarity exist inside and outside of contemporary society simultaneously. They construct free society in the here-and-now and thus act as an example for wider society to see that alternatives are actually possible. Such spaces, Angelo adds, can also 'act to assemble people and ideas together' thus 'creating something new'. And so, for Lowanna, love has become her 'weapon of choice'. She recalls with a smile one occasion in which her and a fellow Indigenous activist 'love-bombed' an unsuspecting government official as a way of resetting the ingrained relations of domination between their two communities and creating something new:

> Me and a sister girl asked ourselves 'what if we don't hate?' And we decided that we would go to the extremes of love … So here we were – two black fellas – and we told the guy 'we have great news for you – we love you! Thank you for your dispossession. Thank you for your exile. Thank you for your discrimination and your colonisation. We love you.' And the guy was like 'but …

what do you want?' And we were like 'nothing, we just love you.' It was so counterintuitive. It didn't make sense. It was about resetting the relationship. It's not about ignoring or forgetting the past. It's saying that we need new futures, and new futures can't be built on hate. It's about finding new relationships with each other as individuals and communities right now.

And so, as Jack explains: 'if love is what we are bringing into perception in this moment, then that is the world we are living in, and that is the relationship'. Thus, a political praxis of (r)evolutionary love is prefigurative of itself. Its activation animates a radical solidarity grounded in the deep commons, through which it is free to circulate in a contagious manner without fear of capitalist enclosure – suffusing individual subjectivities through an entangled (intersubjective) matrix in the here-and-now. And it is in the immanence of this deep commons that spaces of freedom might be opened which are at once autonomous from the forces of domination and transformative of them, with our rediscovery and activation of the Agapeic web extending these moments onward through a co-constitutive process grounded in a radical ethic of love and care – the community of communities that we will explore at more depth in the next chapter. But of course, as we have now established, any such utopia must remain grounded. There will be no end point, and no eventual transcendence. And even if like Lowanna we find ourselves to be adept at 'love bombing' our oppressors, there is no guarantee of them loving us back! It would therefore be a denial of objective material conditions for us, before we proceed, not to acknowledge and discuss the ongoing potential for conflict and violence latent in any future society that we co-constitute. And it is to this we now turn

Prefiguration and violence: from antagonism to agonistic pluralism

If we are indeed to accept the need for our movements to develop new forms of praxis grounded in (r)evolutionary love, then what of the question of violence? Knabb argues that acts of violence by activists can actually work to reinforce the state – and even confirm the need to strengthen it.[108] In fact, it can be evidenced historically that if during the revolutionary moment the required spectacles of violence do not break out spontaneously, the state itself will produce them by means of provocateurs in order to break the momentum of the event and legitimate the use of state force. And as we witness further increases in policing, state repression and media-induced xenophobic nationalisms, Tom argues that resilient organisations will be required that are capable of self-defence – not necessarily through confrontation, but through the ability to sustain themselves despite being under attack. He gives an example from his own experience: 'In the 1990s and the early 2000s there was a group in Toronto called the Heritage Front which was an open neo-Nazi organisation and there were street fights and confrontations with the fascists threatening to assassinate anarchist activists. So, there are people who are going to be hurt. People are going to be targeted and attacked'.

Thus, it would be naïve to think that as we collectively bring new worlds into being, state capitalism will not use increasingly violent means to maintain a hold on its current political and social hegemony, and to protect private property interests against the opening up of the commons. Would therefore, as Robyn Marasco fears, a movement that 'gives itself over to love' be one that 'perpetually risks becoming Empire's bitch'?[109] 'Not necessarily', responds Alice. She argues that by adopting such (r)evolutionary loving praxes as part of the wider struggle, well established (and often unquestioned) patterns of interaction between activists and the forces of state and capital might be interrupted, and oppressive methods illuminated and delegitimised. Alice describes how when occupying Westminster Bridge as part of environmental protests in London there seemed to be a collective 'infusion of love' which made it difficult for the police to adopt tactics of violence to suppress the activists. 'There was anger', she acknowledges, but it didn't come out in ways that were destructive: 'we were able to access the anger and the energy and be creative with it rather than destructive' – and thus developed creative alternatives which 'avoided legitimising aggressive responses from the authorities'. As Martin Luther King Jr. reminded us: 'This does not mean that we have to abandon our militant efforts. With every ounce of our energy we must continue … But we need not in the process relinquish our privilege and obligation to love'.[110] Todd May similarly argues that for a (r)evolutionary movement to be successful it will need to remain largely non-violent for more pragmatic reasons. As he points out, the targets of campaigns against modern-day capitalism are often institutions and practices rather than individuals. And, as he explains:

> It is impossible to oppose practices with violence, because practices only exist in their instantiation by people's behaviour, and many of the people who instantiate neoliberalism are its victims rather than its beneficiaries. And even those who are its beneficiaries are often more a product of neoliberalism rather than its producer.[111]

Yet it requires effort and commitment to cultivate and maintain such ways of organising, and there is always a danger of reverting to default ingrained patterns of conflict and violence. After many months of being part of the Preston New Road anti-fracking camp in the UK, Jack reflected how difficult maintaining a grounding of love in the midst of struggle can be, and how damaging it becomes without it:

In the heat of the moment, when as a group you might be intimidated by
police, in conflict with police, it takes a very strong person to keep coming
back to that place of love. And after two years of being there that mode of
aversion and conflict was really entrenched and the two sides were just bat-
tling against each other over and over. It was painful to see, and to consider
how different it would have been if there had been a web of love underneath
all of that.

And so, hate creates separation. And hate magnifies *the other* to sometimes
monstrous proportions. Lowanna describes her relationship with hate as a
member of a colonised people and reflects upon its impact on her personally:

I grew up with protest and activism, and I've waved a flag and banged a drum
and I've taken to the streets. And I realised that the hate that I had was like a
stone in my gut. It was making me unhealthy. I think the hate was going to kill
me. Hate is really easy. You don't have to think about hate. Hate is all encompassing, and it's exciting. But hate made me sick – physically sick, culturally
sick, spiritually sick.

But while contemporary forms of movement organisation largely agree
on a preference for adopting non-violent tactics over more violent alternatives, this might be more easily said than done for community activists
at the sharp end of state violence within which their lives and the lives of
those closest to them might be in danger. As Katie reflects: 'Should I tell
African Americans that they shouldn't use violence to protect themselves
from the police in the United States when there is systemic state sponsored
violence against their community?' And as Gordon points out, although the
indiscriminate violence by legal state forces has certainly declined in most
Western societies (replaced to a lesser extent with legitimised violent tactics
utilised by the police and in prison settings – now normalised by the rule
of law), they do continue to be overtly employed 'by proxy' in the postcolonial world.[112] He therefore makes the argument that violence against the
state is in fact precisely prefigurative of the stateless society we might wish
to inhabit, because even in a free society a defence would need to be made,
with violence if necessary, against attempts at domination and the reconstitution of hierarchical social order.[113]

A contemporary example of this can be seen in the Autonomous
Administration of North and East Syria where they attempt to defend
their commitment towards principles of ecology, direct democracy and
democratic confederalism against multiple hostile forces: the Turkish state,
which aims to supress Kurdish autonomy, Islamic organisations seeking to
extend their territory, and the Syrian state itself. Interestingly, rather than
framing their choice as between violence and non-violence, the Rojavans
have posited the choice as between the *monopolisation* of violence and the

democratisation of violence. As Christiaan Boonen explains, this democratisation of how their defence is organised, which includes equal gender participation across all councils, institutions and positions of authority, and a guaranteed veto for women and youths on any decision affecting them, defends against the monopolisation of violence in the hands of the few (mainly men and the elderly).[114] Thus Boonen warns against succumbing to the 'allure of military heroism', and reminds us that 'while violence might play a role in the defence of what are sometimes fragile, new forms of life, it should not overtake them'.[115] This justification for violence in certain limited conditions does therefore possess a compelling logic. Yet even if constrained by such strong ethical considerations, it is difficult to envisage how any act of violence, however theoretically defensible, would not have implications prefiguratively – as the seeds of future violence. There are no easy answers. While certain acts of violence might be understood as a legitimate response to injustice, especially when faced with a state apparatus with infinitely more power than those who struggle to challenge it, there seems to be no logical escape from the fact that violent struggle will in turn prefigure violent society. To quote the title of a 1979 pamphlet printed in the aftermath of the Sydney Hilton Hotel bombing – *You Can't Blow Up a Social Relationship*.[116]

And even if, as this book contends, political praxes grounded in (r)evolutionary love *will* constitute a radically less-violent society, if we are to truly replace domination with freedom then what political processes can be constructed that maintain such a freedom? It is here that the multiple examples of horizontal, flexible and fluid democratic practices that can be found across contemporary left-libertarian movements are of crucial importance, not only as a liberatory way of relating with one another as activists, but as making visible in a material way legitimate, workable alternatives to our capitalist, market-driven, 'representative' politics as usual.[117] But with regards to finally realising such alternatives, Maria asks an important question:

> Can we even have a political system where people are not corrupted? We can have a better model of politics, sure. But if the people involved are thinking only of themselves, and of their own, then it's going to be corrupted again, right? People craving power, craving money. How can we ensure that in the new politics it's not just all going to change back again to the way it was?

Gordon claims that the wielding of such power within free organisations can be resolved through a 'culture of solidarity' which serves as a positive motivation for modifying behaviour.[118] And while this collective visioning has similarly argued that a radical solidarity borne of an experiential understanding of the deep commons will be an essential cohesive ground on which free society can be built, this must not lead to a denial of the efficacy of structure itself – thus throwing the proverbial baby out with the bath water. In the influential article 'The tyranny of structurelessness', Jo Freeman warns that however much we might wish for it, 'there is no such thing as a structureless group'.[119] For her, any group of people coming together for any length of time will inevitably structure itself in some way. Thus, an apparently 'unstructured' group always has an 'informal' or 'covert' structure, with the performance of structurelessness often a way of masking power relations of domination. But if, as Freeman argues, structure is not only necessary but inevitable, is that not antithetical to a free society existing at all? Alex Prichard believes not – he argues from an anarchist perspective that freedom from domination can be realised through 'a set of rules and principles, rights and duties that members of a community agree among themselves in order to constitute an order that will be the best means for them to realise their vision for the good'.[120] In fact, throughout history radical communities have been sustained by such structures, from the Paris Commune to the syndicalist unions, and in the countless intentional communities, cooperatives and federations that have strived for a free society.[121] It is hard to conceive of a move to direct participatory democracy of any significant scale that will not require the construction of sizable deliberative structures and assemblies. And thus a return to familiar and well-known problems inherent in such formations such as competitiveness, egotism, charismatic leadership, aggression, factionalism and majoritarianism will be a persistent danger which must be faced.[122] Therefore, in order for any new system(s) to forestall such characteristics, or to dissolve them as they emerge, two core conditions will be foundational: the communities through which the system(s) are co-constituted must themselves be grounded in the ethics, values and affective relationships which support this – a politics of immanence grounded in (r)evolutionary love as previously outlined; and the forms of deliberation adopted must be robust enough to sustain (and even celebrate) an agonistic plurality of voices with divergent perspectives as an ongoing process in order to avoid reverting to such problems.

Anyone who has been involved in processes of consensus-based decision making will concede that such processes can be long, demanding and labour intensive. And of course, in the end consensus is not always achievable. As Emma notes: 'when people get together to work on a particular area, I notice that interpersonal relationships get really sticky and difficult. And if you mix that with ideological differences it's really tricky stuff'. Therefore, in a free society, such an ongoing, open process of co-constitution will no doubt continue to experience contestation ad infinitum as it is continually reimagined by a plurality of subjects. Epstein has argued that assumptions common in contemporary movement organisations – that conflict automatically equates to power, and power to domination – should be re-examined.

The task for such organisations, she suggests, is not to 'abolish power and conflict' but to find 'egalitarian forms of power and nonviolent means of conflict'.[123] And so Rosie asks: 'How can we bring more love, compassion and care to the ways in which we work with each other not just as activists, but with those we meet in our activism who are opponents? How can we do that in a way that is really creating the world that we want to see and is making the transformations we want to create?' From Msizi's perspective: 'we can have different arguments, and this is important for developing the community, but once we have argued we don't have to become enemies – we still need each other'. And so rather than an inevitable re-emergence of domination and hierarchy formations as rival actors attempt to institute their own values and negate diversity, such agonism might alternatively be utilised as constructive of the free society. Vivien Lowndes and Marie Paxton argue that such an agonistic process is possible if it adheres to five characteristics: it is (1) *processual* – maintaining an ongoing process of discussion, questioning and collective problem solving, while resisting the formulation of universal norms; (2) *collective* – engaging a multiplicity of actors in the active, open-ended construction of a collective will; (3) *contextual* – acknowledging the embedded nature of democratic formation and the distinctive forms of local agency and environments; (4) *contestable* – valuing conflict and making spaces for agonistic contests, allowing for passionate expression of differences; and always (5) *provisional* – harnessing rather than suppressing open-ended processes of political reflection, understood as necessarily incomplete, and rejecting any endpoint.[124]

A contemporary example of such an agonistic process can be found in the Autonomous Administration of North and East Syria and their practice of *Tekmîl* – a form of 'revolutionary constructive criticism'.[125] Tekmîl involves giving critique, receiving critique and engaging in self-critique, and is grounded in the concept of *Hevaltî* which translates as friendship or comradeship. Processes of Tekmîl generally follow military operations, training sessions and civil projects, and can be called by anyone in either the civil or military structures of Rojava. In order to prevent the process descending into antagonism and polemics, the process of Tekmîl provides each participant with the opportunity to provide both critique and self-critique without interruption from the other participants. And in order to avoid the perception of a participant being singled out and attacked by the group, the overt repetition of any one critique is avoided. The process then ends with a group reflexive process which seeks to discover improved ways of approaching the issue in the future. Philip Argeş O'Keeffe, who worked with *Saziya Yekiti u Pistgiriya Gelan* (the Association for the Unity and Solidarity of Peoples) in Qamishlo, describes the importance of this approach to their co-constitutive processes:

> By establishing the culture of Hevaltî as the basis of revolutionary life we cre-
> ate the alternative environment and society conducive to constructive criticism
> and the means by which, together, we improve ourselves and the collective.
> This is critical to Tekmîl because it allows us to respectfully give criticisms
> and more importantly, accept, absorb and address the criticisms in an efficient
> manner, free of ego, fear, mistrust or conflict.[126]

Such fluid, responsive processes of agonistic pluralism resonate with the entangled contingency of the deep commons. And the cultivation of such political decision-making processes provides an essential complementary factor to consensus-based organisational forms in pursuit of practical, long-term sustainable political systems. Furthermore, there is every reason to believe that Gordon's 'culture of solidarity' would indeed replace more antagonistic forms of social relations as the existing societal structures of hierarchy and domination are deconstructed. By way of an example, in 2021 a delegation of Zapatistas toured Europe, holding dialogues with social movements and communities in struggle 'from below and to the left' in order to share experiences, articulate social practices and organise collective resistance. At one such dialogue in which I participated, a young Zapatista woman who had grown up in one of the free Caracoles had explained their horizontal organisational structures (which will be explored at more depth in the following chapter). Once she had finished, one Irish comrade asked: 'But what stops a community representative to one of your autonomous municipal councils from attempting to use their position to accumulate personal power?' Perplexed, the woman replied: 'but why would they do that? What would be the point?' This served as a poignant lesson in not only how embedded in hierarchical-dominator thinking we have become in capitalist society, but also how rapidly such ways of thinking and being can be deconstructed and replaced by new egalitarian paradigms – as had been the case for this woman and her community. Bookchin expressed a similar optimism regarding human potentiality:

> We have no reason to be disenchanted by history. As barbarous as its most
> warlike, cruel, exploitative, and authoritarian periods have been, humanity
> has soared to radiant heights in its great periods of social reconstruction,
> thought, and art – despite the burdens of domination and egotism. Once these
> burdens have been removed, we have every reason to hope for a degree of per-
> sonal and social enlightenment for which there are no historical precedents.[127]

But even for the most optimistic among us, given the bleak political reality we currently inhabit, it might still seem an insurmountable task for us to actualise the framework of plurality this book argues will be borne from the (r)evolutionary love it has examined. And so, a useful way of thinking about this conundrum might be the one offered by Emily Kawano – who uses the metamorphosis of the caterpillar into a butterfly as a metaphor for how such a transformation might occur.[128] She describes how the caterpillar is born with 'imaginal cells' which contain the markers for the future butterfly to emerge. Then (mirroring hegemonic capitalism) the residual immune system seeks to attack and kill these imaginal cells, so different are they to their host surroundings. Yet in spite of this onslaught, the imaginal cells that survive begin to locate each other and form into clusters, preparing the ground for metamorphosis. Ultimately, as we know, these clusters of imaginal cells then work together to transform the caterpillar into an entirely new creature. And applying this metaphor to our own contemporary struggles – with the sheer scale and diversity of activists, groups, communities and movements organising today, and the active co-imagining of so many new worlds, dare we now imagine such a metamorphosis for ourselves?

Notes

1 Reclaim The Streets, *Poster for the M41 street party* – July 1996, London. Available online: http://rts.gn.apc.org/imlib.htm (accessed 13 May 2022).
2 John P. Clark and Camille Martin. *Anarchy, geography, modernity: Selected writings of Élisée Reclus* (Oakland, CA: PM Press, 2013), p. 100.
3 Reclus, 'The extended family', p. 137.
4 Landauer, 'Through separation to community', in *Revolution and other writings: A political reader*, p. 96.
5 Goldman, 'Anarchism: What it really stands for', p. 11.
6 Errico Malatesta, *Anarchy* (Cambridge: Dog's Tail Books, 2018), p. 21.
7 Gordon, *Anarchy alive!* pp. 30–34.
8 Combahee River Collective, 'The Combahee River Collective statement'.
9 David N. Pellow and Hollie Nyseth Brehm, 'From the new ecological paradigm to total liberation: The emergence of a social movement frame'. *The Sociological Quarterly* 56 (2015), 185–212.
10 Earth Liberation Front, Communiqué – 5 March 2001, cited in: Pellow and Nyseth Brehm, 'From the new ecological paradigm to total liberation', p. 185.
11 hooks, *Outlaw culture: Resisting representations* (New York: Routledge, 2006), p. 244.
12 Ibid.
13 Olli Tammilehto, 'The present is pregnant with a new future', in F. Venturini, E. Değirmenci and I. Morales (eds) *Social ecology and the right to the city* (Montreal: Black Rose Books, 2019), p. 142.
14 Reclus, 'Anarchy', p. 128.
15 Kropotkin, *Mutual aid: A factor in evolution*, p. 8.
16 Ibid.
17 Iain McKay, *Direct struggle against capital: A Peter Kropotkin anthology* (Oakland, CA: AK Press, 2014), p. 50.
18 Peter Kropotkin, *Ethics: Origin and development*, trans. L. S. Friedland and J. R. Piroshnikof, 1922, 25. Available online: https://theanarchistlibrary.org/

library/petr-kropotkin-ethics-origin-and-development.pdf (accessed 16 May 2022).

19 Pamela Sue Anderson, 'Towards a new philosophical imaginary'. *ANGELAKI* 25:1–2 (2020), 11.

20 Ibid, p. 15.

21 Arundhati Roy, *The god of small things* (New York: Harper Perennial, 1998), p. 311.

22 Carol Gilligan, 'Moral injury and the ethic of care: Reframing the conversation about differences'. *Social Philosophy* 45:1 (2014), 95–100.

23 Anderson, 'Towards a new philosophical imaginary', p. 8.

24 Peter Kropotkin, 'From expropriation', in I. McKay (ed.) *Direct struggle against capital: A Peter Kropotkin anthology* (Oakland, CA: AK Press, 2014), p, 531.

25 Goldman, 'Marriage and love', p. 102.

26 Murray Bookchin, *The third revolution: Popular movements in the revolutionary era, vol. 1.* (London: Cassell, 1996), p. 294.

27 Tammilehto, 'The present is pregnant with a new future'.

28 Lesley Bellau, 'Pauwauwaein: Idle no more to the indigenous nationhood movement', in Kind-nda-niimi Collective (eds) *The winter we danced* (Winnepeg, CA: Arbeiter Ring, 2014), p. 351.

29 Montgomery and Bergman, *Joyful militancy*, pp. 108–109.

30 David Graeber, 'Afterword', in K. Khatib, M. Killjoy and M. McGuire (eds) *We are many: Reflections on movement strategy from occupation to liberation* (Oakland, CA: AK Press, 2012), p. 426.

31 Marina Sitrin, 'Anarchism and the newest social movements', in C. Levy and M. Adams (eds) *The Palgrave handbook of anarchism* (Cham, Switzerland: Palgrave Macmillan, 2019, p. 660.

32 Gordon, *Anarchy alive!* p. 15.

33 Hansard Society, 'Audit of political engagement 16: The 2019 Report'. Available online: www.johnsmithcentre.com/research/audit-of-political-eng agement-16-the-2019-report/ (accessed 10 May 2022).

34 Kenneth Roth, 'How authoritarians are exploiting the COVID-19 crisis to grab power'. *Human Rights Watch*, 2020. Available online: www.hrw.org/news/ 2020/04/03/how-authoritarians-are-exploiting-covid-19-crisis-grab-power (accessed 16 March 2022).

35 Knabb, *The joy of revolution*, p. 2.

36 Emma Goldman, *My disillusionment in Russia*, 1925, p. 433. Available online: http://libcom.org/files/Emma%20Goldman-%20My%20Disillusionm ent%20in%20Russia.pdf (accessed 22 April 2022).

37 John Holloway, 'Twelve theses on changing the world without taking power'. *The Commoner* 4 (2002), 1–6.

38 Reclus, 'Evolution, revolution, and the anarchist ideal', p. 145.

39 Bookchin, *The third revolution, vol. 1*, p. 7.

40 Ibid., p. 128.

41 Ibid, p. 9.

42 Jerome R. Mintz, *The anarchists of Casas Viejas* (Chicago, IL: University of Chicago Press, 1982), pp. 1–9.

43 Murray Bookchin, 'Introductory essay', in S. Dolgoff (ed.) *The anarchist collectives: Workers' self-management in the Spanish revolution 1936–1939* (Montreal: Black Rose Books, 1990), pp. xi–xxxix.

44 Gaston Leval, *Collectives in the Spanish revolution*, trans. V. Richards (Oakland, CA: PM Press, 2018), p. 270.

45 George Orwell, *Homage to Catalonia*, 1938, p. 7. Available online: https://gutenberg.net.au/ebooks02/0201111h.html (accessed 16 May 2022).

46 James Michael Yeoman, 'The Spanish civil war', in C. Levy and M. Adams (eds) *The Palgrave handbook of anarchism* (Cham, Switzerland: Palgrave Macmillan, 2019), p. 438.

47 Ibid., p. 439.

48 José Peirats, *Anarchists in the Spanish revolution* (London: Freedom Press, 1998), p. 286.

49 Cited in: Peirats, *Anarchists in the Spanish revolution*, p. 292.

50 Ibid., p. 290.

51 Yeoman, 'The Spanish civil war', pp. 437–442.

52 Vernon Richards, *Lessons of the Spanish revolution 1936–1939* (Oakland, CA: PM Press, 2019), p. 225.

53 Ibid., p. 232.

54 Hannah Arendt, *On revolution* (London: Faber & Faber, 2016), p. 268.

55 Jason Del Gandio and A.K. Thompson, *Spontaneous combustion: The Eros Effect and global revolution* (Albany, NY: SUNY Press, 2017), p. 2.

56 Eduardo Romanos, 'From Tahrir to Puerta del Sol to Wall Street: The transnational diffusion of social movements in comparative perspective'. *Revista Española de Investigaciones Sociologicas* 154 (2016), 106.

57 Laura Galián, 'Squares, occupy movements and the Arab revolutions', in C. Levy and M. Adams (eds) *The Palgrave handbook of anarchism* (Cham, Switzerland: Palgrave Macmillan, 2019), p. 716.

58 Sungur Savran, 'The first victory for the Sudanese revolution: Will the people be able to override the "orderly transition"?'. *The Bullet*, 16 April 2019.

59 Bookchin, *The third revolution, vol. 1*, pp. 9–10.

60 Murray Bookchin, *The third revolution: Popular movements in the revolutionary era, vol. 2*. (London: Cassell, 1998), p. 118.

61 Maurice Duverger, cited in: Arendt, *On revolution*, p. 281.

62 Pierre-Joseph Proudhon, *Confessions of a revolutionary, to serve as a history of the February revolution*, 1849, p. 3. Available online: https://en.wikisource.org/wiki/Translation:Confessions_of_a_Revolutionary/3 (accessed 8 May 2022).

63 See: Marx and Engels, 'Address of the central committee to the communist league'; and Trotsky, *The permanent revolution*.

64 Proudhon, *Toast to the revolution*, p. 9.

65 Peter Kropotkin, *The great French revolution 1789–1793* (St Petersburg, FL: Red and Black Publishing, 2010), pp. 360–361.

66 Ibid., p. 361.

67 Kroptkin, 'From expropriation', p. 531.

68 Ibid.

69 Gustav Landauer, 'Revolution', in *Revolution and other writings: A political reader*, pp. 168–170.

70 Sam Dolgoff, *Bakunin on anarchy* (New York: Vintage Books, 1973), p. 357.

71 Paul Raekstad and Sofa Saio Gradin, *Prefigurative politics* (Cambridge: Polity Press, 2020), p. 36.

72 Davis, 'History, politics, and utopia', pp. 130–132.

73 Abram, *The spell of the sensuous*, p. 272.

74 Jernej Kaluža, 'Anarchism in Deleuze'. *Deleuze and Guattari Studies* 13:2 (2019), 289.

75 Ibid., p. 290.

76 Bager Nûjiyan, 'From the free mountains of Kurdistan to the southeast of Mexico: Towards a revolutionary culture of the global freedom struggle'. *Internationalist Commune*, 2019. Available online: https://internationalist commune.com/from-the-free-mountains-of-kurdistan-to-the-southeast-of-mex ico-towards-a-revolutionary-culture-of-the-global-freedom-struggle/ (accessed 1 May 2022).

77 Barbara Epstein, *Political protest and cultural revolution: Nonviolent direct action in the 1970s and 1980s* (Berkeley, CA: University of California Press, 1991), p. 192.

78 Ibid., p. 269.

79 Ibid., p. 192.

80 Gordon, 'Prefigurative politics between ethical practice and absent promise', p. 521.

81 Gordon, 'Utopia in contemporary anarchism', p. 261.

82 Gordon, 'Prefigurative politics between ethical practice and absent promise', p. 522.

83 Ibid., p. 532.

84 Darren Webb, 'Where's the vision? The concept of utopia in contemporary educational theory'. *Oxford Review of Education* 35:6 (2009), 757.

85 Darren Webb, 'Critical pedagogy, utopia and political (dis)engagement'. *Power and Education* 5:3 (2013), 280–290.

86 Ibid., p. 287.

87 Darren Webb, 'Here we stand: The pedagogy of Occupy Wall Street'. *Australian Journal of Adult Learning* 59:3 (2019), 358.

88 Newman, 'Anarchism, utopianism and the politics of emancipation', p. 211.

89 Braidotti, *The posthuman*, p. 104.

90 Dan Swain, 'Not not but not yet: Present and future in prefigurative politics'. *Political Studies* 67:1 (2019), 59.

91 Benjamin Franks, *Rebel alliances: The means and ends of contemporary British anarchisms* (Oakland, CA: AK Press, 2006), p. 114.

92 Landauer, 'Through separation to community', p. 100.

93 Ibid., p. 103.

94 Uri Gordon and CrimethInc, 'Prefigurative politics, catastrophe, and hope: Does the idea of "prefiguration" offer false reassurance?' *The Anarchist Library*,

2018, p. 14. Available online: https://theanarchistlibrary.org/library/uri-gor don-prefigurative-politics-catastrophe-and-hope (accessed 16 May 2022).

95 Élisée Reclus, 'Why we are anarchists', 1889. Available online: https://autonomies. org/2019/08/elisee-reclus-why-we-are-anarchists/ (accessed 12 May 2022).

96 Escobar, 'Thinking-feeling with the Earth', p. 18.

97 Braidotti, *The posthuman*, p. 191.

98 Bookchin, *The ecology of freedom*, p. 421.

99 Marianne Maeckelbergh, 'Doing is believing: Prefiguration as strategic practice in the alterglobalization movement'. *Social Movement Studies* 10:1 (2011), 2.

100 See: Joshua Clover, 'The coming occupation', in K. Khatib, M. Killjoy, and M. McGuire (eds) *We are many: Reflections on movement strategy from occupation to liberation* (Oakland, CA: AK Press, 2012), 98.

101 Benjamin Franks, 'Prefiguration', in B. Franks, N. Jun, and L. Williams (eds) *Anarchism: A conceptual approach* (London: Routledge, 2018), p. 34.

102 Braidotti, *The posthuman*, p. 193.

103 Springer, 'Space, time, and the politics of immanence', p. 161.

104 Saul Newman, 'Postanarchism', in C. Levy and M. Adams (eds) *The Palgrave handbook of anarchism* (Cham, Switzerland: Palgrave Macmillan, 2019), p. 298.

105 Sitrin, 'Anarchism and the newest social movements', p. 674.

106 Gordon, 'Utopia in contemporary anarchism', p. 269.

107 Nathan Eisenstadt, 'Non-domination, governmentality, and care of the self', in M. Lopes de Souza, R. J. White and S. Springer (eds) *Theories of resistance: Anarchism, geography, and the spirit of revolt* (London: Rowman and Littlefield, 2016), p. 36.

108 Knabb, *The joy of revolution*, p. 94.

109 Robyn Marasco, 'I would rather wait for you than believe that you are not coming at all: Revolutionary love in a post-revolutionary time'. *Philosophy and Social Criticism* 36:6 (2010), 651.

110 Cited in: Chabot, 'Love and revolution', p. 804.

111 Todd May, *Nonviolent resistance: A philosophical introduction* (Cambridge: Polity Press, 2015), p. 175.

112 Gordon, *Anarchy Alive!* p. 83.

113 Ibid., p. 99.

114 Christiaan Boonen, 'A (non-)violent revolution? Strategies of civility for the politics of the common', in S. Cogolati and J. Wouters (eds) *The commons and a new global governance* (Cheltenham, UK: Edward Elgar Publishing, 2018), pp. 71–72.

115 Ibid., p. 72.

116 Libertarian Socialist Organisation, *You can't blow up a social relationship* (Brisbane, Australia: Anarres Books Collective, 1979).

117 See Maeckelbergh, 'Doing is believing'.

118 Gordon, *Anarchy Alive!* p. 76.

119 Jo Freeman, 'The tyranny of structurelessness'. *The Women's Liberation Movement, USA*, 1970. Available online: http://struggle.ws/pdfs/tyranny.pdf (accessed 27 February 2022).

120 Alex Prichard, 'Freedom', in C. Levy and M. Adams (eds) *The Palgrave handbook of anarchism* (Cham, Switzerland: Palgrave Macmillan, 2019), p. 71.

121 Ibid., p. 86.

122 Clark, *The impossible community*, p. 278.

123 Epstein, *Political protest and cultural revolution*, pp. 269–270.

124 Vivien Lowndes and Marie Paxton, 'Can agonism be institutionalised? Can institutions be agonised? Prospects for democratic design'. *The British Journal of Politics and International Relations* 20:3 (2018), 705–707.

125 Philip Argeş O'Keeffe, 'Tekmîl: Creating a culture of constructive criticism'. *Komun Academy for Democratic Modernity*, 2018. Available online: https://theanarchistlibrary.org/library/philip-arge-o-keeffe-tekmil (accessed 13 May 2022).

126 Ibid.

127 Bookchin, *The ecology of freedom*, p. 439.

128 Emily Kawano, 'Solidarity economy: Building an economy for people and planet'. *The Next System Project*, 2018, p. 12. Available online: www.solidarityeconomy.coop/wp-content/uploads/2017/06/Kawano-E.-2018_Solidarity-Economy.pdf (accessed 11 May 2022).

6

The collective heart: Co-constituting free society

'Only life, delivered from all its governmental and doctrinaire barriers, and given full liberty of action, can create.'

– Mikhail Bakunin[1]

Introduction

At this point in our enquiry, it might be useful to revisit the four distinct conceptions of love found in classical Greek philosophy – *Éros*, *Storgē*, *Philía* and *Agápe*. While the boundaries between these qualities of love are not always easy to define, we have established in earlier chapters how *éros* (desire/passion) and *storgē* (familial affection) possess acutely divergent potentialities – the potential for abuse, inequality and domination, or the potential to encourage alternative and liberatory forms of relationship beyond separateness and competition. And similarly, we have seen how *philía* (friendship/kinship) and *agápe* (charity/empathetic love for the many) at once offer the potential to act as a basis for building a radical solidarity, or of being subverted to legitimise xenophobic nationalisms, patriotisms and fascisms. In the opening pages of this book, it was suggested that while these four facets of love clearly possess liberatory potential in their own right, it is the (r)evolutionary love examined throughout this enquiry that might prove the most politically transformative due to its catalytic relationship with each of them. And having explored at depth the entangled relationality of the deep commons, and the consequent onto-epistemological shift in the way we might frame subject–object relations, we are now in a position to expand on this argument somewhat.

From this new perspective we can understand *éros*, *storgē*, *philía* and *agápe* to function on what we might broadly call the egoic level, requiring a degree of separation between subject and object as reference points for the loving relation to exist. *Agápe* for example, even at its most expansive, still involves the subject taking 'all beings' as its object. Therefore, as much as they might (and of course frequently do) potentiate free relations, they are also prone to power imbalances and the emergence of domination as the subject clings to, and fixates on, that which is beloved. By contrast, (r)evolutionary love in this same sense might be seen as non-referential as it requires no such fixation. It is love without an object – the post-egoic embodied experience of our radical interdependence as described by the activists involved in this enquiry. It is a signifier of the deep commons. And in the easing of this conceptual split there is a consequential abatement of the ground on which power imbalances might configure. It is at once free and freeing.

This argument in no way seeks a negation of individual experience in favour of the universal/communal or vice versa, for they are – as we have repeatedly discovered – intimately entangled. From the perspective of this enquiry, it is more a question of agency. For instance, Sigmund Freud's conceptualisation of *éros* as one of two fundamental life drives (Éros and Thanatos)[2] has been taken up by a number of Marxist scholars, most notably Fromm, Marcuse and, later, Katsiaficas, as a powerful libidinal force capable of generating mass political awakenings and spontaneous rebellions.[3] However, scholars such as Katsiaficas and most recently the autonomist political philosopher Richard Gilman-Opalsky have concluded that this 'Eros Effect' cannot be continuously activated: 'We cannot keep our affection going in energetic movements indefinitely. Human energy can be exhausted and recharged variously for different causes, but not "kept on" for a lifetime'.[4] And to a large extent this is true. The erotic drive alone can never quite fully obtain its imagined object of desire, and thus risks the perpetuation of impossible/unreachable utopias. Therefore, however powerful a political force it might be (and this book would argue that it most certainly is), such manifestations of *éros* cannot energise a movement – or free society – indefinitely, as the tragic history of counterrevolution and defeat explored at depth in the previous chapter confirms. For as we have now established, it is ultimately when our love is re-joined with(in) the deep commons that we are able to realise freedom as an actually existing immanent quality of the here-and-now. In fact, Marcuse's original theorisation of *éros* fully agrees on the importance of this return to immanence in order to close our endless cycles of alienation: 'Man comes to himself only when transcendence has been conquered – when eternity has become present in the here-and-now ... This is the total affirmation of the life instincts, repelling all escape and negation'.[5] Our task then is to (r)evolutionise *éros* – to unbind it from this constant propulsion towards a desired future, and thus free it to permeate immanent being and illuminate the potentiality of the moment. In so doing, we discover a potent generative force: an *agápe* beyond 'all beings' and an *éros* unhooked from ego. Life bursting forth as a profoundly intimate process of co-arising.

The aim here is thus to illuminate how such a grounded, immanent (r)evolutionary love offers a direct (and directable) causal effect on our multiple entangled relations, and therefore to the extent to which they will lead to intimate or social relations of domination or liberation. As explored in previous chapters, this radical interrelationality thus serves as the basis for a co-emergent relational ethics grounded in a web of profoundly immanent normativities – a generative process through which a living ethos of solidarity and care is perpetually co-created and renewed. Such an ethics is therefore uniquely anarchistic as it eschews both the conformation of rigid norms, constraining rules and forms of coercion that are otherwise required for the maintenance of an ethical universality, and the abstractions of more transcendent ethical forms. Furthermore, this grounding in the deep commons acts to unsettle the usual anthropocentrism of ethical enquiry in ways that demand a fuller acknowledgement of our entanglement in a more-than-human world. In *Matters of Care*, María Puig de la Bellacasa uses the philosophy and practice of permaculture to make this very point:

> Embedded in the interdependency of all forms of life – humans and their technologies, animals, plants, microorganisms, elemental resources such as air and water, as well as the soil we feed on – permaculture ethics is an attempt to decentre human ethical subjectivity by not considering humans as masters or even as protectors of but as participants in the web of Earth's living beings. And yet, or actually, *correlatively*, in spite of this nonhuman-centred stance, of the affirmation that humans are not separated from the natural worlds, permaculture ethics cultivate specific ethical obligations for humans.[6]

And once again, rather than this vision of a living relational ethics belonging to an entirely new postmodern imaginary, it is found to be firmly rooted in classical anarchist thought. More than a century ago, Kropotkin conceived of such mutual relations as 'not petrified by law, routine, or superstition, but continually developing and continually readjusted, in accordance with the ever-growing requirements of a free life ... a continual evolution – such as we see in nature'.[7]

We have seen how this love materialises as political direct action in moments where our collective psycho-socio-material entanglement is realised, experienced and embodied. Conversely, we have seen how its power can be invoked as long-term processes of struggle, activating a radical solidarity embedded in this deep commons. Strategically developing political praxes grounded in this love might therefore provide the basis upon which to co-constitute free society here-and-now – as an imaginative/responsive ongoing process rather than reverting to default capitalistic, patriarchal, racist or anthropocentric modes of reproduction, and thus provide a means for sustaining such a system in the absence of domination. But (many will undoubtedly ask) how realistic can such a profound reconfiguration actually be? And the answer, somewhat unsurprisingly given the sheer scale of struggle visible today, is that it is entirely possible to find living, vibrant examples of such societal formations across the world right now that might inspire us. Perhaps, as Salleh suggests, political theorists have simply been 'too culturally blinkered to see it'.[8] This chapter will now turn to the Zapatista revolution as one such example, and specifically the Indigenous concept of *O'on* or 'collective heart', examining its central role in the social reproduction of their communities and anarchistic organisational structures. A critique of contemporary international relations theory and its reification of the state as sole political actor will follow. Finally, using the example of the extraordinary experiment in horizontal participatory democracy taking place in the Autonomous Administration of North and East Syria as a starting point, the deep commons will be proposed as a location in which to co-constitute the global 'community of communities' envisaged by generations of anarchist thinkers as a liberatory alternative to the current system.

The Zapatistas' (r)evolutionary love

'Where did you get those strange rhythms that you sing and dance to?
...The heart.'
                                                      – Subcomandante Marcos.[9]

The *Ejército Zapatista de Liberación Nacional* (EZLN) was born in a camp in Chiapas, the southernmost state of Mexico, on 17 November 1983. Six urban revolutionaries from *Fuerzas de Liberación Nacional* (FLN) – a Marxist insurgent group – had arrived in the mountains with the intention of organising and radicalising the local *campesino* communities for an armed revolution. But the events that followed did not proceed according to this preordained script. Indeed, rather than the Indigenous population being transformed by Marxist ideology as had been the plan, it was the insurgents themselves who were transformed – by the radically different worldview they encountered in the Indigenous communities of Chiapas.[10] What took place instead has been described by Clark as an 'extraordinary dialectical reversal' in which the militants were converted from a view of revolution as 'the imposition of an ideological paradigm led by an enlightened vanguard' to one of (r)evolution as a 'socially and ecologically regenerative activity' grounded in local autonomy and self-determination.[11] Reflecting on this ideological journey Marcos described this 'evolution of thinking' as their most important development to date: 'From revolutionary vanguardism to governing by obeying; from taking power above to the creation of power below; from political politics to everyday politics; from the leaders to the people; from the marginalisation of gender to the direct participation of women; from the mocking of the other to the celebration of difference'.[12] It was this ideological transformation that prefigured what the Zapatista revolution would soon become. And in this pivotal moment Marcos describes how they found themselves with the need to answer some decisive questions: 'What's next? Prepare those who are next on the road of death? Train more and better soldiers? Invest our efforts in improving our battered machinery of war?' In the end, rather than embarking on 'the path that others direct towards power', the revolutionaries decided to turn their 'hearts' towards the 'native peoples, guardians of the earth and memory'.[13] And thus, explains Marcos, they made their choice:

> Instead of devoting ourselves to training guerrilla warriors, soldiers, and squadrons, we trained health and education promoters, and the foundations were laid for the autonomy that amazes the world today. Instead of building barracks, improving our weaponry, erecting walls and trenches, we built schools, hospitals, and health centres; we improved our living conditions. Instead of fighting to have a place in the Parthenon of individualized deaths below, *we chose to build life* [emphasis added].[14]

And so, what was this Indigenous onto-epistemology that so radically transformed both these original insurgents and consequently the entire trajectory of the Zapatista experiment to date? Central to the Zapatista understanding of what it means to live in the world is the Indigenous Tsotsil concept of *O'on* or 'collective heart' – a concept masterfully translated for a non-Tsotsil audience in Dylan Eldredge Fitzwater's book *Autonomy Is in Our Hearts*.[15] In the Tsotsil language, thoughts and feelings are considered to be one and the same, thus better framed as *thought-feeling*, and are understood to manifest in this collective heart as the realisation of its 'inherent potentialities'. This underlying potentiality is called *ch'ulel*, often translated as soul or spirit – and a spirit located in the heart.[16] But *ch'ulel* does not easily fit into contemporary Western understandings of spirit. Rather than existing apart from our day-to-day material world, *ch'ulel* is a means of describing the 'inherent or immanent potentialities' that are always present and ready to shape and form the 'dynamic relationships that compose reality'.[17] Xuno López Intzin, a contemporary Tzetsal scholar and activist, explains how *ch'ulel* potentiates a profound interrelationality that resonates with our previous conceptualisations of the deep commons:

> From this understanding of the ch'ulel in everything, the human being establishes relations with all that exists, in other words the human being interacts with their environment and the environment with the human being on a material and immaterial plane. From this plane or universe of ch'ulel existence is ordered, and social relations are ordered with all that exists.[18]

Intzin further argues that capitalism, along with hegemonic rational thought, has distanced *ch'ulel* from nature. And thus he claims that only by 'building a collective heart in order to recover the meaning of our humanity can we reconnect with the forgotten sacred'.[19] A common way of greeting one another in Tsotsil is to ask *k'usi javo'on* which literally means 'what is the state of your heart?' with the respondent's wholeness or fragmentation of heart describing their own or their community's emotional, spiritual and physical state.[20] Therefore, as the collective heart (*O'on*) and its underlying potentiality (*ch'ulel*) share a reciprocal interrelationality, the wholeness of the collective heart indicates the conscious embodiment of the underlying potentiality, and its fragmentation indicates an obscuration. Thus, if we equate *O'on* to (r)evolutionary love and *ch'ulel* to the deep commons, we can see once again how *O'on*, like (r)evolutionary love, materialises in moments where our collective psycho-socio-material entanglement is realised, experienced and embodied, and likewise how it can be invoked, activating a radical solidarity embedded in its *ch'ulel* or the deep commons. The creation of free society from a Tsotsil perspective can therefore be seen as an ongoing reciprocal process of nurturing and developing both this underlying potentiality and our collective heart. And this process of 'bringing one another to greatness' (*ichbail ta muk*) in turn creates 'the life that is good for everyone' (*lekil kuxlejal*), as Fitzwater explains: 'For the Zapatistas, dignity, autonomy, and democracy for each people, as well as the creation of this people as a collectivity, arises through the growth of the heart, through bringing one another into one collective heart, through ichbail ta muk'.[21] And so more than mere abstract theory, the Agapeic web as envisioned in the previous chapters can be seen as animate in the actually existing anarchistic practices of the ongoing Zapatista revolution – a political project that has been described by Clark as 'one of the most radical and far-reaching conceptions of democracy yet to appear'.[22]

The centre of Zapatista autonomous governance is in 'every Zapatista community', existing as multiple dialogical processes that work openly on the tensions between different actors while simultaneously constructing a framework of 'shared aspirations born from a collective heart'.[23] And this process includes at its centre an ongoing radical reconfiguration of gender relations within these communities. Taking the shared commitment to engage in struggle *juntos y a la par* ('together and side by side') seriously, there is a shared recognition that any struggle against colonialism and capitalism is also 'necessarily a struggle against patriarchy'.[24] Material results of this can be seen in the increased engagement by Zapatista men in reproductive work and emotional labour, and the increased involvement of women in positions of responsibility and decision making in community life, political organising and autonomous governance.[25] And while (as in all contemporary societies) there remains a long way to go in terms of fully overcoming masculine domination and machismo forms of masculinity, the strides they are making in these communities towards women's collective empowerment, claims Levi Gahman, are 'nothing short of miraculous': 'Rebel women, and the socially reproductive labour they do each day, are at the heart of both the movement and lifegiving world they are creating'.[26]

The Zapatista governance structures have no central constitution, only principles arrived at through collective agreement. Community representatives who serve in the MAREZ (Zapatista Autonomous Rebel Municipalities), for instance, follow the seven principles of autonomous government or 'Command by Obeying' which are: (1) serve and not be served; (2) represent and not supersede; (3) build and not destroy; (4) obey and not command; (5) propose and not impose; (6) convince and not defeat; and (7) come down and not go up.[27] Thus the system of assembly (*Ichbail ta muk*) maintains a 'constant process of creation and re-creation' in order to remain free and open, with each community free to imagine for themselves what unique form their democracy might take. And so, when the smaller collectives that constitute the collective heart find themselves in disagreement or imbalance, an assembly is convened in order for all constituents to participate in the formulation of a new agreement, resulting in the co-creation of a new collective heart, and so on and so forth. It is this process of direct community approval of all decisions that ensures the flow of communication (and power) between the various levels of autonomous government remains in perpetual movement, and thus continuously weaving the multiple collective hearts of the communities into the one collective heart of the Zapatista organisation.[28] Moreover, as a further tactic for combatting the ever present danger of the accumulation of power in any one community or by a new governing elite, a complex rotation system for assembly representatives has been established that ensures no one person has the opportunity to develop disproportionate power or influence – with the governance structures and communities thus remaining part of 'the same social body'.[29] And in congruence with this book, Fitzwater concludes that autonomous structures of government such as this cannot/must not have an end point. Such structures, he argues, must be created by the 'constant creation and re-creation' of governing systems that respond to the 'desires and problems experienced by the communities themselves'[30] – utopia as process.

Perhaps just as extraordinary as the collective heart of the Zapatista revolution in Chiapas has been the transnational impact of *Zapatismo* on other struggles around the world – towards the formation of a planetary collective heart. When the Mexican government appealed to the machismo culture that exists in the country by attempting to discredit Subcomandante Marcos by accusing him of being gay, he famously responded by describing this expansive affinity which is grounded in the interdependent and entangled nature of their own and others struggles:

> Yes, Marcos is gay. Marcos is gay in San Francisco, Black in South Africa, an Asian in Europe, a Chicano in San Ysidro, an anarchist in Spain, a Palestinian in Israel, a Mayan Indian in the streets of San Cristobal, a Jew in Germany, a Gypsy in Poland, a Mohawk in Quebec, a pacifist in Bosnia, a single woman on the Metro at 10pm, a peasant without land, a gang member in the slums, an unemployed worker, an unhappy student and, of course, a Zapatista in the mountains.[31]

This radical solidarity had not occurred by chance. The EZLN had deliberately chosen to begin their resistance against the Mexican government on the same day the North Atlantic Free Trade Agreement (NAFTA) came into effect, leading to the emergence of a decentralised global web of solidarity groups in Mexico and around the world.[32] In 1996, the Zapatistas hosted 3,000 activists from around the world at La Realidad in Chiapas for the First Intercontinental Encuentro for Humanity and Against Neoliberalism. And at the second *encuentro*, in Spain, in 1997, organised by the Ya Basta! network, and the subsequent gathering in Geneva in 1998, the People's Global Action was founded as a decentralised and leaderless global anti-capitalist coordinating network. The Zapatistas have continued to play a central role in the anarchistic turn which has been taken by the global anti-capitalist left, resulting in an increased autonomy from the 'traditional triad' of political representation: party, state and vanguard.[33] The Second Declaration of La Realidad described this decentralised, non-hierarchical nature of their emergent organisation thus: 'We are the network, all of us who resist'.[34] And in a 2018 speech, Subcomandante Galeano (one of Marcos' many pseudonyms) addressed this ongoing global network of struggle and the Zapatistas' unwavering commitment to achieving free society for themselves and others:

> All over the world rebellions are being born and are growing. They refuse to accept the limits of schemes, laws and precepts. For there are not only two genders, only seven colours, only four cardinal points. There is not only one world. As Zapatista Defence, our sole aim is to take care of Zapatista hope. If this world is unable to deliver this much, then we will have to build another one – one in which many worlds can fit.[35]

But in our current globalised world, constrained by capitalist hegemony, can such spaces of free society really hope to co-exist, let alone replace the current systems of domination? Rather than submitting to the One World project of neoliberal globalisation, this book proposes that by repositioning ourselves ontologically in the deep commons, an infinite number of worlds can indeed coexist simultaneously, realising this vision of *un mundo donde quepan muchos mundos* – 'a world where many worlds fit'.[36]

The communitarian anarchist ideas of Reclus, Kropotkin, Landauer and, more recently, theorists such as Bookchin and Clark have likewise shared this central contention that our human nature, the history of human community and the structure of cooperative activity all indicate that the creation of a 'community of free communities' at the global level is an entirely reasonable and viable proposition.[37] And it is towards this expansive liberatory ideal that we will now direct our attention.

Towards a global community of communities

(R)evolutionary love as a force in global politics will of course be considered a naivety by most international relations scholars and theorists. And as the field currently strongly favours a determinist approach limited to the interactions and tensions occurring between nation-states, we can fully understand why. But it is this reification of the state as primary actor in international politics that leads to a self-perpetuating reinforcement of state-centric systemic features – thus denying the potential for humanity's 'self-creation', and ultimately privileging 'structure over agency'.[38] The very term 'international relations' obscures the complexity of social relations which co-produce global society, deferring rather to states themselves as sole actants. Consequently, the ascendance of the state system has tended to be viewed as a natural process in which smaller groups consolidate through time into ever larger totalities. But this model becomes problematic when, as this book argues, the process of social formation occurs immanently in the here-and-now through a profoundly entangled interrelationality, rather than through the abstract theorisation of a 'fixed political monism'.[39] And so it is this denial of complexity, and the states' attempts at regulating and suppressing its constituent diversity, that inhibit the 'plural possibilities for emergence and becoming'[40] of which the deep commons is pregnant.

Yet ironically it is the state system itself which has facilitated the process of neoliberal globalisation, leading to the increasing conditions of global pluralism in which we have seen horizontal networked relationships interlink individuals and groups across multiple sites of (unevenly distributed) power – ironic because it is this very anarchic plurality that is rapidly dislodging the state-centric global order.[41] Of course, as we have already seen, these current conditions are being appropriated, shaped and utilised by the forces of capital with incredible force and at a disorienting pace. Yet it is within this anarchic plurality – embodying the entangled conditions explored throughout this book, where free society can be co-constituted and lived. As Chris Sciabarra argues, rather than simply a collection of abstracted state elements, world politics is in fact a 'complex nexus of interrelated institutions and processes, of volitionally conscious and acting individuals and their dynamic relations'.[42] A 'social-relational dialectic' for world politics would therefore understand that the intersubjective engagements between human (and we might add more-than-human) beings position us as entirely capable of, and responsible for, social self-production without the state as intermediary.[43] And as Kinna and Prichard point out, without revisiting this question of constitutionalising beyond the limitations of the state, 'domination and tyranny are all we can expect'.[44]

Through studying the organisational practices of three iconic Occupy camps (Wall Street, Oakland and London) Kinna, Prichard and Swann argue that not only are such horizontal and participatory forms of 'grassroots, post-statist constitutional politics' effective, but they can be 'mimicked and linked up' en masse.[45] Similarly for Alice, although living and organising in communities with a more 'collective sense of democracy' can be 'hard work' and often with 'difficult dynamics' to navigate, she agrees that there is 'real value in those kinds of communities as a model for larger populations'. Rather than forming a closed, consolidating institution, such praxes offer a constitutionalising process which is open and dynamic – a 'fluid structural form' that operates in the absence of a nation-state. And rather than thinking in usual terms of scaling up, such forms of anarchist constitutionalising concentrate on 'linking across, imitating, multiplying, and hybridising'.[46] As far back as the founding of the First International in 1864, Proudhon was calling for such a federalism built on direct democracy and grassroots organising. In the economic sphere it was envisaged that people would freely associate into groups for production, distribution and consumption, and in turn compose larger groups coordinating federally. Political federations would then complement this process based on municipalities and communes, further federating into regional and even global organisations.[47] In the collective visioning process, Dembe suggested that replacing the current system with such cooperative-based models might end the compulsion to produce and consume which has characterised the modern era. And Alice similarly proposed a decentralisation of power towards more 'community-centred forms of collaboration and sharing of goods' – first working together in localised ways, and then more expansively through 'interlocking federations that network globally'. We have already seen how the Zapatista revolution has adopted such a municipal/federal model – animated by (r)evolutionary love and grounded in the deep commons. But, as previously noted, they are not alone in this endeavour. There are in fact many such experiments in anarchistic direct democracy taking place across the globe right now. And, while these struggles are under constant threat of enclosure by state powers, they collectively keep this dream of actualising a global community of communities alive.

Perhaps the most striking contemporary example of such a model, and certainly the largest, is that of the Autonomous Administration of North and East Syria, also known as Rojava – an extraordinary experiment in horizontal participatory democracy involving a multicultural population of around three million people. Tracing a similar trajectory to that of the Zapatistas in Mexico, sections of the Kurdish Workers Party (PKK) – a Marxist guerrilla movement at war with the Turkish state since the 1970s, and their comrades in the Syrian Democratic Union Party (PYD) founded in 2003 – underwent their own political transformation from a vanguardist top-down Leninist party to the more anarchistic governance structure we see today. Drawing on Bookchin's concepts of *communalism*[48] and *libertarian municipalism*,[49] and inspired by the writings of Abdullah Öcalan – the PKK leader imprisoned by the Turkish state since 1999 – the revolutionaries of Rojava realised that the creation of a free society could only be determined by 'the free will of moral and political society'.[50] As Öcalan explains:

> In contrast to the nation-state's centralist, linear and bureaucratic understanding of administration and the exercise of power, democratic federalism poses a type of political formation where society governs itself and where all societal groups and cultural identities can express themselves in local meetings, general conventions, and councils. What is important is the ability to take decisions through councils and discussions. Administration that is elite and not grounded in these are deemed invalid.[51]

At the heart of the Rojavan governance structure are the communes, of which in 2020 there were an estimated 4,000.[52] For Öcalan it is these free and democratic communities that act as the 'main school' in which the individual member of a truly democratic society can be shaped and fully realised because, he argues, in order for democratic society to flourish the individual must be 'communal as well as free'.[53] Each commune makes its own decisions autonomously concerning issues, disputes and developments directly affecting its members. The communes are then organised into districts, with two delegates from each commune – one female, one male – composing a district peoples council to deliberate on matters of administration and economics such as cooperative enterprises, waste disposal and sewage, land distribution and resource distribution. And for matters concerning the entire federation of communes/districts, delegates gather at one further level of decision making in the legislative assembly and public council. Importantly, no decisions are made or departments organised by any external or higher authorities. It is only and always the citizens in the communal assemblies that make decisions on matters of policy.[54]

Also, in common with the Zapatista revolution, anti-patriarchal praxes have been central to this process. Öcalan has described the need for a 'total divorce' from the 5,000-year-old culture of masculine domination, making clear that the 'most permanent and comprehensive component of democratisation' is that of women's freedom.[55] In this determination to revolutionise traditional gender relations, autonomous women's councils have been established in parallel to each level of decision making. These councils determine policy on matters of particular concern to women such as forced marriages, polygamy, sexual violence and discrimination. More than a mere token gesture, the women's councils hold genuine power to overrule the mixed decision-making bodies on any conflict on a decision concerning women.[56] And in line with the posthumanist critique made earlier, this is also a more-than-human (r)evolution. There are now 12 ecological councils active within the federation, with the Mesopotamian Ecology Movement – who have been instrumental in the creation and facilitation of these councils – expressing a vision of achieving a 'dialectical connection' with the natural environment that is 'beyond conventional anthropocentrism'.[57] Agricultural cooperatives for instance are engaged in a process of converting the previous system of industrial farming into an ecologically sound system of production based on 'cooperating with complex living systems' instead of dominating them.[58]

This is not to claim that the process is without its difficulties. Private property relations continue to exist, as do gender, social class, and traditional tribal systems and structures. And as one Rojavan activist recently acknowledged: 'the difficulties of changing a system [without resorting to repressive means] where the majority of the population is used to delegating to state powers is actually the biggest challenge'.[59] This will undoubtedly remain a key challenge to be tackled in any (r)evolutionary process – in Rojava or anywhere else in the world. But interestingly, yet perhaps at this stage not surprisingly, we discover that love has once again played an important role in seeking responses to such issues in their struggle. Clearly a (r)evolution of this scale and depth is no easy task, and the construction of a truly free democratic society, argues Öcalan, will therefore require a 'devotion at the level of real love'.[60] In fact, for him the system of capitalist modernity itself has been based on a denial of love: 'The denial of society, the uncontrollability of individualism, pervasive sexism, the deification of money, the substitution of nation-state for God and the transformation of women into unwaged or low paid workers also means denial of the material basis of love'.[61] This Rojavan (r)evolutionary love, like many of the examples already examined, remains deeply rooted in the cultural imaginary of the region. Nazan Üstündağ argues that Öcalan's thought has thus been influenced by the Indigenous epistemologies transmitted through religious-cultural traditions such as Alevism and Sufism, and can be crystallised by the aphorism, 'Truth is Love; Love is Free Life'.[62] And once again reflecting the interrelationality of (r)evolutionary love with(in) the deep commons, Üstündağ describes an expansive more-than-human matrix containing an inherent promise of freedom:

> This love is not a form of love that can be sexually consummated, contained by household, property, and nation, or reproduce a lineage. Love and eroticism are lived in relation to nature, the world, and revolution, in people, living matter, and society – in other words, in all kinds of relationships – as a movement and a flow.[63]

What makes this democratic (r)evolution all the more astonishing are the precarious conditions in which it has been taking place. Shortly after the start of the Syrian civil war in 2011, Rojavan forces drove out the agents of the Assad regime only to then be forced to defend the region against multiple Islamist groups, including the Islamic State of Iraq and the Levant (ISIL). After a successful defence of the region for a number of years and the collapse of ISIL as a force on the ground, in 2019 the Turkish state – backed by the Russian state and facilitated by the US army – invaded the Rojavan regions of Serkekaniye and Gire Spî, with the regions of Shehba, Minbic, Ain Issa and Till Temir continuing to be regularly bombed at the time of writing. As a recent communiqué from the Internationalist Commune of Rojava confirms: 'the war never stops'.[64] The non-interventionist stance taken by the international community regarding the continued aggression and military incursions that persist against Rojava was likened by Graeber as reminiscent of the inaction shown as the forces of Hitler and Mussolini poured troops and weapons into Spain to arm the fascists against the social revolution underway in the republic, with Graeber moved to say: 'we cannot let it end the same way again'.[65] And without doubt, the scale of Rojava's intended socio-cultural-ecological transformation – especially under such conditions – is a radical utopia by anyone's reckoning. But as discussed in previous chapters, this is a utopia of the here-and-now – a politics of immanence firmly grounded in (and generative of) the day-to-day life and struggles of the communes. It is a process of free society continually creating and recreating itself. As Öcalan explains:

> On this voyage, the question of when the construction of the democratic nation will be completed is a redundant one. This is a construction that will never be finished: it is an ongoing process. The construction of a democratic nation has the freedom to recreate itself at every instant. In societal terms, there can be no utopia or reality that is more ambitious than this.[66]

And resonating with '*la grande famille*' envisaged by Reclus, and Landauer's 'complete community', Öcalan similarly imagines an eventual expansion of confederated communities from the local and regional levels to a 'world democratic confederal union' as a superior form of association to that of the current United Nations which is composed of nation-states and dominated by superpowers and corporations.[67]

But as inspiring as the examples of the Rojavan and Zapatista (r)evolutions might be for many of us around the world, we must remain vigilant. As specific federalised networks achieve a certain level of success, we must consciously resist the temptation to overly reify and essentialise them and thus abstract yet more fixed blueprints for future social formations. As we have already established, it will remain crucial that the co-constitution of free society remains an ongoing process – pluralised, open, responsive and grounded in the here-and-now. Furthermore, what is to stop these new localised democratic territories consolidating over time into ever larger totalities, and thus reproducing yet another state system? The clear answer that has emerged through the collective visioning process is to consciously frame such constitutional processes in the context of the deep commons. Resonating with this idea, Bookchin described an 'active, concrete, existential nature' that develops and expands through complex stages into equally complex and dynamic ecosystems.[68] These systems in turn interlink into similarly complex and dynamic bioregions – constituting the ground for very specific forms of society to emerge in relation to the unique climatic conditions, land, plants, animals and human cultures that have developed within this ecological web. Rediscovering our own unique socio-ecological systems and our place with(in) them might then potentiate the emergence of more-than-human free community. As Alice explains:

> We can see a natural homeostasis as all that constitutes that region inter-relate and accommodate the needs of the other. If we take the example of a forest, there are millions of complex systems at work that support each other, from the mycelium networks underground to the bees that pollinate the flowers of the trees, and they do so with a natural reciprocity that comes from an innate understanding of our interdependence. If humans can learn to develop communities in this way there could be a shift from the current model towards a culture of care and reciprocity, valuing what each individual brings to the community as they recognise the distinct needs of the land they live upon.

And similarly for Lowanna it is important that we 'place-base' love. She explains how as an Indigenous person she is 'nothing without the land', that it is the 'base of our kinship and reciprocity'. Yet once again, as we embark on this deep reconnection, and as we escape the abstracted boundaries and controls of state formations, we must take great care not to then – out of sheer habit – re-territorialise our ecosystems and bioregions and concretise their integrative ecotones into yet more borders. Let us not forget, as Angelo reminds us, the interweaving 'historical, cultural and language relations' that cut across such partial boundaries. A more holistic reintegration into our socio-ecological systems will thus unlock the freedom to fully embody, enjoy and creatively express our more-than-human psycho-socio-material becomings which are at once unique to time and place *and* connected expansively.

The deep commons thus offers an alternative frame of reference to that of the state by eradicating arbitrary static borders (in fact making them an absurdity), and by honouring both the local and the global without reifying either. The concept potentiates the formation of multiple coherent local identities, communities and regions, developing in unique forms according to localised conditions, yet avoiding isolationism due to the need for mutual aid and cooperation with neighbouring communities in order to survive and flourish. Top-down governance becomes nonsensical in relation to this locally responsive ongoing co-production of the world, as does any form of homogenous culture. Such a community of communities is what Sian Sullivan has referred to as *holonic* in the sense that each community is part of the broader scales of a more global organisation while at the same time a localised autonomous whole.[69] Thus power flows bi-directionally across this spectrum, avoiding the accumulation of power at any point of the scale. This 'enfolding-unfolding, implicate-explicate' model of social organisation potentiates a 'proliferation of democratic processes' in which distribution and emergence can occur simultaneously.[70] It realises Reclus' vision of a 'globalisation from below' in which humanity might finally undertake an 'open ended and creative project of liberatory self-realisation'.[71] And mirroring Proudhon's vision of anarchist society in which the 'centre is everywhere, its circumference nowhere',[72] it is literally impossible to find a medial point or a periphery as each socio-ecological system flows into the next in dynamic interconnectedness. There is no beginning and no end, no us and no them. It is the ultimate realisation of *O'on* – the flourishing of the global collective heart, and the location for us to finally co-constitute free society grounded in (r)evolutionary love.

Notes

1 Mikhail Bakunin, *God and the state* (New York: Dover Publications, 1970), p. 62.
2 Sigmund Freud, 'Civilisation and its discontents', in I. Smith (ed.) *Freud – Complete works*, 2010, p. 4509. Available online: www.topoi.net/wp-content/uploads/2012/12/Freud-Complete-Works.unlocked.pdf (accessed 15 May 2022).
3 See: Fromm, *The art of loving*; Marcuse, *Eros and civilization*; and Katsiaficas, 'Eros and revolution'.
4 Gilman-Opalsky, *The communism of love*, p. 297.
5 Marcuse, *Eros and civilisation*, p. 122.
6 María Puig de la Bellacasa, *Matters of care: Speculative ethics in more than human worlds* (Minneapolis, MN: University of Minnesota Press, 2017), p. 129.

7 Peter Kropotkin, *Kropotkin's revolutionary pamphlets*, ed. R. Baldwin (New York: Benjamin Blom, 1969), pp. 119–120.

8 Ariel Salleh, *Ecofeminism as politics: Nature, Marx and the postmodern* (London: Zed Books, 2017), p. 269.

9 Subcomandante Marcos, 'Simple answers to complex questions', in N. Henck (ed.) and H. Gales (trans.) *The Zapatistas' dignified rage: Final public speeches of Subcommander Marcos* (Chico, CA: AK Press, 2014), p. 81.

10 Alex Khasnabish, *Zapatistas: Rebellion from the grassroots to the global* (New York: Zed Books, 2010), pp. 68–70.

11 John P. Clark, 'Foreword', in D. E. Fitzwater, *Autonomy is in our hearts: Zapatista autonomous government through the lens of the Tsotsil language* (Oakland, CA: PM Press, 2019), p. xiv.

12 Subcomandante Marcos, *Professionals of hope: The selected writings of Subcomandante Marcos* (Brooklyn, NY: The Song Cave, 2017), p. 222.

13 Marcos, 'Between light and shade', in N. Henck (ed.) and H. Gales (trans.) *The Zapatistas' dignified rage: Final public speeches of Subcommander Marcos* (Chico, CA: AK Press, 2014), p. 213.

14 Ibid.

15 Fitzwater, *Autonomy is in our hearts*.

16 Ibid, 32.

17 Ibid, 32–33.

18 Xuno López Intzin, cited in: Fitzwater, *Autonomy is in our hearts*, 33.

19 López Intzin, 'Rediscovering the sacred and the end of hydra capitalism', speech made at the *Hemispheric Institute of Performance and Politics*, New York, 14 April 2016.

20 Dylan Eldredge Fitzwater, *Autonomy is in our Hearts: Zapatista autonomous government through the lens of the Tsotsil language* (Oakland, CA: PM Press, 2019), p. 35.

21 Ibid., p. 36.

22 John P. Clark, *Between Earth and empire: From the necrocene to the beloved community* (Oakland, CA: PM Press, 2019), p. 103.

23 Fitzwater, *Autonomy is in our hearts*, p. 49.

24 Levi Gahman, 'Contra plantation, prison, and capitalist annihilation: Collective struggle, social reproduction, and the co-creation of lifegiving worlds'. *The Journal of Peasant Studies* 47:3 (2020), 518.

25 Ibid., p. 519.

26 Ibid., p. 521.

27 Subcomandante Moisés, 'Fourth wind: An organized dignified rage', in N. Henck (ed.) and H. Gales (trans.) *The Zapatistas' dignified rage: Final public speeches of Subcommander Marcos* (Chico, CA: AK Press, 2018), pp. 169–170.

28 Fitzwater, *Autonomy is in our hearts*, pp. 69–71.

29 Ibid., p. 136.

30 Ibid., p. 160.

31 Marcos, *Professionals of hope*, fourth cover.

32 Carles Feixa, Inés Pereira and Jeffrey S. Juris, 'Global citizenship and the "New, New" social movements: Iberian connections'. *Nordic Journal of Youth Research* 17:4 (2009), 421–442.

33 Jérôme E. Roos and Leonidas Oikonomakis, 'We are everywhere! The autonomous roots of the real democracy movement'. Paper prepared for the *7th Annual ECPR General Conference*. Bordeaux, 4–7 September 2013, p. 3.

34 Cited in: Roos and Oikonomakis, 'We are everywhere!' p. 10.

35 Galeano, quoted in Ké Huelga, 'Zapatistas: the fight goes on'. *Open Democracy*, 2019. Available online: www.opendemocracy.net/en/democraciaabierta/zap atistas-fight-goes/ (accessed 12 May 2022).

36 Cited in: Escobar, 'Thinking-feeling with the Earth', p. 20.

37 Clark, *The impossible community*, p. 11.

38 Shannon Brincat, 'Towards a social-relational dialectic for world politics'. *European Journal of International Relations* 17:4 (2010), 688.

39 Alex Prichard, 'Collective intentionality, complex pluralism and the problem of anarchy'. *Journal of International Political Theory* 13:3 (2017), 373.

40 Ibid.

41 See: Philip G Cerny and Alex Prichard, 'The new anarchy: Globalisation and fragmentation in world politics'. *Journal of International Political Theory* 13:3 (2017), 378–395.

42 Chris Sciabarra, 'Reply to Roderick Long: Dialectical libertarianism: all benefits, no hazards'. *The Journal of Ayn Rand Studies* 3:2 (2002), 383.

43 Brincat, 'Towards a social-relational dialectic for world politics', p. 691.

44 Ruth Kinna and Alex Prichard, 'Anarchism and non-domination'. *Journal of Political Ideologies* 24:3 (2019), 235.

45 Ruth Kinna, Alex Prichard and Thomas Swann, 'Occupy and the constitution of anarchy'. *Global Constitutionalism* 8:2 (2019), 357–390.

46 Ibid., p. 385.

47 Robert Graham, 'Anarchism and the first international', in C. Levy and M. Adams (eds) *The Palgrave handbook of anarchism* (Cham, Switzerland: Palgrave Macmillan, 2019), pp. 326–327.

48 Murray Bookchin, *Social ecology and anarchism* (Oakland, CA: AK Press, 2009).

49 Murray Bookchin, 'Libertarian municipalism: An overview'. *Green Perspectives*, 1991. Available online: https://theanarchistlibrary.org/library/murray-bookc hin-libertarian-municipalism-an-overview (accessed 14 January 2022).

50 Abdullah Öcalan, 'Democratic confederalism', in A. Öcalan, *The political thought of Abdullah Öcalan* (London: Pluto Press, 2017), p. 41.

51 Ibid., p. 42.

52 Ted Trainer, 'Kurdist Rojava: A social model for our future'. *Resilience*, 2020. Available online: www.resilience.org/stories/2020–01–03/kurdist-rojava-a-soc ial-model-for-our-future/ (accessed 6 May 2022).

53 Abdullah Öcalan, 'Democratic nation', in A. Öcalan, *The political thought of Abdullah Öcalan* (London: Pluto Press, 2017). Original work published 2016, pp. 116–117.

54 Meredith Tax, 'The revolution in Rojova'. *Dissent Magazine*, 2015. Available online: www.dissentmagazine.org/online_articles/the-revolution-in-rojava (accessed 17 March 2022).
55 Abdullah Öcalan, 'Liberating life: Woman's revolution', in A. Öcalan, *The political thought of Abdullah Öcalan* (London: Pluto Press, 2017), p. 89.
56 Tax, 'The revolution in Rojova'.
57 Stephen E Hunt, 'Prospects for Kurdish ecology initiatives in Syria and Turkey: Democratic confederalism and social ecology'. *Capitalism Nature Socialism* 30:3 (2019), 19–20.
58 Fabian Scheidler, 'Rojova or the art of transition in a collapsing civilization', in International Initiative: Freedom for Abdullah Öcalan – Peace in Kurdistan (eds) *Building Free Life: Dialogues with Öcalan* (Oakland, CA: PM Press, 2020), p. 197.
59 Comments made in response to criticisms of the Rojavan revolution made by CNT members in Spain. See: 'Discussion: Abdullah Ocalan and the Kurdish myth'. *Anarchist Communist Group*, 2021. Available online: www.anarchistcommunism.org/2021/03/01/discussion-abdullah-ocalan-and-the-kurdish-myth/ (accessed 29 March 2022).
60 Öcalan, 'Democratic nation', p. 140.
61 Ibid., p. 125.
62 Nazan Üstündağ, 'The theology of democratic modernity', in International initiative: Freedom for Abdullah Öcalan – Peace in Kurdistan (eds) *Building free life: Dialogues with Öcalan* (Oakland, CA: PM Press, 2020), p. 253.
63 Ibid.
64 Internationalist Commune of Rojava, 'Rojava: Current political situation – Increasing Turkish attacks and pressure', 23 April 2020. *Indymedia NL*. Available online: www.indymedia.nl/node/47781 (accessed 15 October 2021).
65 David Graeber, 'Why is the world ignoring the revolutionary Kurds in Syria?' *The Guardian*, 8 October 2014.
66 Öcalan, 'Democratic nation', p. 140.
67 Öcalan, 'Democratic confederalism', p. 45.
68 Bookchin, *The ecology of freedom*, p. 98.
69 Sian Sullivan, 'An *other* world is possible? On representation, rationalism and romanticism in social forums'. *Ephemera* 5:2 (2005), 380.
70 Ibid.
71 Clark and Martin, *Anarchy, geography, modernity*, p. 4.
72 Pierre-Joseph Proudhon, *General idea of the revolution in the nineteenth century*, trans. J. Robinson (New York: Haskell House Publishers, 1989), p. 282.

Conclusion

'Beneath the government machinery, in the shadow of political institutions, out of the sight of statesmen and priests, society is producing its own organism, slowly and silently; and constructing a new order, the expression of its vitality and autonomy.'

– Pierre-Joseph Proudhon[1]

We are living in the midst of an unprecedented planetary emergency. By far the greatest challenge that humanity has faced in its brief history. And one entirely of our own making. This book has illuminated how the ferocity with which human beings are consuming resources is literally destroying our web of life constructed over billions of years, upon which all of us, human and non-human, depend for survival. And to make matters worse, our collective ability to co-imagine a creative, transformative and timely response to this threat is being undermined by the moment-to-moment syphoning and redirection of our attention through the processes of digital capitalism – with our thoughts, desires and even our imaginations, all being limited and shaped by this algorithmic conditioning. But as we have also explored in previous chapters, it is not the entanglement itself that imprisons us, for this is simply the way things are – the underlying condition of being human (or more-than-human). It is the seizure and control by the forces of domination – of the entangled systems and flows within which we continuously reproduce ourselves and society that we must confront. It is here where our freedom can be won or lost. In the face of our current overlapping social and ecological crises, our initial (and entirely understandable) response might well be to flee, to escape. But this enquiry has invited us to attempt the very opposite – to pause and take time to re-orient ourselves in relation to the multitude of other beings with whom we find ourselves entangled, and to start our political project from this basis. As contemporary political subjects, we find ourselves located precariously between localism and globalism, between insular security and expansive growth. And so, if we are to move beyond our current states of bewilderment, disorientation and denial, we will need to establish new (and learn from existing) grounded utopias which rather than being *not-now* and *nowhere*, are co-imagined and lived right *here* and right *now* – a politics of immanence.

By rejecting the limited conception of revolution as merely a brief, explosive and violent insurgence, and questioning the perceived antinomy of revolutionary and evolutionary theories of social change, this book has argued for (r)evolution as an alternative model. And by establishing how social reproduction is grounded in loving-caring relations, and how such relations thus offer a stream of continuation from the old society to the new, we have explored how the usual post-revolutionary vacuum in which the counterrevolution occurs and free society is repeatedly stolen may now be averted. And so rather than repeatedly deferring freedom to an imagined post-revolutionary moment, it becomes impossible to abstract a mode of political praxis that exists anywhere other than the here-and-now. Loving-caring-community building therefore *is* the concrete action that co-constitutes free society. Encouragingly, we have observed a clear pre-figurative turn within contemporary activism. And displaying a remarkable alignment and consistency of vision across a diversity of struggles and contexts, the activists involved in this collective visioning process have argued that it is only through the co-creation of living, vibrant, material alternatives to the current system that we might tangibly express the utopian potentiality that exists as an immanent feature of the present. Such spaces of solidarity exist inside and outside of contemporary society simultaneously. They both configure/prefigure free society and act as exemplars for wider society to see that alternatives are actually possible. And the process has further indicated such spaces to be expanding in both number and capacity. We have seen how contemporary ecological, anti-capitalist, feminist and anti-racist activists are now far less likely to limit their focus to single issue campaigns alone. Rather, their movement frames encompass the interdependent and entangled nature of their own and others' multiple struggles, realising a greatly expanded solidarity through a collective rejection of all forms of domination in their totality. Such affinity will be crucial for us politically as we move forward, in allowing a plurality of actors to build expansive intersecting networks of struggle while maintaining and honouring diversity.

It is important to note however that the alignment and consistency of vision that occurred between the activists involved in this collective visioning must not be taken as representative of all contemporary organising. In fact, the relative absence of contestation between the participants of this process contrasts significantly with many of the more antagonistic and conflictual relations experienced in and across left-libertarian organising today. And so how do we explain the apparent disjuncture between this particular process and the volatility that many who have been involved in political organising may have experienced as the norm? And what lessons might be learned for future praxis? If we start at a very fundamental level, we can see that the vast majority of our daily social interactions require the establishment of a self (subject) and other (object) as reference points for these interactions to take place. This is of course an essential core process through which we co-construct the world(s) we inhabit, and how we are able to both express our individuality and experience ourselves as being in community. But as argued elsewhere in this book (r)evolutionary love is not dependent on this conceptual split. It is non-referential – love without an object – the experience of our more-than-human psycho-socio-material entanglement. And it is this post-egoic nature of (r)evolutionary love that accounts for the remarkable alignment of activist views throughout this process – born of a shared understanding rather than individual concept or opinion. More than abstracted theory, this has been evidenced throughout the book as a common embodied experience, materialising as political direct action, as long-term processes of struggle, and as a radical solidarity embedded in the deep commons.

Clearly, much of our day-to-day forms of political organising remain fundamentally ego-driven processes of contention, simply by virtue of our being human beings in relation to other human beings. And as discussed in earlier chapters, anyone who has been involved in consensus-based decision making will concede that such processes can be long, demanding, and labour intensive, and ultimately agreement may well remain unachievable. There is therefore little doubt that any conceivable future society will continue to experience contestation ad infinitum as it is continually reimagined by a plurality of subjects. This book has argued, however, that where such consensus-based processes are exhausted and conflicts persist (as is both inevitable and healthy for any free society) (r)evolutionary love might then offer the ethical/relational basis for the development of new processes of agonistic pluralism. And therefore, our task is not to abolish power and conflict entirely, but to find 'egalitarian forms of power and nonviolent means of conflict'.[2] And on this point our enquiry has offered important insights. For not only has this process produced a truly grounded utopia based on the lived/felt experience of a diverse group of contemporary activists (and thus squarely avoided a fantasised blueprint for future society and the inevitable coercion/domination that entails), its grounding in (r)evolutionary love has additionally served to infuse the discussion and debate. And consequently, the numerous examples of praxes described by activists in this book that have been consciously grounded in loving-caring relations act to provide us with material examples that may inspire new ways of approaching political organising in the future. Of course, contention is not obligatory, and consensus is often entirely possible, but when disagreements do arise about fundamental matters of principle, rather than accepting as inevitable the re-emergence of domination and hierarchy formations as rival actors attempt to institute their own values, such praxes might provide us with workable liberatory alternatives for co-constituting free society. And this rediscovery of our profound interconnection might further act to relax some of the political and philosophical tension that has existed between individualist and communalist conceptions of societal formation resulting in the misleading either/or dichotomy between the two ideals. Rather, from a posthumanist perspective this apparent binary between individual and community, between personal autonomy and social solidarity, might now be viewed as little more than a political abstraction that has acted to obscure the immanent potential for free society in the here-and-now. And therefore, by removing the need to reify *me* and *mine* over the *other*, or to negate the self in order to reify the communal, the simultaneous flourishing of both modalities is shown to be an entirely reasonable proposition.

Another central aspect of this book has been to build on the long anarchist tradition of positioning humanity as being nature made self-conscious, reimagining the place of the human being in its wider more-than-human ecology, while taking great care to navigate a path that avoids both the potential anthropocentric bias of social ecology and holism of deep ecology. Our struggle for a free society has instead been located in the entangled plurality that has emerged most recently through posthumanism, and over millennia through multiple Indigenous ontologies, in our more-than-human psycho-socio-material relations – in the deep commons. From a left-libertarian perspective this invites us to reimagine our struggles in order to accommodate such post-unitary concepts of the human subject within this newfound entangled complexity. And crucially, such a reimagining must not remain theoretical. It will demand far more from us as humans than we have previously been willing to concede. As we have established, there still remains a bizarre disconnect between the increasing calls for action to protect 'the environment' and 'nature' made by so many, and the daily terror, torture, murder and dismemberment of non-human animals in order to satisfy the insatiable desire for humans to consume their flesh – depersonalised and reimagined as meat. If we are to truly develop political ecologies of solidarity and care, as this book calls on us to do, then there are uncomfortable questions that we must face. As Springer asks:

> How is it that those who hold anti-racist, decolonial, environmentalist, feminist, autonomist, post structuralist, queer, anarchist, and otherwise critical perspectives continue to ignore the horrors perpetuated against the non-human animal "other"? How can they actively participate in the continuation of such massacre and misery, knowing that it means actually suspending and contradicting the essence of the critical theory that they hold so dear?[3]

There is no sidestepping such questions – this widespread cognitive dissonance will have to be addressed, challenged and overcome for any meaningful progress to be made.

Fundamentally, we have argued that by repositioning ourselves ontologically in the deep commons an infinite number of worlds can be co-imagined simultaneously, realising the 'community of free communities' theorised by generations of anarchist scholars. But as we have also established, it will remain crucial that the co-constitution of free society remains an ongoing process – pluralised, open, responsive and grounded in the here-and-now. Any such utopia must remain immanent both in substance and temporality. There will be no end point, and no eventual transcendence. A political praxis of (r)evolutionary love is thus prefigurative of itself, its activation animating a radical solidarity grounded in the deep commons through which it is free to circulate in a contagious manner without fear of capitalist enclosure – suffusing individual subjectivities through an entangled (intersubjective) matrix. And it is in the immanence of this deep commons that spaces of freedom might be opened which are at once autonomous from the forces of domination and transformative of them – with our rediscovery of the Agapeic web extending these moments onwards through a co-constitutive process grounded in a radical ethic of love, solidarity and care.

There are thus two key messages this book would like to leave with the reader. The first is simple: that love deserves to be taken seriously as a political concept by activists and academics alike. Whether we focus on the unequal and exploitative exchanges that manifest in intimate and social relations in the name of love, on the exchanges of love which underpin parenting, caring, friendship and group solidarity, on love as a catalyst for radical social change, or indeed on its entire panorama as this book has strived to do, there is no escaping its central (yet often overlooked) importance for both theory and praxis: love, when (r)evolutionised, transforms our worlds. The second key message is more epistemic. It is that a free society will not be imagined by vanguard intellectuals. It must/can only be imagined in common with those who will constitute it. We have observed how the current waves of ecological, anti-capitalist, feminist and anti-racist political praxes have been prefigured by a strong and vibrant lineage of knowledge co-production through multiple struggles over many years. And consequently, we must further understand that this positions our current movement wave as responsible for prefiguring what comes next. The liberatory epistemologies and forms of knowledge co-production that have grounded this enquiry thus offer significant potential for developing new modes of praxis in pursuit of such a society. This book therefore wishes to encourage activists and academics alike to engage in an ongoing relationship/dance between the kinds of approaches to learning and knowledge (co)production that contemporary activists might seek to advance their struggles, and the theoretical insights that the academy might offer the activist. And most fundamentally, for us to collectively pursue theoretical and conceptual questions in ways that are firmly grounded in the here-and-now of contemporary grassroots activism. Such processes might thus contribute to the ongoing development of a new field of anarchist political ecology to meet the cascading socio-ecological challenges we face today and support the formation of new political praxes which might emerge from such enquiry. As we stand witness to an increasingly globalised network of authoritarian capitalism, its xenophobic nationalisms, its racism and its ongoing ecocide, our ability to collectively envision radical social change has never been so essential both in the academy and out on the streets.

Throughout history we can see that times of global crisis have led to fundamental shifts in the dominant political, economic and social paradigms of the day. And in recent years the COVID-19 pandemic acted to temporarily decelerate linear time and make visible an immanence usually obscured by the disorienting pace of modern capitalist society. In that brief moment it became impossible to ignore the previously devalued work of love, care and solidarity relations as being central to social reproduction and fundamentally constitutive of society. Workers previously considered as 'low-skilled' – the carers, the cleaners, the food producers – were suddenly understood to be 'essential'. And as an empirical manifestation of the Agapeic web, mutual aid groups formed spontaneously in countless communities across the planet: feminist collectives organising soup kitchens and food supply networks in Mexico;[4] relief collectives organising support and resources for migrant workers and slum dwellers in India;[5] social health clinics offering solidarity and support to refugees in Greece;[6] community-based solidarity groups providing medical treatment in Zimbabwe;[7] workers cooperatives creating solidarity kitchens in the UK;[8] and activist groups distributing food and supplies in the favelas of Brazil,[9] to name but a few. Moreover, the urgency, scale and radicality with which governments across the globe responded to the emergency illuminated the fact that the TINA narrative – that There Is No Alternative – was always a falsehood. While the pandemic brought into sharp focus the vast structural inequalities that exist on this planet (and we must therefore take great care not to generalise one global experience), there are at least two universals that might be legitimately drawn from the crisis: for years to come, and as obscured as it might become by the challenges we are yet to face, there will remain a collective lived experience that we are, all of us – both human and more-than-human – profoundly interconnected, and that there are (many) other worlds possible after all.

The academic and climate activist Vishwas Satgar likened the pandemic to a 'dress rehearsal for a world that breaches 2- and 3-degrees Celsius' – by which time the catastrophic effects on our life-supporting socio-ecological systems will be irreversible.[10] In this brief moment, as we have witnessed forgotten social solidarities reconstituted, spaces have been opened for new collective visions to occur. And so, in whatever time we might still have before these affective currents of solidarity and care are redirected and repackaged as patriotisms and nationalisms, our task must be to strengthen and expand them into pockets of free ecological society, and then to link them. For if not us, then who? And if not now, when? (R)evolutionary love thus offers an alternative political response to the multiple crises we now face – to turn outwards, to reconnect, and in that connection to transform ourselves and the worlds we co-create.

Notes

1 Proudhon, *General idea of the revolution in the nineteenth century*, p. 243.

2 Epstein, *Political protest and cultural revolution*, pp. 269–270.

3 Springer, 'Total liberation ecology', p. 275.

4 María José Ventura Alfaro, 'Feminist solidarity networks have multiplied since the COVID-19 outbreak in Mexico'. *Interface* 12:1 (2020), 82–87.

5 Sobhi Mohanty, 'From communal violence to lockdown hunger: emergency responses by civil society networks in Delhi, India'. *Interface* 12:1 (2020), 47–52.

6 EP and TP, 'Solidarity networks in Greece', in M. Sitrin and Colectiva Sembrar (eds) *Pandemic solidarity: Mutual aid during the Covid-19 crisis* (London: Pluto Press, 2020), pp. 155–158.

7 Boaventura Monjane, 'Confronting state authoritarianism: Civil society and community-based solidarity in Southern Africa', in M. Sitrin and Colectiva Sembrar (eds) *Pandemic solidarity: Mutual aid during the Covid-19 crisis* (London: Pluto Press, 2020), pp. 113–115.

8 Sergio Ruiz Cayuela, 'Organising a solidarity kitchen: Reflections from Cooperation Birmingham'. *Interface* 12:1 (2020), 304–309.

9 Vanessa Zettler, 'On grassroots organizing: Excerpts from Brazil', in M. Sitrin and Colectiva Sembrar (eds) *Pandemic solidarity: Mutual aid during the Covid-19 crisis* (London: Pluto Press, 2020).

10 Vishwas Satgar, 'Covid-19, the climate crisis and lockdown: An opportunity to end the war with nature'. *Kafila*, 2020. Available online: https://kafila.online/2020/03/28/covid-19-the-climate-crisis-and-lockdown-an-opportunity-to-end-the-war-with-nature-vishwas-satgar/ (accessed 16 May 2022).

Bibliography

Abram, David. *The spell of the sensuous: Perception and language in a more-than-human world* (New York: Vintage Books, 2017). Original work published 1996.

Ahmed, Sara. *The cultural politics of emotion* (Edinburgh: Edinburgh University Press, 2004).

Alfaro, María José Ventura. 'Feminist solidarity networks have multiplied since the COVID-19 outbreak in Mexico'. *Interface* 12:1 (2020), 82–87.

Altmann, Philip. '*Sumak Kawsay* as an element of local decolonisation in Ecuador'. *Latin American Research Review* 52:5 (2018), 749–759.

American Psychological Association. *Mental health and our changing climate: Impacts, implications and guidance* (San Francisco, CA: ecoAmerica, 2017).

Anderson, Pamela Sue. 'Towards a new philosophical imaginary'. *ANGELAKI* 25:1–2 (2020), 8–22.

Arendt, Hannah. *On revolution* (London: Faber & Faber, 2016). Original work published 1963.

Argeş O'Keeffe, Philip. 'Tekmîl: Creating a culture of constructive criticism'. *Komun Academy for Democratic Modernity*, 2018. Available online: https://theanarchist library.org/library/philip-arge-o-keeffe-tekmil.

Ascaso, Frank. 'Why MLK should be remembered as a revolutionary'. *Black Rose Anarchist Federation*, 2019. Available online: https://blackrosefed.org/why-mlk-should-be-remembered-as-a-revolutionary/.

Bakunin, Mikhail. *God and the state* (New York: Dover Publications, 1970). Original work published 1916.

Balug, Katarzyna. 'The imagination paradox: Participation or performance of visioning the city'. *Geoforum* 102 (2017), 278–286.

Barad, Karen. 'Matter feels, converses, suffers, desires, yearns and remembers', in R. Dolphijn and I. Van der Tuin (eds) *New materialism: Interviews and cartographies* (Ann Arbor, MI: Open Humanities Press, 2012).

Barad, Karen. *Meeting the universe halfway: Quantum physics and the entanglement of matter and meaning* (Durham, NC: Duke University Press, 2007).

Barad, Karen. 'Nature's queer performativity'. *Qui Parle* 19:2 (2011), 121–158.

Barad, Karen. 'Posthumanist performativity: Toward an understanding of how matter comes to matter'. *Gender and Science* 28:3 (2003), 801–831.

Batchelor, Stephen. *Verses from the centre: A Buddhist vision of the sublime* (New York: Riverhead Books, 2001).

Beins, Agatha. 'Radical others: Women of colour and revolutionary feminism'. *Feminist Studies* 41:1 (2015), 150–183.

Bellau, Lesley. 'Pauwauwaein: Idle no more to the indigenous nationhood movement', in Kind-nda-niimi Collective (eds) *The Winter we danced* (Winnepeg: Arbeiter Ring, 2014).

Bendell, Jem. 'Deep adaption: A map for navigating climate tragedy'. IFLAS Occasional Paper 2, 2018.

Bendell, Jem. 'Doom and bloom: Adapting to collapse', in *This is not a drill: An Extinction Rebellion handbook* (London: Penguin, 2019).

Benjamin, Walter. *Selected writings, vol. 4, 1938–1940*, eds H. Eiland and M. W. Jennings (Cambridge, MA: Harvard University Press, 2003).

Berlant, Lauren. 'The commons: Infrastructure for troubling times'. *Environment and Planning D: Society and Space* 34:3 (2016), 393–419.

Berlant, Lauren. *Cruel optimism* (Durham, NC: Duke University Press, 2011).

Berry, David. 'Revolution as redemption: Daniel Guérin, religion and spirituality', in A. Christoyannopoulos and M.S. Adams (eds) *Essays in anarchism and religion, Vol. 3.* (Stockholm: Stockholm University Press, 2020).

Bignall, Simone and Rigney, Daryle. 'Indigeneity, posthumanism and nomadic thought: Transforming colonial ecologies', in R. Braidotti and S. Bignall (eds) *Posthuman ecologies: Complexity and process after Deleuze* (London: Rowman and Littlefield, 2019).

Bloch, Ernst. *The principle of hope*, vol. 1, trans. N. Plaice, S. Plaice and P. Knight (Cambridge, MA: MIT Press, 1986). Original work published 1954.

Bollier, David. 'Commoning as a transformative social paradigm'. *The Next system Project*, 2016. Available online: https://thenextsystem.org/node/187.

Bond, Patrick. 'The right to the city and the eco-social commoning of water: Discursive and political lessons from South Africa', in F. Sultana and A. Loftus (eds) *The right to water: Politics, governance and social struggles* (New York: Earthscan, 2012).

Bondurant, Joan V. *Conquest of violence: The Gandhian philosophy of conflict* (Berkeley, CA: University of California Press, 1971).

Bookchin, Murray. 'Deep ecology, anarchosyndicalism and the future of anarchist thought', in M. Bookchin, G. Purchase, B. Morris, R. Aitchtey, R. Hart and C. Wilb (eds) *Deep ecology and anarchism* (London: Freedom Press, 1997).

Bookchin, Murray. *The ecology of freedom: The emergence and dissolution of hierarchy* (Stirling: AK Press, 2005).

Bookchin, Murray. 'Introductory essay', in S. Dolgoff (ed.) *The anarchist collectives: Workers' Self-management in the Spanish Revolution 1936–1939* (Montreal: Black Rose Books, 1990).

Bookchin, Murray. 'Libertarian municipalism: An overview'. *Green Perspectives*, 1991. Available online: https://theanarchistlibrary.org/library/murray-bookchin-libertarian-municipalism-an-overview.

Bookchin, Murray. *Post-scarcity anarchism* (Berkeley, CA: Ramparts press, 1971).

Bookchin, Murray. *Social ecology and anarchism* (Oakland, CA: AK Press, 2009).

Bookchin, Murray. *Social ecology and communalism*, ed. Eirik Eiglad (Edinburgh: AK Press, 2007).

Bookchin, Murray. *The third revolution: Popular movements in the revolutionary era, vol. 1.* (London: Cassell, 1996).

Bookchin, Murray. *The third revolution: Popular movements in the revolutionary era, vol. 2.* (London: Cassell, 1998).

Boonen, Christiaan. 'A (non-)violent revolution? Strategies of civility for the politics of the common', in S. Cogolati and J. Wouters (eds) *The commons and a new global governance* (Cheltenham: Edward Elgar Publishing, 2018).

Bosker, Bianca. 'The binge breaker'. *The Atlantic,* 2016. Available online: www.theatlantic.com/magazine/archive/2016/11/the-binge-breaker/501122/.

Bottici, Chiara. *Anarchafeminism* (London: Bloomsbury Academic, 2021).

Bottici, Chiara. 'Imagination, imaginary, imaginal: Towards a new social ontology?'. *Social Epistemology* 33:5 (2019), 433–441.

Braidotti, Rosi. 'The critical posthumanities; or, is Medianatures to Naturecultures as Zoe is to Bios?' *Cultural Politics* 12:3 (2016), 380–390.

Braidotti, Rosi. 'Generative futures: On affirmative ethics', in A. Radman and H. Sohn (eds) *Critical and clinical cartographies: Architecture, robotics, medicine, philosophy* (Edinburgh: Edinburgh University Press, 2017).

Braidotti, Rosi. 'The politics of "life" itself and new ways of dying', in D. Coole and S. Frost (eds) *New materialisms: Ontology, agency, politics* (Durham, NC: Duke University Press, 2010).

Braidotti, Rosi. *The posthuman* (Cambridge: Polity Press, 2013).

Braidotti, Rosi. 'Posthuman affirmative politics', in S. E. Wilmer and A. Žukauskaitė (eds) *Resisting biopolitics: Philosophical, political, and performative strategies* (New York: Routledge, 2016).

Braidotti, Rosi. 'Posthuman relational subjectivity and the politics of affirmation', in P. Rawes (ed.) *Relational architectural ecologies: Architecture, nature and subjectivity* (London: Routledge, 2013).

Brincat, Shannon. 'Reclaiming the utopian imaginary in IR theory'. *Review of International Studies* 35 (2009), 581–609.

Brincat, Shannon. 'Towards a social-relational dialectic for world politics'. *European Journal of International Relations* 17:4 (2010), 679–703.

Brooks, John. 'Tech insiders call out Facebook for literally manipulating your brain'. *KQED Science*, 2017. Available online: www.kqed.org/futureofyou/379828/tech-insiders-call-out-facebook-for-literally-manipulating-your-brain.

Brooks, Libby. 'Hundreds of global civil society representatives walk out of COP26 in protest'. *The Guardian*, 12 November 2021.

Brown, Judith. 'Ernst Bloch and the utopian imagination'. *Eras Journal* 5, 2003. Available online: www.monash.edu/arts/philosophical-historical-international-studies/eras/past-editions/edition-five-2003-november/ernst-bloch-and-the-utopian-imagination.

Brulle, Robert J. 'The climate lobby: A sectoral analysis of lobbying spending on climate change in the USA, 2000 to 2016'. *Climatic Change* 149 (2018), 289–303.

Bryant, Miranda. 'Is Facebook leading us on a journey to the metaverse?' *The Guardian*, 26 September 2021.

Camacho, Jorge. 'A tragic note: On Negri and Deleuze in the light of the Argentinazo'. *New Formations* 68 (2010), 58–76.

Carrington, Damian. 'Huge reduction in meat-eating 'essential' to avoid climate breakdown'. *The Guardian*, 10 October 2018.

Cayuela, Sergio Ruiz. 'Organising a solidarity kitchen: Reflections from Cooperation Birmingham', *Interface* 12:1 (2020), 304–309.

Cerny, Philip G and Prichard, Alex. 'The new anarchy: Globalisation and fragmentation in world politics'. *Journal of International Political Theory* 13:3 (2017), 378–395.

Chabot, Sean. 'Love and revolution'. *Critical Sociology* 34:6 (2008), 803–828.

Chandler, David and Fuchs, Christian. *Digital objects, digital subjects: Interdisciplinary perspectives on capitalism, labour and politics in the age of Big Data* (London: University of Westminster Press, 2019).

Chatterton, Paul. 'The zero-carbon city', in *This is not a drill: An Extinction Rebellion handbook* (London: Penguin, 2019).

Chesters, Graeme. 'Social movements and the ethics of knowledge production'. *Social Movement Studies* 11:2 (2012), 145–160.

Christoyannopoulos, Alexandre. *Christian anarchism: A political commentary on the gospel*, abridged edition (Exeter: Imprint Academic, 2011).

Clark, John P. 'Anarchy and the dialectic of utopia', in L. Davis and R. Kinna (eds) *Anarchism and utopianism* (Manchester: Manchester University Press, 2009).

Clark, John P. *Between Earth and empire: From the necrocene to the beloved community* (Oakland, CA: PM Press, 2019).

Clark, John P. 'Foreword', in D. E. Fitzwater, *Autonomy is in our hearts: Zapatista Autonomous Government through the lens of the Tsotsil language* (Oakland, CA: PM Press, 2019).

Clark, John P. *The impossible community: Realizing communitarian anarchism* (New York: Bloomsbury, 2013).

Clark, John P. and Martin, Camille. *Anarchy, geography, modernity: Selected writings of Élisée Reclus* (Oakland, CA: PM Press, 2013).

Climate Action Tracker. *Temperatures: Addressing global warming*, 2021. Available online: https://climateactiontracker.org/global/temperatures/.

Clover, Joshua. 'The coming occupation', in K. Khatib, M. Killjoy and M. McGuire (eds) *We are many: Reflections on movement strategy from occupation to liberation* (Oakland, CA: AK Press, 2012).

Combahee River Collective. 'The Combahee River Collective statement', 1977. Available online: https://americanstudies.yale.edu/sites/default/files/files/Keyword%20Coalition_Readings.pdf.

Cozolino, Louis. *The neuroscience of human relationships: Attachment and the developing social brain* (New York: W. W. Norton & Company, 2014).

Croeser, Sky. 'Post-industrial and digital society', in C. Levy and M. Adams (eds) *The Palgrave handbook of anarchism* (Cham, Switzerland: Palgrave Macmillan, 2019).

Cudworth, Erika. 'Farming and food', in C. Levy and M. Adams (eds) *The Palgrave handbook of anarchism* (Cham, Switzerland: Palgrave Macmillan, 2019).

Curran, Giorel. *21st century dissent: Anarchism, anti-globalisation and environmentalism* (New York: Palgrave Macmillan, 2006).

Dalla Costa, Mariarosa and James, Selma. *The power of women and the subversion of community* (Brooklyn, NY: Pétroleuse Press, 1971).

Daly, Herman. *Beyond growth: The economics of sustainable development* (Boston, MA: Beacon Press, 1997).

Dardot, Pierre and Laval, Christian. *Common: On revolution in the 21st century*, trans. M. MacLellan (London: Bloomsbury, 2019).

Davis, Laurence. 'Everyone an artist: art, labour, anarchy, and utopia', in L. Davis and R. Kinna (eds) *Anarchism and utopianism* (Manchester: Manchester University Press, 2009).

Davis, Laurence. 'History, politics, and utopia: Toward a synthesis of social theory and practice', in P. Vieira and M. Marder (eds) *Existential utopia: New perspectives on utopian thought* (New York: Continuum, 2012).

Davis, Laurence. 'Individual and community', in C. Levy and M. Adams (eds) *The Palgrave handbook of anarchism* (Cham, Switzerland: Palgrave Macmillan, 2019).

Davis, Laurence. 'Love and revolution in Ursula Le Guin's *Four Ways to Forgiveness*', in J. Heckert and R. Cleminson (eds) *Anarchism and sexuality: Ethics, relationships and power* (New York: Routledge, 2011).

Davis, Laurence. 'Social anarchism or lifestyle anarchism: An unhelpful dichotomy'. *Anarchist Studies* 18:1 (2010), 62–82.

Day, Dorothy. *From Union Square to Rome*, 1939. Available online: www.catholic worker.org/dorothyday/articles/201.pdf.

De Angelis, Massimo. *Omnia sunt communia: On the commons and the transformation to postcapitalism* (London: Zed Books, 2017).

De Beauvoir, Simone. *The second sex*, trans. H.M. Parshley (London: Vintage, 1997). Original work published 1949.

De La Boétie, Étienne. *The politics of obedience: The discourse of voluntary servitude*, trans. H. Kurz (Auburn, AL: Mises Institute, 2015). Original work published 1577.

De Waal, Frans. *The age of empathy: Nature's lessons for a kinder society* (London: Souvenir Press, 2019).

Del Gandio, Jason. 'Rethinking the Eros Effect', in J. Del Gandio and A.K. Thompson (eds) *Spontaneous combustion: The Eros Effect and global revolution* (Albany, NY: SUNY Press, 2017).

Del Gandio, Jason and Thompson, AK. *Spontaneous combustion: The Eros Effect and global revolution* (Albany, NY: SUNY Press, 2017).

Díaz, Sandra, Settele, Josef and Brondízio, Eduardo. 'Summary for policymakers of the global assessment report on biodiversity and ecosystem services'. *IPBES*, 2019.

Dolgoff, Sam. *Bakunin on anarchy* (New York: Vintage Books, 1973).

Donson, Fiona, Chesters, Graeme, Welsh, Ian and Tickle, Andrew. 'Rebels with a cause, folk devils without a panic: Press jingoism, policing tactics and anti-capitalist protest in London and Prague'. Internet Journal of Criminology, 2004. Available online: http://orca.cf.ac.uk/60834/1/Rebel%20with%20a%20ca use%20.

Do Or Die. 'Reclaim the Streets!'. *Do or die – Voices from Earth First!* 6 (2003), 1–6.

Doran, Peter. 'Climate change and the attention economy'. *Open Democracy*, 2019. Available online: www.opendemocracy.net/en/transformation/climate-change-and-attention-economy/.

Drinnon, Richard. 'Introduction', in E. Goldman, *Anarchism and other essays* (New York: Dover Publishers, 1969).

Ebert, Teresa L. 'Alexandra Kollontai and red love'. *Solidarity US*, 1999. Available online: www.solidarity-us.org/site/node/1724.

Eisenstadt, Nathan. 'Non-domination, governmentality, and care of the self', in M. Lopes de Souza, R. J. White, and S. Springer (eds) *Theories of resistance: Anarchism, geography, and the spirit of revolt* (London: Rowman and Littlefield, 2016).

EP and TP. 'Solidarity networks in Greece', in M. Sitrin and Colectiva Sembrar (eds) *Pandemic solidarity: Mutual aid during the Covid-19 crisis* (London: Pluto Press, 2020).

Epstein, Barbara. *Political protest and cultural revolution: Nonviolent direct action in the 1970s and 1980s* (Berkeley, CA: University of California Press, 1991).

Escobar, Arturo. 'Thinking-feeling with the Earth: Territorial struggles and the ontological dimension of the epistemologies of the South'. *Revista de Antropología Iberoamericana* 11:1 (2016), 11–32.

Extinction Rebellion. 'Extinction Rebellion launch plans for UK rebellion'. *Popular Resistance*, 2021. Available online: https://popularresistance.org/extinction-rebellion-launch-plans-for-uk-rebellion/.

Fabrizio, Eva. 'Social movements are political movements. What's geopolitics?' *Geopolitics* 9:2 (2010), 478–483.

Falk, Candace. *Love, anarchy and Emma Goldman: A biography* (New York: Holt, Rinehart, and Winston, 1984).

Faulconbridge, Guy and Marshall, Andrew. 'Extinction Rebellion has a message for the world – We've only just begun'. *Reuters World News*, 1 May 2019.

Federici, Silvia. *Re-enchanting the world: Feminism and the politics of the commons* (Oakland, CA: PM Press, 2019).

Federici, Silvia. *Revolution at point zero: Housework, reproduction, and feminist struggle* (Oakland, CA: PM Press, 2020).

Federici, Silvia. *Witches, witch-hunting and women* (Oakland, CA: PM Press, 2018).

Federici, Silvia. 'Women, land struggles, and the reconstruction of the commons'. *WorkingUSA* 14:1 (2011), 41–56.

Feixa, Carles, Pereira, Inés, and Juris, Jeffrey S. 'Global citizenship and the "New, New" social movements: Iberian connections'. *Nordic Journal of Youth Research* 17:4 (2009), 421–442.

Ferguson, Ann. 'Feminist love politics: Romance, care, and solidarity', in A. G. Jónasdóttir and A. Ferguson (eds) *Love: A question for feminism in the twenty-first century* (London: Routledge, 2014).

Ferguson, Ann and Toye, Margaret. 'Feminist love studies – Editors' introduction'. *Hypatia* 32:1 (2017), 5–18.

Ferguson, Kathy E. *Emma Goldman: Political thinking in the streets* (Plymouth: Rowman and Littlefield, 2013).

Firestone, Shulamith. *The dialectic of sex: The case for feminist revolution* (New York: Bantam Books, 1971).

Fitzwater, Dylan Eldredge. *Autonomy is in our hearts: Zapatista autonomous government through the Lens of the Tsotsil Language* (Oakland, CA: PM Press, 2019).

Foran, John. *Taking power: On the origins of Third World revolutions* (Cambridge: Cambridge University Press, 2005).

Franks, Benjamin. 'Prefiguration', in B. Franks, N. Jun and L. Williams (eds) *Anarchism: A conceptual approach* (London: Routledge, 2018).

Franks, Benjamin. *Rebel alliances: The means and ends of contemporary British anarchisms* (Oakland, CA: AK Press, 2006).

Franks, Benjamin and Kinna, Ruth. 'Contemporary British anarchism'. *La Revue LISA* 7:8 (2014), 338–371.

Frassinelli, Pier Paulo. 'Biopolitical production, the common, and a happy ending: on Michael Hardt and Antonio Negri's *Commonwealth*'. *Critical Arts* 25:2 (2011), 119–131.

Freeman, Jo. 'The tyranny of structurelessness'. *The Women's Liberation Movement, USA*, 1970. Available online: http://struggle.ws/pdfs/tyranny.pdf.

Freire, Paulo. *Pedagogy of the oppressed* (Harmondsworth: Penguin, 1996). Original work published 1968.

Freud, Sigmund. 'Civilisation and its discontents', in I. Smith (ed.) *Freud – Complete works*, 2010. Original work published 1930. Available online: www.topoi.net/wp-content/uploads/2012/12/Freud-Complete-Works.unlocked.pdf.

Friedlingstein, Pierre and 51 co-authors. 'Global carbon budget 2019'. *Earth System Science Data* 11:4 (2019), 1783–1838.

Friedlingstein, Pierre and 83 co-authors. 'Global carbon budget 2021'. *Earth System Science Data*, 2021 [Preprint]. Available online: https://essd.copernicus.org/preprints/essd-2021–386/.

Fromm, Erich. *The art of loving* (London: Thorsons, 1995). Original work published 1957.

Fukuyama, Francis. 'The end of history?' *The National Interest* 16:3 (1989), 1–18.

Gahman, Levi. 'Contra plantation, prison, and capitalist annihilation: Collective struggle, social reproduction, and the co-creation of lifegiving worlds'. *The Journal of Peasant Studies* 47:3 (2020), 513–524.

Galián, Laura. 'Squares, occupy movements and the Arab revolutions', in C. Levy and M. Adams (eds) *The Palgrave handbook of anarchism* (Cham, Switzerland: Palgrave Macmillan, 2019).

Gayle, Damien, and Carrington, Damian. 'Extinction Rebellion eyes shift in tactics as police crackdown on protests'. *The Guardian*, 3 September 2021.

Gilligan, Carol. 'Moral injury and the ethic of care: Reframing the conversation about differences'. *Social Philosophy* 45:1 (2014), 89–106.

Gilman-Opalsky, Richard. *The communism of love: An inquiry into the poverty of exchange value* (Chico, CA: AK Press, 2020).

Glassgold, Peter. 'Introduction: The life and death of *Mother Earth*', in P. Glassgold (ed.) *Anarchy! An anthology of Emma Goldman's Mother Earth* (Washington, DC: Counterpoint, 2001).

Goldman, Emma. 'Anarchism: What it really stands for', in E. Goldman, *Anarchism and other essays* (Los Angeles, CA: Enhanced Media Publishing, 2017). Original work published 1911.

Goldman, Emma. 'Anarchy and the sex question', in T. Anderson (ed.) *Publications by Emma Goldman* (CreateSpace Independent Publishing Platform, 2017). Original work published 1896.

Goldman, Emma. *Living my life* (London: Penguin Books, 2006). Original work published 1931.

Goldman, Emma. 'Marriage and love', in E. Goldman, *Anarchism and other essays* (Los Angeles, CA: Enhanced Media Publishing, 2017). Original work published 1911.

Goldman, Emma. *My disillusionment in Russia*, 1925. Available online: http://lib com.org/files/Emma%20Goldman-%20My%20Disillusionment%20in%20Rus sia.pdf.

Goldman, Emma. 'Patriotism: A menace to liberty', in E. Goldman, *Anarchism and other essays* (Los Angeles, CA: Enhanced Media Publishing, 2017). Original work published 1908.

Goldman, Emma. 'The tragedy of women's emancipation', in A. K. Shulman (ed.) *Red Emma speaks: An Emma Goldman reader* (Amherst, MA: Humanity Books, 1998). Original work published 1911.

Goldman, Emma. 'What I believe', in T. Anderson (ed.) *Publications by Emma Goldman* (CreateSpace Independent Publishing Platform, 2017). Original work published 1908.

Gordon, Uri. *Anarchy alive!* (London: Pluto Press, 2008).

Gordon, Uri. 'Prefigurative politics between ethical practice and absent promise'. *Political Studies* 66:2 (2017), 521–537.

Gordon, Uri. 'Utopia in contemporary anarchism', in L. Davis and R. Kinna (eds) *Anarchism and utopianism* (Manchester: Manchester University Press, 2009).

Gordon, Uri, and CrimethInc. 'Prefigurative politics, catastrophe, and hope: Does the idea of "prefiguration" offer false reassurance?' *The Anarchist Library*, 2018. Available online: https://theanarchistlibrary.org/library/uri-gordon-prefigurative-politics-catastrophe-and-hope.

Gornick, Vivian. 'Love and anarchy: Emma Goldman's passion for free expression burns on'. *The Chronicle of Higher Education*, 2011. Available online: www.chronicle.com/article/love-and-anarchy/.

Gorski, Paul C. 'Relieving burnout and the "Martyr Syndrome" among social justice education activists: The implications and effects of mindfulness'. *Urban Review* 47 (2015), 696–716.

Graeber, David. 'Afterword', in K. Khatib, M. Killjoy and M. McGuire (eds) *We are many: Reflections on movement strategy from occupation to liberation* (Oakland, CA: AK Press, 2012).

Graeber, David. 'Why is the world ignoring the revolutionary Kurds in Syria?' *The Guardian*, 8 October 2014.

Graham, Robert. 'Anarchism and the first international', in C. Levy and M. Adams (eds) *The Palgrave handbook of anarchism* (Cham, Switzerland: Palgrave Macmillan, 2019).

Griffin, Paul. 'The carbon majors database CDP carbon majors report'. *Climate Accountability Institute*, 2017.

Gruen, Lori. *Entangled empathy: An alternative ethic for our relationships with animals* (New York: Lantern Books, 2015).

Gruen, Lori. 'Expressing entangled empathy: A reply'. *Hypatia* 32:2 (2017), 452–462.

Gruening, Martha. 'Speaking of democracy', in P. Glassgold (ed.) *Anarchy! An anthology of Emma Goldman's Mother Earth* (Washington, DC: Counterpoint, 2001).

Guerin, Daniel. 'Anarchism in the Russian revolution'. *Libcom, 2005*. Available online: https://libcom.org/library/anarchism-daniel-guerin-4.

Guevara, Ernesto Che. *Che Guevara reader: Writings on politics and revolutions*, ed. David Deutschmann (Melbourne: Open Press, 2003).

Gurstein, Rochelle. 'Emma Goldman and the tragedy of modern love'. *Salmagundi* 135/136 (2002), 67–89.

Haiven, Max and Khasnabish, Alex. *The radical imagination* (London: Zed Books, 2014).

Hansard Society. 'Audit of political engagement 16: The 2019 Report'. Available online: www.johnsmithcentre.com/research/audit-of-political-engagement-16-the-2019-report/.

Hardt, Michael. 'For love or money'. *Cultural Anthropology* 26:4 (2011), 676–682.

Hardt, Michael. 'Pasolini discovers love outside'. *Diacritics* 39:4 (2009), 113–129.

Hardt, Michael. *The procedures of love* (Ostfildern, Germany: Hatje Cantz Verlag, 2012).

Hardt, Michael and Negri, Antonio. *Commonwealth* (Cambridge: Harvard University Press, 2011).

Hardt, Michael and Negri, Antonio. *Multitude: War and democracy in the age of empire* (London: Penguin Books, 2005).

Harvey, Fiona. 'Destruction of world's forests increased sharply in 2020'. *The Guardian*, 31 March 2021.

Heckert, Jamie, and Cleminson, Richard. *Anarchism and sexuality: Ethics, relationships and power* (New York: Routledge, 2012).

Heckert, Jamie, Shannon, Deric Michael and Willis, Abbey. 'Loving-teaching: Notes for queering anarchist pedagogies'. *Educational Studies* 48:1 (2012), 12–29.

Heckert, Vishwam. 'Loving politics: On the art of living together', in C. Levy and S. Newman (eds) *The Anarchist Imagination: Anarchism encounters the Humanities and Social Sciences* (London: Routledge, 2019).

Hemmings, Clare. *Considering Emma Goldman: Feminist political ambivalence and the imaginative archive* (Durham, NC: Duke University Press, 2018).

Hemmings, Clare. 'In the mood for revolution: Emma Goldman's Passion'. *New Literary History* 43 (2012), 527–545.

Hennessy, Rosemary. 'Bread and roses in the common', in A. G. Jónasdóttir and A. Ferguson (eds) *Love: a question for feminism in the twenty-first century* (London: Routledge, 2014).

Hewitt, Marsha. 'Emma Goldman: The case for anarcho-feminism', in D. Roussopoulos (ed.) *The anarchist papers* (Montreal: Black Rose Books, 1986).

Hick, Steven, and Furlotte, Charles. 'Mindfulness and social justice approaches: Bridging the mind and society in social work practice'. *Canadian Social Work Review* 26:1 (2009), 5–24.

Hill, Julia Butterfly. 'The Taoist and the activist'. Interview with Dr Benjamin Tong for *Lunch with Bokara*, KCET Television, 7 July 2005. Available online: www.kcet.org/shows/lunch-with-bokara/episodes/the-taoist-and-the-activist.

Hipp, Jack. 'The Eros Effect and the embodied mind', in J. Del Gandio and A.K. Thompson (eds) *Spontaneous combustion: The Eros Effect and global revolution* (Albany, NY: SUNY Press, 2017).

Hobbes, Thomas. *Man and citizen: 'De Homine' and 'De Cive'*, ed. Bernard Gert (Indianapolis, IN: Hackett Publishing Company, 1991). Original works published 1658 and 1642 respectively.

Hollender, Rebecca. 'A politics of the commons or commoning the political? Distinct possibilities for post-capitalist transformation'. *SPECTRA* 5:1 (2016), 1–15.

Holloway, John. 'Twelve theses on changing the world without taking power'. *The Commoner* 4 (2002), 1–6.

hooks, bell. *All about love: New visions* (New York: Harper Collins, 2000).

hooks, bell. *Outlaw culture: Resisting representations* (New York: Routledge, 2006).

hooks, bell. 'Toward a worldwide culture of love'. *Lion's Roar*, 2018. Available online: www.lionsroar.com/toward-a-worldwide-culture-of-love/.

Hopkins, Rob. 'From what is to what if? Unleashing the power of imagination'. *STIR* 28 (2020), 16–19.

Horvat, Srećko. *The radicality of love* (Cambridge: Polity Press, 2016).

Huelga, Ké. 'Zapatistas: the fight goes on'. *Open Democracy*, 2019. Available online: www.opendemocracy.net/en/democraciaabierta/zapatistas-fight-goes/.

Hunt, Stephen E. 'Prospects for Kurdish ecology initiatives in Syria and Turkey: Democratic confederalism and social ecology'. *Capitalism Nature Socialism* 30:3 (2019), 7–26.

Ibáñez, Tomás. *Anarchism is movement* (London: Freedom Press, 2019).

Illouz, Eva. *The end of love: A sociology of negative relations* (New York: Oxford University Press, 2019).

Internationalist Commune of Rojava. 'Rojava: Current political situation – Increasing Turkish attacks and pressure', 23 April 2020. Available online: www.indymedia.nl/node/47781.

IPCC. 'Summary for Policymakers', in *Global Warming of 1.5°C. An IPCC Special Report on the impacts of global warming of 1.5°C above pre-industrial levels and related global greenhouse gas emission pathways, in the context of strengthening the global response to the threat of climate change, sustainable development, and efforts to eradicate poverty* (World Meteorological Organization: Geneva, Switzerland, 2018).

IPCC. 'Summary for Policymakers', in *Climate change 2022: Mitigation of climate change. Contribution of Working Group III to the Sixth Assessment Report of the Intergovernmental Panel on Climate Change* (New York: Cambridge University Press, 2022).

Janning, Finn. 'Deep ecology movement: Love and care in the present moment – The philosophy of Arne Næss'. *The Mindful Word*, 2017. Available online: www.the mindfulword.org/2017/deep-ecology-movement-naess.

Kallis, Giorgos. 'The degrowth alternative'. *The Great Transition Initiative*, 2015. Available online: https://greattransition.org/images/GTI_publications/Kallis-The-Degrowth-Alternative.pdf.

Kalpokas, Ignas. *Algorithmic governance: Politics and law in the post-human era* (Cham, Switzerland: Palgrave Macmillan, 2019).

Kaluža, Jernej. 'Anarchism in Deleuze'. *Deleuze and Guattari Studies* 13:2 (2019), 267–292.

Kasser, Tim, Rosenblum, Katherine L., Sameroff, Arnold J., Deci, Edward L., Niemiec, Christopher P., Ryan, Richard M., Árnadóttir, Osp, Bond, Rod, Dittmar, Helga, Dungan, Nathan and Hawks, Susan. 'Changes in materialism, changes in psychological well-being: Evidence from three longitudinal studies and an intervention experiment'. *Motivation and Emotion* 38 (2014), 1–22.

Katsiaficas, George. 'Eros and revolution'. Paper prepared for the *Critical Refusals Conference of the International Herbert Marcuse Society*. Philadelphia, 28 October 2011.

Katsiaficas, George. 'From Marcuse's "political eros" to the Eros Effect', in J. Del Gandio and A.K. Thompson (eds) *Spontaneous combustion: The Eros Effect and global revolution* (New York: SUNY Press, 2017).

Kawano, Emily. 'Solidarity economy: Building an economy for people and planet'. *The Next System Project*, 2018. Available online: www.solidarityeconomy.coop/wp-content/uploads/2017/06/Kawano-E.-2018_Solidarity-Economy.pdf.

Kelley, Robin. *Freedom dreams: The black radical imagination* (Boston, MA: Beacon Press, 2003).

Khasnabish, Alex. *Zapatistas: Rebellion from the grassroots to the global* (New York: Zed Books, 2010).

King, Martin Luther, Jr. 'Where do we go from here?'. Speech made at the *11th Annual Southern Christian Leadership Conference*. Atlanta, Georgia, 16 August 1967.

Kinna, Ruth. 'Utopianism and prefiguration', in S. Chrostowska and J. Ingram (eds) *Political uses of utopia: New marxist, anarchist, and radical democratic perspectives* (New York: Columbia University Press, 2016).

Kinna, Ruth and Prichard, Alex. 'Anarchism and non-domination'. *Journal of Political Ideologies* 24:3 (2019), 221–240.

Kinna, Ruth, Prichard, Alex and Swann, Thomas. 'Occupy and the constitution of anarchy'. *Global Constitutionalism* 8:2 (2019), 357–390.

Klein, Hilary. 'The Zapatista movement: Blending indigenous traditions with revolutionary praxis', in B. Maxwell and R. Craib (eds) *No gods, no masters, no peripheries: Global anarchisms* (Oakland, CA: PM Press, 2015).

Knabb, Ken. *The joy of revolution* (Berkeley, CA: Bureau of Public Secrets, 1997).

Koenig, Brigitte. 'Visions of the future: reproduction, revolution, and regeneration in American anarchist utopian fiction', in L. Davis and R. Kinna (eds) *Anarchism and utopianism* (Manchester: Manchester University Press, 2009).

Kollontai, Alexandra. *Selected writings of Alexandra Kollontai*, ed. and trans. A. Holt (New York: Horton, 1977).

Kovel, Joel. *History and spirit: An inquiry into the philosophy of liberation* (Boston, MA: Beacon Press, 1991).

Kropotkin, Peter. *Ethics: Origin and development*, trans. L. S. Friedland and J. R. Piroshnikof, 1922. Available online: https://theanarchistlibrary.org/library/petr-kropotkin-ethics-origin-and-development.pdf.

Kropotkin, Peter. 'From expropriation', in I. McKay (ed.) *Direct struggle against capital: A Peter Kropotkin anthology* (Oakland, CA: AK Press, 2014). Original work published 1886.

Kropotkin, Peter. *The great French revolution 1789–1793* (St Petersburg, FL: Red and Black Publishing, 2010). Original work published 1909.

Kropotkin, Peter. *Kropotkin's revolutionary pamphlets*, ed. R. Baldwin (New York: Benjamin Blom, 1969). Original work published 1927.

Kropotkin, Peter. *Mutual aid: A factor in evolution*, ed. W. Jonson (Marston Gate: Amazon, 2018). Original work published 1902.

Kümmel, Friedrich. 'Time as succession and the problem of duration', in J. T. Fraser (ed.) *The voices of time* (London: Penguin Press, 1968). Original work published 1952.

La Revue Socialiste. 'A workers' enquiry', trans. C. Price, 1997. Works of Karl Marx 1880. Available online: www.marxists.org/archive/marx/works/1880/04/20.htm.

Landauer, Gustav. 'Revolution', in *Revolution and other writings: A political reader*, ed. and trans. G. Kuhn (Oakland, CA: PM Press, 2010). Original work published 1907.

Landauer, Gustav. 'Weak statesmen, weaker people!', in *Revolution and other writings: A political reader*, ed. and trans. G. Kuhn (Oakland, CA: PM Press, 2010). Original work published 1910.

Landauer, Gustav. 'Through separation to community', in *Revolution and other writings: A political reader*, ed. and trans. G. Kuhn (Oakland, CA: PM Press, 2010). Original work published 1901.

Latour, Bruno. *Down to earth: Politics in the new climate regime* (Cambridge: Polity Press, 2018).

Lenton, Timothy, Rockström, Johan, Gaffney, Owen, Rahmstorf, Stefan, Richardson, Katherine, Steffen, Will and Schellnhuber, Hans Joachim. 'Climate tipping points – Too risky to bet against'. *Nature* 575 (2019), 592–595.

Leval, Gaston. *Collectives in the Spanish revolution*, trans. V. Richards (Oakland, CA: PM Press, 2018). Original work published 1972.

Levitas, Ruth. *Utopia as method: The imaginary reconstitution of society* (London: Palgrave Macmillan, 2013).

Libertarian Socialist Organisation. *You can't blow up a social relationship* (Brisbane, Australia: Anarres Books Collective, 1979).

López Intzin, Xuno. 'Rediscovering the sacred and the end of hydra capitalism'. Speech made at the *Hemispheric Institute of Performance & Politics*. New York, 14 April 2016.

Lowe, Leyna. 'Revolutionary love: feminism, love, and the transformative politics of freedom in the works of Wollstonecraft, Beauvoir, and Goldman', in A. G. Jónasdóttir and A. Ferguson (eds) *Love: a question for feminism in the twenty-first century* (London: Routledge, 2014).

Lowndes, Vivien and Paxton, Marie. 'Can agonism be institutionalised? Can institutions be agonised? Prospects for democratic design'. *The British Journal of Politics and International Relations* 20:3 (2018), 693–710.

Maeckelbergh, Marianne. 'Doing is believing: Prefiguration as strategic practice in the alterglobalization movement'. *Social Movement Studies* 10:1 (2011), 1–20.

Majewska, Ewa. 'Love in translation: Neoliberal availability or a solidarity practice?', in A. G. Jonasdottir and A. Ferguson (eds) *Love: A question for feminism in the twenty-first century* (London: Routledge, 2014).

Majewska, Ewa. 'Precarity and gender: What's love got to do with it?'. *Praktyka Teoretyczna* 4:38 (2020), 19–48.

Malatesta, Errico. *Anarchy* (Cambridge: Dog's Tail Books, 2018). Original work published 1891.

Malatesta, Errico. *Life and ideas: The anarchist writings of Errico Malatesta*, ed. V. Richards (Oakland, CA: PM Press, 2015). Original work published 1965.

Malmquist, David. 'Sea-level report cards: 2019 data adds to trend in acceleration'. *Virginia Institute of Marine Science,* 2020. Available online: www.vims.edu/newsandevents/topstories/2020/slrc_2019.php.

Malo de Molina, Marta. 'Common notions, part 1: Workers-inquiry, co-research, consciousness-raising', trans. Maribel Casas-Cortés and Sebastian Cobarrubias, of the Notas Rojas Collective Chapel Hill. *European Institute for Progressive Cultural Policies,* 2004. Available online: http://transform.eipcp.net/transversal/0406/malo/en.html.

Malo de Molina, Marta. 'Common notions, part 2: Institutional analysis, participatory action-research, militant research', trans. Maribel Casas-Cortés and Sebastian Cobarrubias, of the Notas Rojas Collective Chapel Hill, August 2005, ed. by other members of Notas Rojas, online, February 2006. *European Institute for Progressive Cultural Policies.* Available online: http://transform.eipcp.net/transversal/0406/malo/en.html.

Mannermaa, Mika. 'Introduction', in M. Mannermaa, J. Dator and P. Tiihonen (eds) *Democracy and futures* (Helsinki: Committee for the Future, Parliament of Finland, 2006).

Marasco, Robyn. 'I would rather wait for you than believe that you are not coming at all: Revolutionary love in a post-revolutionary time'. *Philosophy and Social Criticism* 36:6 (2010), 643–662.

Marcos, Subcomandante. 'Between light and shade', in N. Henck (ed.) and H. Gales (trans.) *The Zapatistas' dignified rage: Final public speeches of Subcommander Marcos* (Chico, CA: AK Press, 2014).

Marcos, Subcomandante. 'Introduction', in N. Henck (ed.) and H. Gales (trans.) *The Zapatistas' dignified rage: Final public speeches of Subcommander Marcos* (Chico, CA: AK Press, 2014).

Marcos, Subcomandante. *Professionals of hope: The selected writings of Subcommander Marcos* (Brooklyn, NY: The Song Cave, 2017).

Marcos, Subcomandante. 'Simple answers to complex questions', in N. Henck (ed.) and H. Gales (trans.) *The Zapatistas' dignified rage: Final public speeches of Subcommander Marcos* (Chico, CA: AK Press, 2014).

Marcuse, Herbert. *Counterrevolution and revolt* (Boston, MA: Beacon Press, 1972).

Marcuse, Herbert. *Eros and civilization: A philosophical enquiry into Freud* (Boston, MA: Beacon Press, 1966).

Marshall, Peter. 'Preface', in L. Davis and R. Kinna (eds) *Anarchism and utopianism* (Manchester: Manchester University Press, 2009).

Marx, Karl. 'Economic and philosophical manuscripts', in *Early writings*, trans. R. Livingstone and G. Benton (London: Penguin, 1975). Original work written 1844, and first published 1932.

Marx, Karl and Engels, Frederick. 'Address of the central committee to the communist league', London, March 1850.

Matthews, David. 'Capitalism and mental health'. *Monthly Review* 70:8 (2019), 49–62.

Mau, Steffen. *The metric society: On the quantification of the social* (Cambridge: Polity Press, 2019).

May, Todd. *Nonviolent resistance: A philosophical introduction* (Cambridge: Polity Press, 2015).

McBride, Keally. 'Emma Goldman and the power of revolutionary love', in J. Casas Klausen and J. Martel (eds) *How not to be governed: Readings and interpretations from a critical anarchist left* (Plymouth: Lexington Books, 2011).

McDonald, Rachel, Chai, Hui Yi and Newell, Ben R. 'Personal experience and the "psychological distance" of climate change: An integrative review'. *Journal of Environmental Psychology* 44 (2015), 109–118.

McKay, Iain. *Direct struggle against capital: A Peter Kropotkin anthology* (Oakland, CA: AK Press, 2014).

Mintz, Jerome R. *The anarchists of Casas Viejas* (Chicago, IL: University of Chicago Press, 1982).

Mitchell, Juliet. *Psychoanalysis and feminism* (New York: Pantheon Books, 1974).

Mohanty, Sobhi. 'From communal violence to lockdown hunger: emergency responses by civil society networks in Delhi, India'. *Interface* 12:1 (2020), 47–52.

Moisés, Subcomandante. 'Fourth wind: An organized dignified rage', in N. Henck (ed.) and H. Gales (trans.) *The Zapatistas' dignified rage: Final public speeches of Subcommander Marcos* (Chico, CA: AK Press, 2018).

Monjane, Boaventura. 'Confronting state authoritarianism: Civil society and community-based solidarity in Southern Africa', in M. Sitrin and Colectiva Sembrar (eds) *Pandemic solidarity: Mutual aid during the Covid-19 crisis* (London: Pluto Press, 2020).

Montgomery, Nick and Bergman, Carla. *Joyful militancy: Building thriving resistance in toxic times* (Chico, CA: AK Press, 2017).

Morton, Timothy. 'The Mesh', in S. Lemenager, T. Shewry and K. Hiltner (eds) *Environmental criticism for the twenty-first century* (New York: Routledge, 2011).

Naess, Arne. 'The shallow and the deep, long-range ecology movement: A summary'. *Inquiry* 16 (1973), 95–100.

Nash, Jennifer C. 'Practicing love: Black feminism, love-politics, and postintersectionality'. *Meridians: feminism, race, transnationalism* 2:2 (2013), 1–24.

Negri, Antonio. 'Logic and theory of enquiry: Militant praxis as subject and episteme', in D. Graeber, S. Shukaitis and E. Biddle (eds) *Constituent imagination: Militant investigations, collective theorization* (Oakland, CA: AK Press, 2007).

Newman, Saul. 'Anarchism, utopianism and the politics of emancipation', in L. Davis and R. Kinna (eds) *Anarchism and utopianism* (Manchester: Manchester University Press, 2009).

Newman, Saul. 'Postanarchism', in C. Levy and M. Adams (eds) *The Palgrave handbook of anarchism* (Cham, Switzerland: Palgrave Macmillan, 2019).

Nocella, Anthony J., Sorenson, John, Socha, Kim and Matsuoka, Atsuko. *Defining critical animal studies: An intersectional social justice approach for liberation* (New York: Peter Lang, 2014).

NSIDC/NASA. 'Vital signs of the planet: Arctic sea ice minimum'. *NASA global climate change vital signs of the planet*, 2020. Available online: https://climate.nasa.gov/vital-signs/arctic-sea-ice/.

Nûjiyan, Bager. 'From the free mountains of Kurdistan to the southeast of Mexico: Towards a revolutionary culture of the global freedom struggle'. *Internationalist Commune*, 2019. Available online: https://internationalistcommune. com/from-the-free-mountains-of-kurdistan-to-the-southeast-of-mexico-towards-a-revolutionary-culture-of-the-global-freedom-struggle/.

Öcalan, Abdullah. 'Democratic confederalism', in A. Öcalan, *The political thought of Abdullah Öcalan* (London: Pluto Press, 2017). Original work published 2011.

Öcalan, Abdullah. 'Democratic nation', in A. Öcalan, *The political thought of Abdullah Öcalan* (London: Pluto Press, 2017). Original work published 2016.

Öcalan, Abdullah. *Manifesto for a democratic civilization, vol. 1, Civilization. The age of masked gods and disguised kings* (Porsgrunn, Norway: New Compass Press, 2015).

Öcalan, Abdullah. 'Liberating life: Woman's revolution', in A. Öcalan, *The political thought of Abdullah Öcalan* (London: Pluto Press, 2017). Original work published 2013.

OHCHR. 'Climate change and poverty: Report of the Special Rapporteur on extreme poverty and human rights', delivered to *the Human Rights Council Forty-first session*, 24 June – 12 July 2019.

Oliver, Kelly. *Earth and world* (New York: Columbia University Press, 2015).

Orwell, George. *Homage to Catalonia*, 1938. Available online: https://gutenberg. net.au/ebooks02/0201111h.html.

Özselçuk, Ceren. 'Fifteen years after the Empire: An interview with Michael Hardt'. *Rethinking Marxism* 28:1 (2016), 124–138.

Peirats, José. *Anarchists in the Spanish revolution* (London: Freedom Press, 1998).

Pellow, David N and Nyseth Brehm, Hollie. 'From the new ecological paradigm to total liberation: The emergence of a social movement frame'. *The Sociological Quarterly* 56 (2015), 185–212.

Pieters, Rik. 'Bidirectional dynamics of materialism and loneliness: Not just a vicious cycle'. *Journal of Consumer Research* 40:4 (2014), 615–631.

Pollin, Robert. 'De-growth vs a green new deal'. *New Left Review* 112 (2018), 5–25.

Pötz, Martin. 'Utopian imagination in activism: Making the case for social dreaming in change from the grassroots'. *Interface* 11:1 (2019), 123–146.

Power, Nina. 'Feminism and the Eros Effect', in J. Del Gandio and A.K. Thompson (eds) *Spontaneous combustion: The Eros Effect and global revolution* (Albany, NY: SUNY Press, 2017).

Prashad, Vijay. 'This concerns everyone', in K. Khatib, M. Killjoy and M. McGuire (eds) *We are many: Reflections on movement strategy from occupation to liberation* (Oakland, CA: AK Press, 2012).

Preciado, Paul B. *Counter-sexual manifesto* (New York: Columbia University Press, 2018).

Price, Andy. 'Green anarchism', in C. Levy and M. Adams (eds) *The Palgrave handbook of anarchism* (Cham, Switzerland: Palgrave Macmillan, 2019).

Prichard, Alex. 'Collective intentionality, complex pluralism and the problem of anarchy'. *Journal of International Political Theory* 13:3 (2017), 360–377.

Prichard, Alex. 'Freedom', in C. Levy and M. Adams (eds) *The Palgrave handbook of anarchism* (Cham, Switzerland: Palgrave Macmillan, 2019).

Proudhon, Pierre-Joseph. *Confessions of a revolutionary, to serve as a history of the February revolution*, 1849. Available online: https://en.wikisource.org/wiki/Translation:Confessions_of_a_Revolutionary/3.

Proudhon, Pierre-Joseph. *General idea of the revolution in the nineteenth century*, trans. J. Robinson (New York: Haskell House Publishers, 1989). Original work published 1851.

Proudhon, Pierre-Joseph. *Système des contradictions économiques ou Philosophie de la misère* (Paris: Garnier Frères, 1850).

Proudhon, Pierre-Joseph. *Toast to the revolution*, 1848. The Anarchist Library. Available online: https://libcom.org/files/pierre-joseph-proudhon-toast-to-the-revolution.pdf.

Proudhon, Pierre-Joseph. *What is property?* 1876. Available online: https://libcom.org/files/Proudhon%20-%20What%20is%20Property.pdf.

Puig de la Bellacasa, María. *Matters of care: Speculative ethics in more than human worlds* (Minneapolis, MN: University of Minnesota Press, 2017).

Raekstad, Paul and Gradin, Sofa Saio. *Prefigurative politics* (Cambridge: Polity Press, 2020).

Ramnath, Maia. *Decolonising anarchism: An antiauthoritarian history of India's liberation struggle* (Oakland, CA: AK Press, 2016).

Rebel City. 'Climate change is not a single issue'. *Rebel City* 12 (2019), 3–4.

Reclus, Élisée. 'Anarchy', in J. Clark and C. Martin (eds) *Anarchy, geography, modernity: Selected writings of Élisée Reclus* (Oakland, CA: PM Press, 2013). Original work published 1894.

Reclus, Élisée. 'Evolution, revolution, and the anarchist ideal', in J. Clark and C. Martin (eds) *Anarchy, geography, modernity: Selected writings of Élisée Reclus* (Oakland, CA: PM Press, 2013). Original work published 1898.

Reclus, Élisée. 'The extended family', in J. Clark and C. Martin (eds) *Anarchy, geography, modernity: Selected writings of Élisée Reclus* (Oakland, CA: PM Press, 2013). Original work published 1896.

Reclus, Élisée. 'On vegetarianism', in J. Clark and C. Martin (eds) *Anarchy, geography, modernity: Selected writings of Élisée Reclus* (Oakland, CA: PM Press, 2013). Original work published 1901.

Reclus, Élisée. 'Why we are anarchists', 1889. *Autonomies*. Available online: https://autonomies.org/2019/08/elisee-reclus-why-we-are-anarchists/.

Richards, Vernon. *Lessons of the Spanish revolution 1936–1939* (Oakland, CA: PM Press, 2019). Original work published 1953.

Rigaud, Kanta Kumari, de Sherbinin, Alex, Jones, Bryan, Bergmann, Jonas, Clement, Viviane, Ober, Kayly, Schewe, Jacob, Adamo, Susana, McCusker, Brent, Heuser, Silke and Midgley, Amelia. *Groundswell: Preparing for internal climate migration* (Washington, DC: The World Bank, 2018).

Ripple, William J., Wolf, Christopher, Newsome, Thomas M, Barnard, Phoebe, Moomaw, William R. and 11,258 scientist signatories from 153 countries. 'World scientists' warning of a climate emergency'. *BioScience* 70:1 (2020), 8–12.

Rojava Azadi Madrid. 'One thought on the discussion: Abdullah Ocalan and the Kurdish myth', in online discussion: 'Abdullah Öcalan and the Kurdish myth'. *Anarchist Communist Group*, 2021. Available online: www.anarchistcommunism.org/2021/03/01/discussion-abdullah-ocalan-and-the-kurdish-myth/.

Romanos, Eduardo. 'From Tahrir to Puerta del Sol to Wall Street: The transnational diffusion of social movements in comparative perspective'. *Revista Española de Investigaciones Sociologicas* 154 (2016), 103–118.

Román-Palacios, Cristian and Wiens, John J. 'Recent responses to climate change reveal the drivers of species extinction and survival'. *Proceedings of the National Academy of Sciences of the United States of America*, 10 February 2020. Available online: www.pnas.org/content/early/2020/02/04/1913007117.

Roos, Jérôme E. and Oikonomakis, Leonidas. 'We are everywhere! The autonomous roots of the real democracy movement'. Paper prepared for the *7th Annual ECPR General Conference*. Bordeaux, 4–7 September 2013.

Rossdale, Chris. 'Dancing ourselves to death: The subject of Emma Goldman's Nietzschean anarchism'. *Globalizations* 12:1 (2015), 116–133.

Roth, Kenneth. 'How authoritarians are exploiting the COVID-19 crisis to grab power'. *Human Rights Watch*, 2020. Available online: www.hrw.org/news/2020/04/03/how-authoritarians-are-exploiting-covid-19-crisis-grab-power.

Rousseau, Jean-Jacques. *On the Origin of the Inequality of Mankind*, 1754. Available online: www.marxists.org/reference/subject/economics/rousseau/inequality/ch02.htm.

Rowe, James K. 'Zen and the art of social movement maintenance'. *Waging Nonviolence*, 2015. Available online: https://wagingnonviolence.org/feature/mindfulness-and-the-art-of-social-movement-maintenance/.

Rowe, James K. and Simpson, Mike. 'Lessons from the front lines of anti-colonial pipeline resistance'. *Waging Nonviolence*, 2017. Available online: https://waging nonviolence.org/2017/10/lessons-front-lines-anti-colonial-unistoten-pipeline-resistance/.

Roy, Arundhati. *The god of small things* (New York: Harper Perennial, 1998).

Roy, Arundhati. 'The Mahatma Ayyankali lecture'. Presentation given to the international seminar – *Re-imagining struggles at the margins: A history of the unconquered and the oppressed*. University of Kerala, Thiruvananthapuram, 17 July 2014.

Ruivenkamp, Guido and Hilton, Andy. *Perspectives on commoning: Autonomist principles and practices* (London: Zed Books, 2017).

Rushkoff, Douglas. 'Survival of the richest', in *This is not a drill: An Extinction Rebellion handbook* (London: Penguin, 2019).

Salleh, Ariel. *Ecofeminism as politics: Nature, Marx and the postmodern* (London: Zed Books, 2017). Original work published 1997.

Salleh, Ariel. 'Re-worlding – With a pluriversal new deal'. *Arena*, 2020. Available online: https://arena.org.au/re-worlding-with-a-pluriversal-new-deal/.

Sandilands, Catriona. 'Feminism and biopolitics: A cyborg account', in S. MacGregor (ed.) *Routledge handbook of gender and environment* (New York: Routledge, 2017).

Sandoval, Chela. *Methodology of the oppressed* (Minneapolis, MN: University of Minnesota Press, 2000).

Santos, Boaventura de Sousa. *The end of the cognitive empire: The coming of age of epistemologies of the South* (Durham, NC: Duke University Press, 2018).

Santos, Boaventura de Sousa, Nunes, João Arriscado and Meneses, Maria Paula. 'Introduction: Opening up the canon of knowledge and recognition of difference', in B. Santos (ed.) *Another knowledge is possible: Beyond northern epistemologies* (London: Verso, 2008).

Satgar, Vishwas. 'Covid-19, the climate crisis and lockdown: An opportunity to end the war with nature'. *Kafila*, 2020. Available online: https://kafila.online/2020/03/28/covid-19-the-climate-crisis-and-lockdown-an-opportunity-to-end-the-war-with-nature-vishwas-satgar/.

Savran, Sungur. 'The first victory for the Sudanese revolution: Will the people be able to override the "orderly transition"?'. *The Bullet*, 16 April 2019.

Scheidler, Fabian. 'Rojova or the art of transition in a collapsing civilization', in International Initiative: Freedom for Abdullah Öcalan – Peace in Kurdistan (eds) *Building free life: Dialogues with Öcalan* (Oakland, CA: PM Press, 2020).

Sciabarra, Chris. 'Reply to Roderick Long: Dialectical libertarianism: all benefits, no hazards'. *The Journal of Ayn Rand Studies* 3:2 (2002), 381–399.

Seshan, Suprabha. 'From this wounded forest: A dispatch'. *Counter Currents*, 2019. Available online: https://countercurrents.org/2019/04/from-this-wounded-forest-a-dispatch.

Sethness-Castro, Javier. *Imperilled life: Revolution against climate catastrophe* (Oakland, CA: AK Press, 2012).

Shiva, Vandana. 'Foreword', in *This is not a drill: An Extinction Rebellion handbook* (London: Penguin, 2019).

Shukaitis, Stevphen. 'Nobody knows what an insurgent body can do: Questions for affective resistance', in J. Heckert and R. Cleminson (eds) *Anarchism and sexuality: Ethics, relationships and power* (Abingdon: Routledge, 2011).

Shukaitis, Stevphen and Graeber, David. *Constituent imagination: Militant investigations – Collective theorization* (Oakland, CA: AK Press, 2007).

Silva, Grant J. 'Racism as self-love'. *Radical Philosophy Review* 22:1 (2019), 85–112.

Singh, Neera. 'Becoming a commoner: The commons as sites for affective socio-nature encounters and co-becomings'. *Ephemera* 17:4 (2017), 751–776.

Singh Chaudhary, Ajay. 'The extractive circuit: An exhausted planet at the end of growth'. *The Baffler* 60 (2021). Available online: https://thebaffler.com/salvos/the-extractive-circuit-singh-chaudhary.

Sitrin, Marina. 'Anarchism and the newest social movements', in C. Levy and M. Adams (eds) *The Palgrave handbook of anarchism* (Cham, Switzerland: Palgrave Macmillan, 2019).

Situationist International. *Situationist international anthology*, ed. and trans. K. Knabb (Berkeley, CA: Bureau of Public Secrets, 2006). Original work published 1981.

Springer, Simon. 'Abandoning our humanity'. *DOPE Magazine,* 2021. Available online: https://dogsection.org/abandoning-our-humanity/.

Springer, Simon. 'Space, time, and the politics of immanence'. *Global Discourse* 4:2–3 (2014), 159–162.

Springer, Simon. 'Total liberation ecology: Integral anarchism, anthroparchy, and the violence of indifference', in S. Springer, J. Mateer, M. Locret-Collet and M. Acke (eds) *Undoing human supremacy: Anarchist political ecology in the face of anthroparchy* (New York: Rowman and Littlefield, 2021).

Springmann, Marco, Clark, Michael, Mason-D'Croz, Daniel, Wiebe, Keith, Bodirsky, Benjamin Leon, Lassaletta, Luis, de Vries, Wim, Vermeulen, Sonja J., Herrero, Mario, Carlson, Kimberly M., Jonell, Malin, Troell, Max, DeClerck, Fabrice, Gordon, Line J., Zurayk, Rami, Scarborough, Peter, Rayner, Mike, Loken, Brent, Fanzo, Jess, Godrfay, Charles J., Tilman, David, Rockström, Johan and Willett, Walter. 'Options for keeping the food system within environmental limits'. *Nature* 562 (2018), 519–525.

Stansell, Christine. *American moderns: Bohemian New York and the creation of a new century* (New York: Henry Holt and Co, 2000).

Stout, Linda. *Collective visioning: How groups can work together for a just and sustainable future* (San Francisco, CA: Berrett-Koehler Publishers, 2011).

Stronzake, Janaina. 'People make the occupation and the occupation makes the people', in K. Khatib, M. Killjoy and M. McGuire (eds) *We are many: Reflections on movement strategy from occupation to liberation* (Oakland, CA: AK Press, 2012).

Sullivan, Sian. 'An *other* world is possible? On representation, rationalism and romanticism in social forums'. *Ephemera* 5:2 (2005), 370–392.

Swain, Dan. 'Not not but not yet: Present and future in prefigurative politics'. *Political Studies* 67:1 (2019), 47–62.

Tabuchi, Hiroko. 'A Trump insider embeds climate denial in scientific research'. *The New York Times*, 2 March 2020.

TallBear, Kim. 'An indigenous reflection on working beyond the human/not human'. *GLQ: A Journal of Lesbian and Gay Studies* 21:2–3 (2015), 230–235.

Tammilehto, Olli. 'The present is pregnant with a new future', in F. Venturini, E. Değirmenci and I. Morales (eds) *Social ecology and the right to the city* (Montreal: Black Rose Books, 2019).

Tax, Meredith. 'The revolution in Rojova'. *Dissent Magazine*, 2015. Available online: www.dissentmagazine.org/online_articles/the-revolution-in-rojava.

Tillman, Rachel. 'Toward a new materialism: Matter as dynamic'. *Minding Nature* 8:1 (2015), 30–35.

Tolstoy, Leo. *What I believe*, trans. C. Popoff (n.p., 2005 [1886]). Available online: https://archive.org/details/WhatIBelieve_109.

Toye, Margaret E. 'Towards a poethics of love: Poststructuralist feminist ethics and literary creation'. *Feminist Theory* 11:1 (2010), 39–55.

Trainer, Ted. 'Kurdist Rojava: A social model for our future'. *Resilience*, 2020. Available online: www.resilience.org/stories/2020–01–03/kurdist-rojava-a-social-model-for-our-future/.

Trotsky, Leon. *The permanent revolution*, 1931. Available online: www.marxists.org/archive/trotsky/1931/tpr/pr-index.htm.

Tweedy, Rod. 'A mad world: capitalism and the rise of mental illness'. *Red Pepper*, 2017. Available online: www.redpepper.org.uk/a-mad-world-capitalism-and-the-rise-of-mental-illness/.

Ureña, Carolyn. 'Loving from below: Of (de)colonial love and other demons'. *Hypatia* 32:1 (2017), 86–102.

Üstündağ, Nazan. 'The theology of democratic modernity', in International initiative: Freedom for Abdullah Öcalan – Peace in Kurdistan (eds) *Building free life: Dialogues with Öcalan* (Oakland, CA: PM Press, 2020).

Van Dijck, José, Poell, Thomas and Waal, Martijn. *The platform society: Public values in a connective world* (Oxford: Oxford University Press, 2018).

Veltman, Andrea. 'Transcendence and immanence in the ethics of Simone De Beauvoir', in M. A. Simons (ed.) *Philosophy of Simone De Beauvoir: Critical essays* (Bloomington, IN: Indiana University Press, 2006).

Watts, Jonathan. 'Arctic warming: scientists alarmed by "crazy" temperature rises'. *The Guardian*, 27 February 2018.

We Mean Business Coalition. '87 major companies lead the way towards a 1.5°C future at UN Climate Action Summit'. Press release, 22 September 2019. Available online: www.wemeanbusinesscoalition.org/press-release/87-major-companies-lead-the-way-towards-a-1–5c-future-at-un-climate-action-summit/.

Webb, Darren. 'Critical pedagogy, utopia and political (dis)engagement'. *Power and Education* 5:3 (2013), 280–290.

Webb, Darren. 'Here we stand: The pedagogy of Occupy Wall Street'. *Australian Journal of Adult Learning* 59:3 (2019), 342–364.

Webb, Darren. 'Where's the vision? The concept of utopia in contemporary educational theory'. *Oxford Review of Education* 35:6 (2009), 743–760.

Wexler, Alice. *Emma Goldman: An intimate life* (New York: Pantheon, 1984).

White, Richard J. and Gunderman, Hannah C. 'Kindness and compassion for mutual flourishing in post-human worlds: Re-imagining our relationships with insects'. *EuropeNow* 45, 2021. Available online: www.europenowjournal.org/2021/11/07/kindness-and-compassion-for-mutual-flourishing-in-post-human-worlds-re-imagining-our-relationships-with-insects/.

Wiley, Terrance A. *Angelic troublemakers: Religion and anarchism in America* (New York: Bloomsbury Academic, 2014).

Wilkinson, Eleanor. 'On love as an (im)properly political concept'. *D: Society and Space* 35:1 (2017), 57–71.

Wilkinson, Eleanor. 'Love in the multitude? A feminist critique of love as a political concept', in A. G. Jónasdóttir and A. Ferguson (eds) *Love: A question for feminism in the twenty-first century* (London: Routledge, 2014).

Wilson, Edward O. *Biophilia* (Cambridge, MA: Harvard University Press, 1984).

Woodcock, Jamie. 'The workers' inquiry from Trotskyism to Operaismo: A political methodology for investigating the workplace'. *Ephemera* 14:3 (2014), 489–509.

World Wildlife Fund. *Living planet report*, M. Grooten and R. Almond (eds) (Gland, Switzerland: WWF, 2018).

Xu, Xiaoming, Sharma, Prateek, Shu, Shijie, Lin, Tzu-Shun, Ciais, Philippe, Tubiello, Francesco N., Smith, Pete, Campbell, Nelson and Jain, Atul K. 'Global greenhouse gas emissions from animal-based foods are twice those of plant-based foods'. *Nature Food* 2 (2021), 724–732.

Yeoman, James Michael. 'The Spanish civil war', in C. Levy and M. Adams (eds) *The Palgrave handbook of anarchism* (Cham, Switzerland: Palgrave Macmillan, 2019).

York, Matt. 'Transforming masculinities: A qualitative study of a transformative education programme for young Zulu men and boys in rural Kwazulu-Natal'. *Journal of Pan African Studies* 7:7 (2014), 55–78.

Zettler, Vanessa. 'On grassroots organizing: Excerpts from Brazil', in M. Sitrin and Colectiva Sembrar (eds) *Pandemic solidarity: Mutual aid during the Covid-19 crisis* (London: Pluto Press, 2020).

Zittlow-Rogness, Kate and Foust, Christina R. 'Beyond rights and virtues as foundation for women's agency: Emma Goldman's rhetoric of free love'. *Western Journal of Communication* 75:2 (2011), 148–167.

Index

Aanikobijiganag 102
Abram, David 85, 129
affective domination 57
affective entanglement 89, 117
affinity group 4, 48, 121
agápe 4, 149
Agapeic web 9, 85, 114
agonistic pluralism 10, 116, 136,
    142, 169
algorithmic governance 57–61
    and degrowth 107
anarchism 13, 17, 23, 33, 49, 76, 98,
    146, 147
anarchist 6–7, 9, 10, 13–14, 19, 21–22,
    27, 30, 33, 43, 45–47, 67, 76, 87,
    89, 92, 98, 100, 114–115, 117,
    120–122, 124, 131, 137, 140,
    151, 156–158, 163,
    170–171, 172
Anderson, Pamela Sue 117
animal industrial complex 63, 96
anthropocentrism 31
anthroprivilege 97
anti-nuclear movements 121
Arab Spring 6, 29, 45, 119, 122, 126
Argentinazo 8, 42
Autogestion 134
Autonomous Administration of North
    and East Syria 10, 126, 138, 141,
    152, 159
    see also Rojava

Bakunin, Mikhail 128, 149
Barad, Karen 11, 31
Beins, Agatha 25
Bellacasa, Maria Puig de la 151

Berlant, Lauren 25
Big Data Capitalism 58
    see also algorithmic governance
biophilia 97
bioregions 162
black feminism 17
Bloch, Ernst 43
Bollier, David 92
Bolsheviks 119, 124
Bookchin, Murray 92, 123, 127, 133,
    142, 157, 159, 162
Boonen, Christiaan 139
    see also Rojava
Borda, Fals 42
    see also Participatory Action
        Research
Bottici, Chiara 94
Braidotti, Rosi 11, 24, 55, 56, 77,
    94, 131
Buen Vivir 102
Butterfly Hill, Julia 31

ch'ulel 153–4
Chatterton, Paul 97
    see also biophilia
Chaudhary, Ajay Singh 68
Clark, John P xii, 55–56, 83, 88, 98,
    100, 152, 154, 157
Cleminson, Richard 17
collective heart 4, 10, 149, 152,
    153–155, 163
    see also O'on
collective visioning 6, 41–49
    and mindfulness 48
    participants 45–48
Combahee River Collective 16, 115

communalism 124, 159
Communiqué from an Absent Future
    133
    see also US Student Occupation
        Movement
Confederación Nacional del Trabajo
    (CNT) 124
    see also Spanish Revolution
connection to nature 7
consensus-based decision making
    140, 169
COVID-19 pandemic 75, 118, 122, 172
Cozolino, Louis 89
    see also love becomes flesh

Davis, Laurence 18, 44, 50, 98, 100, 129
Day, Dorothy 14
De Angelis, Massimo 88, 90
De Beauvoir, Simone 24
De Waal, Frans 89
    see also mirror neurons
deep commons 7, 90–95
    and bioregionalism 162–163
    and international relations 157–158
    and temporality 129–130
    indigenous conceptions of 100–106
    post-egoic embodied
        experience of 150
    Zapatista conception of 154
deep ecology 9, 92, 170
degrowth 106–108
Diggers 124
direct action 4, 6, 16, 18, 31, 47, 67,
    116, 127, 135, 151, 169
direct democracy 6, 8, 42, 118, 138, 158

Eagleman, David 89
Earth First! 3
Earth Liberation Front 115
eco-la-la 92
    see also Bookchin, Murray
Ecodharma Centre 48
ecological crises 61–68
empathic entanglement 9, 31, 85, 118
encuentros 43
English Revolution 124
entangled empathy 31
Epstein, Barbara 130
éros ix, 4, 149–150
Eros effect 29, 150
    see also Katsiaficas, George

ethics 5
    and immanence 151
    and mutual aid 117
    more-than-human 30
    of permaculture 151
Extinction Rebellion 66–68

Falk, Candace 21
fascisms ix, 4, 19–20, 149
Federación Anarquista Ibérica (FAI) 124
    see also Spanish Revolution
Federici, Silvia 72, 91, 105
fēmina implexa 98
feminist collectives, Mexico 172
Ferguson, Ann 23
First Intercontinental Encuentro
        for Humanity and Against
        Neoliberalism 156
    see also La Realidad
Fitzwater, Dylan Eldredge 153
Foran, John 12
Franks, Benjamin 132
freedom
    as an actually-existing immanent
        quality 150
    as an essential prerequisite for the
        manifestation of life 93
    etymology of 5
Freeman, Jo 140, 147
French Revolution 119, 124, 145
Freud, Sigmund 15, 150, 185
Fromm, Erich 15, 150
Fuerzas de Liberación Nacional 152
    see also Zapatista

G20 protests 4, 120
Gahman, Levi 155
Gandhi, Mahātmā xi, 16
Generative Somatics 48
Gilligan, Carol 117
Gilman-Opalsky, Richard 18, 150
Goldman, Emma 12, 14, 18
    and Alexander Berkman 27
    and Edward Brady (Sasha) 22
    and free love 22
    and racial oppression 22
    critique of marriage 19–20
    critique of patriotic love 21
    feminist criticisms of 21
Gordon, Uri 130, 132,
        138–139, 142–143

Gorski, Paul 48
Graeber, David 120, 161
ground zero for revolution 92
    see also Federici, Silvia
grounded utopias 44, 85, 129, 168
    critique of 130–132
Guevara, Ernesto Che 16
Gunderman, Hannah 97

Hardt and Negri 18
Hardt, Michael 15, 18
    critique of patriotic love 20
    critique of romantic love 20
    feminist critique of 23–25
    on the Gezi encampment 28
Heckert, Jamie 18
Hemmings, Clare 26
Hennessy, Rosemary 23
Heritage Front 137
    see also xenophobic nationalisms
Hevaltî 141
    see also Rojava
Hilton, Andy 91
Hollender, Rebecca 91
hooks, bell 17, 70, 82, 115
horizontalism 6, 134
Horvat, Srećko 28
Hungarian Revolution 119
Huuy-ay-aht 101

Ibáñez, Tomás 33
Idle No More 119
Ilima 103
    see also Ubuntu
immanence 23, 32
    a politics of 132–136
    an ethics of 151
    an ontology of 77
    and anarchism 33
    and 'nature time' 108
    critique of 130–131
    versus transcendence 32
individual and community 98,
    135, 170
international relations theory, critique
    of 157–158
intersectionality 26
Iranian Revolution 119
Italian autonomism 42

Jacobins 124

Kallis, Giorgos 107
    see also degrowth
Kaluža, Jernej 129
Katsiaficas, George x, 29,
    98, 150
Kawano, Emily 142
King, Martin Luther Jr. 16, 137
Kinna, Ruth 77, 158
Knabb, Ken 122
Kollantai, Alexandra 14
Kovel, Joel 32
Kropotkin, Peter 89, 92, 117–118, 127,
    151, 157
Kümmel, Friedrich 44, 129

La Boétie, Étienne de 57, 93
    see also voluntary servitude
Landauer, Gustav x, 13, 33,
    87, 114, 127–128, 132,
    157, 161
La Realidad 156
    see also First Intercontinental
        Encuentro for Humanity and
        Against Neoliberalism
Latour, Bruno 84
le contr'État 128
    see also Landauer, Gustav
la grande famille 114
    see also Landauer, Gustav
Le Guin, Ursula K 36, 75
Levellers 124
Levitas, Ruth 44, 87
libertarian municipalism 159
    see also Bookchin, Murray
López Intzin, Xuno 153
love 12
    and co-constituting free
        society 149–163
    and creating the 'other' 70
    and mutual aid 117–118
    as a political concept 4
    as affinity 116–122
    as domination 19
    as force 128
    as freedom 27–30
    as post-egoic 150
    as transformative 21–26
    becomes flesh 89
    beyond anthropos 30–34
    communism of 18
    decolonial 17

Index

love (*continued*)
    more-than-human 95–100
    of the world 30
love code 61
love laws 118
    see also Roy, Arundhati
love-bombing 135
loving-caring relations 5, 23, 128,
    168–169

Majewska, Ewa 15, 17
Malatesta, Errico 13, 114
Marcuse, Herbert x, 15, 61, 150
Marxist 5, 7, 12, 15–16, 18, 42, 101,
    125, 127, 150, 152, 159
materialism and mental health 68–70
May, Todd 137
McKay, Iain 117
    see also Kropotkin, Peter
Mesopotamian Ecology Movement 160
    see also Rojava
mirror neurons 88, 89
    see also De Waal, Frans
more-than-human psycho-socio-material
    relations ix, 7, 9, 85, 93, 170
Morton, Timothy 33
Movement of Landless Workers 72
Mūlamadhyamakakārikā 33
    see also Nāgārjuna
mutual aid x, xi, 6, 10, 60, 67, 72, 89,
    116–117, 118–119, 120, 163, 172

Naess, Arne 93
Nāgārjuna 33
Nash, Jennifer 26, 87
nature-culture continuum 31
new materiality 24
Newman, Saul 78, 134
North Atlantic Free Trade
    Agreement 156
Nûjiyan, Bager 130
    see also Rojava
Nyoni, Sithembiso 42
    see also Participatory Action Research

Öcalan, Abdullah 4, 57, 159–162
Occupy 6, 28, 43, 45–46, 48, 131,
    133, 158
O'Keeffe, Philip Arges 141
    *see also Saziya Yekiti u Pistgiriya
    Gelan* (Rojava)

onto-epistem-ology 31
ontology of separation 77
O'on 4, 10, 152–154, 163
    see also collective heart
Operaismo 8, 42
Orwell, George 125

Participatory Action Research 42
patriotisms ix, 4, 8, 19, 57, 70,
    149, 173
Pauwauwaein 119–120
People's Global Action 156
permaculture xi, 4, 6, 45, 76, 135, 151
permanent revolution 5, 127
    see also (r)evolution
philía 4, 149
plasma of being 32
posthumanist 7, 30, 93, 118, 160, 170
Powaqqatsi 62
    see also ecological crises
Prashad, Vijay 75
prefigurative politics 6, 58, 130
    and the question of violence 136–143
    critique of 132
Prichard, Alex 140, 158
property relations 90
Proudhon, Pierre-Joseph 3, 5, 11, 91,
    127, 158, 163, 167

radical imagination 22, 133
radical interdependence 150
radical solidarity ix, 4, 10, 32, 73, 77,
    116, 119–120, 136, 139, 149,
    151, 154, 156, 169, 171
Rahman, Mohammed Anisar 42
    see also Participatory Action Research
Ramnath, Maia 100
reciprocal effect 132
    see also Landauer
Reclaim the Streets 3
Reclus, Élisée 70, 86, 95, 114, 117, 123,
    127, 132, 143, 157, 161, 163
relief collectives, India 172
(r)evolution 6, 122–132
(r)evolutionary love 4, 85–90, 149–151
    and the Indian independence
        movement 16
    in Rojava 160–161
    lineage of 13–18
    of the Zapatistas 152–155
Richards, Vernon 125

Rojava 6, 119, 130, 141, 159
  governance structure 159–160
  Internationalist Commune 161
Rossdale, Chris 23
Rousseau, Jean-Jacques 84
Rowe, James 104
Roy, Arundhati 117
Ruivenkamp, Guido 91

Salleh, Ariel 87, 152
Sandoval, Chela 17
Santos, Boaventura de Sousa 100
Satgar, Vishwas 172
Saziya Yekiti u Pistgiriya Gelan 141
  see also Rojava
Second Spring 126
  see also Arab Spring
Seshan, Suprabha 90
Shoras 119
  see also Iranian Revolution
Shukaitis, Stevphen 86
Singh, Neera 92
Sitrin, Marina 134, 173
Situationist International 55
sixth mass extinction event 61
  see also ecological crises
social change, revolutionary and
  evolutionary theories of 5, 126–8
Social Ecology xiii, 92, 165
social health clinics, Greece 172
social reproduction 4–5, 10, 128, 152,
  168, 172
Solastalgia 69
solidarity and care 5, 151, 171, 173
solidarity kitchens, UK 172
Spanish Indignados 6
Spanish Revolution 121, 124–126
Springer 86, 96, 98, 134, 170, 178
storgē ix, 4, 149
Subcomandante Marcos 55, 152, 155
Sullivan, Sian 163
Sumak Kawsay 102
Swann, Thomas 158

Tahrir Square 123, 126
  see also Arab Spring
TallBear, Kim 32
Tammilehto, Olli 116
Tekmîl 141
  see also Rojava
temporary autonomous zones 3

'tyranny of structurelessness, The' 140
  see also Freeman, Jo
Thompson, Mike 104
Tillman, Rachel 24
Tolstoy 13, 34
total field image 92
  see also Naess, Arne
Total Liberation 115
transindividuality 94
  see also Bottici, Chiara

Ubuntu 26, 73, 103
Ulex Project 48
Unión General de Trabajadores
  (UGT) 125
  see also Spanish Revolution
Unist' ot' en 104
Ureña, Carolyn 17
US Student Occupation Movement 133
Üstündağ, Nazan 160
  see also Rojava
utopia 43–45
  see also grounded utopias
  as method 44
  as process 45, 132–136, 155

veganism 95–96, 170
voluntary servitude 57
  see also La Boétie, Étienne de

Wages for Housework
  campaigns 42
Webb, Darren 130
Wexler, Alice 21
Whakapapa 101
White, Richard 97
  see also veganism
Wilkinson, Eleanor 19
witch hunts 105–6
World Social Forum 8, 43

xenophobic nationalisms ix, 4, 8, 32,
  56–57, 122, 136, 149, 172

Ya Basta! 156

Zapatista 4, 8, 10, 101, 142, 152–157,
  159, 162
  seven principles of autonomous
  government 155
Zuccotti Park 120

EU authorised representative for GPSR:
Easy Access System Europe, Mustamäe tee 50,
10621 Tallinn, Estonia
gpsr.requests@easproject.com